Teaching Elementary School Mathematics

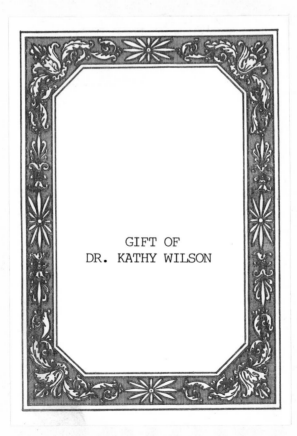

Teaching Elementary School Mathematics:

An Active Learning Approach

Harold H. Lerch *University of Illinois at Urbana–Champaign*

90-1322

Houghton Mifflin Company   *Boston*

Dallas   Geneva, Illinois   Hopewell, New Jersey   Palo Alto   London

Printed in the U.S.A.
Library of Congress Catalog Card Number: 80-82845
ISBN: 0-395-29762-1

Contents

v

Preface

Teaching Elementary School Mathematics: An Active Learning Approach discusses the development and implementation of an active laboratory-type program for elementary mathematics. A major premise of the text is that school administrators, consultants, program coordinators, and classroom teachers are continually involved in efforts to modify and improve programs of instruction. The responsibilities they face are complex and demanding. Decisions influencing the instructional program in elementary mathematics must be based on knowledge that encompasses all aspects of the mathematical content to be presented as well as the instructional procedures to be employed. This volume and the accompanying handbook, *Active Learning Experiences for Teaching Elementary School Mathematics*, are intended to provide professional educators with assistance in making instructional decisions.

Approach

An active laboratory approach to teaching elementary mathematics may be generally described as having (1) a high degree of informality in classroom organization and learning activities; (2) a curriculum that emphasizes individual and small-group learning activities and that goes beyond pacing children through printed textbooks to establishing objectives, content, materials, procedures, and evaluations which allow for pupil differences; (3) a discovery approach in which children use physical object models to develop and express concepts, ideas, and skills; (4) procedures that develop understanding of the formal operations in ways that are meaningful to the elementary student; and (5) opportunities for children to practice ideas and skills in playlike situations.

Organization and Features

The text is divided into two parts that present a balance between the general issues of teaching mathematics in the elementary grades and the methods of teaching specific content topics. The chapters in Part One, "Considerations in Program Development," focus on the scope and goals of the elementary mathematics program, analysis of existing programs, selection of appropriate learning experiences, and evaluation procedures. Part Two, "Strategies for Teaching in the Major Content Areas," identifies and discusses methods for teaching the basic concepts of mathematics, which are organized into five content areas: numeration and notation, operations on collections of objects, operations on numbers using numerals, geometry, and measurement. Examples of learning experiences and suggested activities for self-study are also included in this part. (The accompanying handbook contains complete descriptions of hundreds of active learning experiences in the major content areas.) In addition, the text includes two appendixes: one provides examples of mathematical learning aids that can be constructed for classroom use by teachers or children, and the other appendix suggests sources of ideas for planning and developing an active elementary mathematics program.

Audience

The text is intended for use by preservice and inservice teachers. Undergraduates majoring in elementary education may use the text in courses for methods of teaching elementary mathematics that are offered or required in teacher preparation programs. Considerations in program development and strategies for teaching in the major content areas are appropriate topics of study for future teachers of elementary mathematics. Inservice teachers may use the text to develop instructional programs for children. As such, the text and the handbook may be used by teachers who are taking graduate-level courses that deal with improving elementary mathematics programs, by teachers in formally conducted inservice education programs, or by teachers in the classroom who wish to modify existing programs. School administrators and program coordinators will also find the book helpful in providing background and direction for encouraging development and modification of elementary mathematics programs.

Acknowledgments

It would be impossible to identify all the individuals who have supported the preparation of this book. Encouragement and assistance came in many forms and I am indebted to the following: the individual teachers and many children of the public schools of Urbana, Illinois, who for more than six years participated in the development and class testing of laboratory ideas and learning experiences and the school administrators who allowed their participation; the teachers and children in the schools of Hickory Hills, Illinois, who for the past several years have incorporated these ideas in the TELLEM project; the students in my undergraduate and graduate courses dealing with elementary mathematics education who participated in the math lab activities, listened, questioned, and accepted the development of this active learning approach; the enthusiastic participants in the many inservice workshop sessions conducted under the auspices of various school districts, educational agencies, curriculum development projects, and professional organizations; my professional colleagues and friends who questioned, discussed, and urged me to get on with it; Judy Swanson, who helped edit and proofread the manuscript; and my family who endured it all. I am also grateful to those reviewers whose criticism helped refine the manuscript. They include James Barnard, Oregon College of Education; Thomas Romberg, University of Wisconsin, Madison; and Robert Rea, University of Missouri–St. Louis. To all these people, and particularly to those who kept asking, "When are you going to write that book?" I express my sincere appreciation.

H.H.L.

Teaching Elementary School Mathematics

Considerations in Program Development

What is known as an *elementary mathematics program* is part of the curriculum of every elementary school system at all levels of instruction. The existence of that program, however well defined, detailed, or vague it may be, is accompanied by a variety of expectations on the parts of classrooms teachers, program directors or coordinators, school administrators, children, parents, and perhaps others. Those expectations generally focus on the mathematical content of the program and pupil attainment of the concepts, ideas, and skills of the content at particular levels. However, serious consideration must also be given to aspects of the total program that influence, either positively or negatively, learning opportunities for children in the program. Program expectations should go beyond the content to be presented and the degree to which that content is to be "learned" by children.

When those concerned with the elementary mathematics program are dissatisfied with the extent to which expectations are reached or with other aspects of the program, efforts to improve the program are intensified. How those efforts are coordinated and organized depends on who is dissatisfied and the degree of dissatisfaction. Regardless of the extent of coordination and organization involved, serious efforts to evaluate and improve elementary mathematics programs involve study of the scope and goals of the program as well as the nature of the existing program: the educational principles that guide it, its organization, the types of learning experiences provided, and the evaluation procedures used.

1

Since classroom teachers are the professional educators responsible for the instructional procedures and operations of the program, they are often the prime motivators, planners, and developers of program modifications. Such efforts are initiated by both new and experienced teachers. It is not uncommon for new teachers of elementary mathematics to become disenchanted with aspects of existing programs because those aspects conflict with the knowledge, ideas, or beliefs about elementary mathematics, materials for instruction, children and learning, or teaching procedures that they acquired in their preservice training. When conflicts or dissatisfactions arise, new teachers begin to modify elementary mathematics programs in accordance with their own beliefs.

The situation is not greatly different for experienced teachers who have grown in their profession. However, because of their professional experiences, their concerns and efforts may be taken more seriously by other teachers and administrators. As teachers expand their knowledge and understanding of children and the learning processes; the content of elementary mathematics; the nature, extent, and uses of available materials; and possible alternative instructional procedures, they often begin to change or modify the program and instructional approaches. Classroom teachers, both new and experienced, are the directors and guardians of elementary mathematics programs. Their professional efforts to initiate improvements in programs should be encouraged and applauded, particularly if those efforts are well planned and conducted. Those individual initial concerns and efforts can be incorporated into organized and coordinated total program considerations by other professional educators and laypersons.

The following chapters present material with a view toward development of an active laboratory-type elementary mathematics program. Regardless of whether the modification and development efforts are at classroom, school, or school district levels, the development of an elementary mathematics program in which children actively participate in laboratory learning experiences appropriate to their own characteristics is a professionally responsible and desirable endeavor. A complete, active, laboratory-type program is not easily achieved. A great deal of self-evaluation, planning, and preparation must go into this effort. Part One attempts to assist new and experienced teachers, program coordinators or directors, and school administrators with the process by discussing those factors that ought to be considered in program modification and development.

The Scope of Elementary Mathematics Programs

It has been several decades since that part of the elementary school program that deals primarily with quantitative concepts and operational skills has been called the arithmetic program. At the urgings of mathematicians, mathematics educators, curriculum developers, researchers in the field, and producers of educational materials, approaches to the development of concepts and skills traditionally within the old arithmetic program were modified and some mathematical content that had not been introduced or developed in the study of arithmetic was added. The term *new math* came to be associated with these program modifications. Teachers, schools, and school systems hastened to adopt program materials and approaches that could be called new math. Not all of the newer suggestions withstood the tests of time, values, and classroom instructional practices. Those aspects were gradually removed from instructional materials or ignored in instructional practices.

Criticisms directed at those suggestions, content, and approaches were varied in both source and nature. Parents appeared to be disturbed because their children were apparently studying what they had not studied and in ways in which they had not studied. Content of the program seemed to have changed and the vocabulary surely was different. Many parents were no longer able to help their children study at home. On the other hand, some teachers refused or were reluctant to modify either the content

3

or their approaches to teaching arithmetic regardless of what was suggested or how it was presented in the newer materials. Many schools purchased the new materials but never really adopted the suggested approaches. Mathematicians and mathematics educators disagreed about the value of some of the new content and suggested approaches. One major point of contention was whether the new math programs should be based on applications or on a set of definitions and rules, the structure of the discipline. Perhaps the most important criticisms were that new math was not working, that children were not acquiring the basic skills and concepts, and that the actual changes were merely superficial.

While the basic concepts and skills of traditional arithmetic continue to be a part of modern elementary programs, significant curricular developments have occurred. The content has been expanded in both depth and breadth, the uses of symbolism have increased, and instructional procedures have been modified. These developments led to the use of *elementary mathematics* as a more appropriate descriptive term for good modern programs.

Elementary classroom teachers today attempt to adjust content and instructional procedures to meet the needs and ability levels of individual children. In order to do this, they must become familiar with the scope of the total elementary mathematics program. Knowledge of the total program is necessary if teachers are to take advantage of what has gone before and prepare children for what is to come. Teachers with a limited knowledge of the scope of the program or a view that restricts attention to the objectives or content generally assigned to their particular grade level in any elementary mathematics program will almost always offer fewer learning opportunities to the children they teach. The opportunities they offer will be restricted to content and learning tasks that are inappropriate for a significant percentage of the children in any classroom, including those who have not achieved the goals or expectations of preceding grade levels as well as the more rapid learners who for one reason or another have already acquired a major portion of the concepts and skills generally dealt with at their current grade level. For instruction to be effective, teachers must present each learning opportunity in its appropriate place within a scope of prior and future concepts, ideas, and skills. The sequential nature of mathematical ideas and skills, the manners in which children develop and acquire a structure of mathematical concepts and skills, the educational principles involved in readiness to learn, and the general goals of the total program all lend support to the belief that classroom teachers at any level must consider the total scope of the mathematics program when planning, developing, or presenting possible learning opportunities or experiences.

Defining the Scope of the Program

The scope of an elementary mathematics program is defined by the stated or implied philosophic beliefs, goals, content, and approaches to instruction. The task of ascertaining the scope of the program varies with the nature of the instructional materials being used, the nature of the study of curriculum activities being conducted by the professional educators in the school or school system, and the nature of the inservice or continuing professional education opportunities that are available to classroom teachers.

Definition by Materials

In some schools or school systems where a commercially published program has been adopted, the scope of the program can be quickly determined by studying the scope and sequence chart that accompanies the program. This two-dimensional chart cites grade levels and categorizes content areas or bits of content areas. It then lists the content and skills that are to be dealt with at each level. Other schools or school systems that adopt commercially published programs go beyond the given scope and sequence chart to develop their own curriculum guides. Those guides may, in fact, be utilized when new materials are considered for adoption. Such guides may also include statements of behavioral objectives for grade levels and/or skills check lists. Other schools or school systems may not adopt or prescribe the printed materials to be used, may or may not have developed a curriculum guide, and may expect classroom teachers to plan and present learning experiences that are appropriate for the children they teach. Those learning experiences are expected to fit into a loosely defined program scheme. Unfortunately, the materials available for defining the total scope of the program are not always perused, and/or the needs and ability levels of children in a classroom are not always analyzed. The learning opportunities presented to children in a classroom may become fragments of content, skills, or tasks that may or may not be related to the general goals of the total program.

Definition by General Goals

General goals of a total program may be used to define the scope of the elementary mathematics program. Those general goals describe areas of content to be included, concepts to be developed, and skills to be practiced toward mastery during children's participation in the program. Because of what is known about how children differ, not one of those general goals can be applied as a specific goal for any large group of children of any particular age or grade level at any one time. It is the classroom teacher's professional responsibility to select and adapt specific goals for individual children in accordance with each child's ability and learning characteristics. Each specific goal must be relevant to the general goals or scope of the program.

The scope of the elementary mathematics program should include the development and study of the main ideas of the real number system, geometry, and algebraic foundations. Children are expected to become familiar with those main ideas and acquire the performance skills associated with them. It is the inclusion of additional content dealing with the real number system and major ideas and skills pertaining to geometry and algebraic foundations that extends the scope of the program beyond the mere study of arithmetic to the study of elementary mathematics. A well-planned, well-developed, and properly presented program relates the concepts and skills that are dealt with in the study of the real number system, geometry, and algebraic foundations. Concepts and skills from each area will be needed or can be utilized when other topics are being emphasized in a parallel, integrated development of concepts and skills.

To better define the scope of the elementary mathematics program, one must attempt to answer the following questions:

1. What is meant by the real number system? geometry? algebraic foundations?

2. What are the main ideas of the real number system? geometry? algebraic foundations?
3. What does familiarity with the main ideas of the real number system, geometry, and algebraic foundations entail?

The Real Number System

The *real number system* comprises those sets or subsets of numerals that are used to describe numbers or quantities or the lack of quantities in realistic or common situations. The complexities of the numerals to be used depends on the maturity of the user, the size of the number or quantity to be described, and the nature of the problem in which a quantity is to be named or renamed. Some confusion may exist for the learner when it is stated that the system comprises numerals and names for numbers and that the sets or subsets of the system are called sets of numbers. Number has been defined by some as an abstraction, but for children in the elementary school, numbers of things are real, and those quantities need to be described. The symbols, both oral and written, used to describe the amount or sizes of quantities are numerals.

Entities of the System

In formal or adult presentations, a Venn diagram is often used to picture the set of real numbers. To help clarify Figure 1.1, definitions, descriptions, and examples of the elements or types of numerals in each subset are also given.

The entities of the real number system are the members or elements of these sets or subsets of numerals. The *nonnegative integers* (A) are the number names used to count objects; in other words, the whole numbers including zero, $\{0, 1, 2, 3, \ldots\}$. The same subset could be defined as the positive integers plus zero. For every positive integer, there is a corresponding negative integer (B), $\{\ldots, -3, -2, -1\}$. The combination or union of those two subsets is the set of all *integers* (C), $\{\ldots, -3, -2, -1, 0, 1, 2, 3, \ldots\}$.

A *rational number* is a number that can be written or described in the form a/b where a and b are integers with one condition:

Figure 1.1 *The Set of Real Numbers*

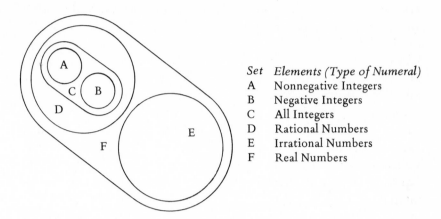

Set	Elements (Type of Numeral)
A	Nonnegative Integers
B	Negative Integers
C	All Integers
D	Rational Numbers
E	Irrational Numbers
F	Real Numbers

b cannot be equal to zero. Rational numbers may be either positive or negative, and they may be less than, equal to, or greater than one. When a rational number that has been written in the form a/b is converted to a decimal fraction, one of two types of decimal fractions emerge. Either the conversion results in a terminating decimal fraction (the quotient of the division operation "comes out even or exact"), or the conversion results in a decimal fraction in which a series of quotient digits repeats in a pattern. Common fractions (which are rational numbers) with denominators of 2, 4, 5, 8, and 10 and all rational numbers whose denominator is a factor of a power of 10 will result in a terminating decimal fraction when the conversion is performed. Since there are many ways to express each of the integers as a rational number in the form a/b, the integers are also rational numbers (for example: $2 = 2/1, 4/2, 8/4, -6/-3$, and so forth). Thus, the set of integers is a subset of the set of rational numbers. When other common fractions are converted to decimal fraction form, a sequence of repeating digits emerges in the decimal fraction. This repeating sequence is easily observed when renaming or converting fractions with denominators of 3, 6, 9, and 11, but persistence in carrying out the division operation is needed to find the repeating sequence when the denominators are 7, 13, or other larger numbers. In notation, one way to indicate the repeating sequence of digits is to overline the repeating sequence (see marginal examples).

$$\frac{1}{6} = 0.1\overline{6} \qquad \frac{5}{6} = 0.8\overline{3}$$

$$\frac{1}{3} = 0.\overline{3} \qquad \frac{2}{3} = 0.\overline{6}$$

$$\frac{1}{9} = 0.\overline{1} \qquad \frac{3}{11} = 0.\overline{27}$$

$$\frac{1}{7} = 0.\overline{142857}$$

Irrational numbers are those numbers that cannot be expressed in the form a/b, $b = 0$. Therefore, irrational numbers are neither terminating nor repeating decimal fractions. Perhaps the more commonly used irrational numbers are π, $\sqrt{2}$, and $\sqrt{3}$. However, irrational numbers can be constructed by merely writing a decimal fraction that neither terminates nor has an ending sequence of repeating digits. There is a pattern in the marginal examples, but not a series of repeating digits. Procedures for dealing with irrational numbers in problem solving or in computational operations are similar to those employed when repeating decimal fractions (rational numbers) or rather long terminating decimal fractions are involved. The numeral is simply rounded off to the required number of decimal places and the problem solved or computation performed with the realization that the resulting answer is not exact. The combination or union of the set of rational numbers and the set of irrational numbers results in the set of real numbers.

0.1234567891011...
0.246810121416...
0.13579111315...

Main Ideas of the System

The main ideas of the real number system involve the elements of the subsets, patterns among the numerals used in describing numbers, and solving problems involving number. Those main ideas are more specifically defined and described in Chapters 7, 8, and 9. The premises are that those main ideas are consistent throughout the study of the real number system regardless of the type of numerals being studied or used and that those main ideas are the content themes of the part of the elementary mathematics program that pertains to the study of the real number system. Learning opportunities or experiences for children and the intended acquisition of concepts and skills are developed around, directed toward, and consistent with those major ideas.

Familiarity with Ideas

Familiarity with the main ideas of the real number system might be best defined in terms of performance skills: the applications of information, ideas, and arithmetical capabilities to problem situations. A child who is familiar with any of the subsets of the sets of numbers previously described would be able to name and rename numbers or quantities utilizing the members or elements of that subset, solve problems involving the number elements of that set, and verify in an appropriate manner the solutions to those problems.

Such familiarity cannot be achieved without emphasis on developing vocabulary and establishing facts, rules, and generalizations. The extent to which familiarity is attained by children at any age, grade, or capability level depends on the complexity of the numerals used to describe the numbers that are being studied. In every instance, regardless of the complexity of the numerals, the major ideas inherent in the set of real numbers will apply. Performance skills and familiarity are extended as the complexity of the numerals increases and as different types or subsets of numbers are introduced and developed.

Geometry

Geometry may be defined as the study of points in space and subsets of points in space. Under that definition, the entities of geometry (points and subsets of points in space) must be considered abstractions because points and subsets of points cannot be seen. Since children at the elementary school level learn best by seeing real things and by manipulating real things, teachers must attempt to make those entities real and seeable through the use of physical object models. The main ideas of geometry pertain to relationships that may exist between geometric entities. An elementary familiarity with those ideas can be introduced and developed through the use of common objects as models for geometric entities.

Entities of Geometry

The entities of geometry (Figure 1.2) may be classified as nondimensional, one-dimensional, two-dimensional, or three-dimensional. Individual points are, of course, nondimensional as they

Figure 1.2 *Drawings of the Entities of Geometry*

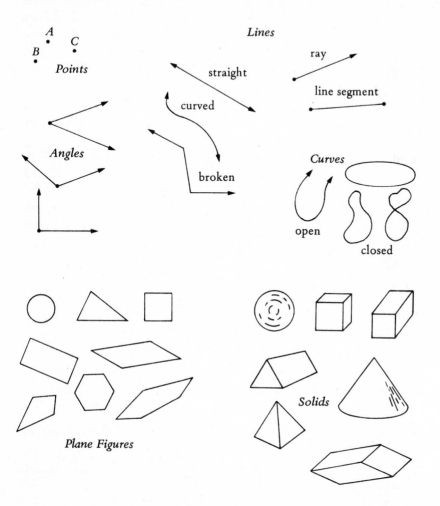

have no length, width, or depth. Each point has only a position, which can be defined or described. Lines and portions of lines (rays and line segments) have only one dimension, length. By a stretch of the imagination, a line or portion of a line may be thought of as the union of a subset of points in which each point touches only two other points. The imagination is necessary because points have no dimensions, no length. Sometimes lines are described as curves. Portions of lines (rays and line segments) are used to imagine, construct, or visualize those geometric entities known as angles and the two-dimensional entities, which are called plane figures (circles, triangles, quadrilaterals, and other polygons). While other more definitive terms may be used, the two general terms for the two dimensions of plane figures are length and width. Plane figures exist in a plane and comprise only the points in or on the line segments that make up the figure. Points outside the plane in which the figure exists are not a part of the entity, and points in the same plane that are inside or outside the figure are not a part of the entity. The three-dimensional entities, solids, can also be thought of as the union of a subset of points with the general dimensions of length, width, and depth or height.

Main Ideas of Geometry

The main ideas of geometry to be introduced and developed in the elementary mathematics program pertain to the characteristics of the entities and the patterns and relationships among those entities. In the language of mathematicians and teachers, but not necessarily the language of children in the program, those major ideas include the concepts of congruence, similarity, symmetry, perpendicularity, and parallelism. Recognition of the entities and specific vocabulary terms are needed if teachers and children are to communicate about the geometric entities and to introduce and develop concepts and skills related to these major ideas; however, recognition and vocabulary skills should not be viewed as the extent of the geometry content at any level of the elementary program. The major ideas of congruence, similarity, symmetry, perpendicularity, and parallelism are further described in Chapter 10. The premise is that these major ideas are content or concept themes that are to prevail throughout the span of the elementary mathematics program and that will be further developed at later levels. Preliminary learning experiences should be planned and presented with these major ideas in mind.

Familiarity with Ideas

The degree of familiarity with the main ideas of geometry may be described in terms of the performance skills that have been acquired or mastered. Mastery of a skill implies successful application of that skill in a problem-centered situation. The simplest performance skills in the area of geometry involve recognizing, describing, naming, and classifying geometric entities. These tasks involve only descriptive communication or vocabulary skills. More complex performance skills require knowledge of geometric relationships and entail comparison skills, construction skills, and abilities to solve problems involving geometric entities. In order to help children develop familiarity with the main ideas of geometry, teachers must present learning opportunities and experiences that involve recognition and vocabulary study, exercises in classification of geometric entities, comparisons of geometric entities from within the same classification, construction activities, and the solution of problems that do and do not include number concepts.

Algebraic Foundations

Algebra may be defined as the mathematical reasoning necessary to solve generalized arithmetical problems or to simplify quantitative relationships by means of a systematized notation including letters and other symbols. Algebra is the study of mathematical expressions, expressions that are descriptions of quantitative relationships. In most instances, the quantitative relationships are stated as *equations*, which are statements of equality or equivalence between two quantitative expressions. In other instances, the relationships are stated as *inequalities*, statements of inequality or nonequivalence between two quantitative expressions. The tasks of algebra require using the basic ideas of arithmetic in analyzing these statements, simplifying the statements, finding one or more solutions for the unknowns or variables in the statements, and solving problems through a process of establishing an equation or expression and solving for the unknowns in the problem.

The foundations of algebra that may be developed more fully in the elementary mathematics program include establishing or describing quantitative relationships in an arithmetical or number sentence form, analyzing those statements, renaming the quantitative expressions by performing indicated operations, simplifying statements, and finding one or more solutions for any unknown in the statement. If developing problem-solving skills is to be a major objective of the elementary mathematics program, those statements should be developed or established from arithmetical problem situations. Learning experiences directed toward the acquisition of algebraic foundations should involve both the development of understanding of problem situations and the development of communication skills in using mathematical symbolism.

The entities of algebraic foundations are the printed symbols utilized in writing quantitative expressions, equations, or number sentences. Since (1) children cannot reasonably be expected to write what they cannot read, (2) children cannot be expected to read what they cannot say, and (3) children cannot be expected to say what they have not heard, the natural development of vocabularies proceeds from listening to speaking to reading to writing. The initial work and study of quantitative expressions must be in the form of oral communication about real problem situations. Only after children can orally describe the quantitative situation should they encounter or be expected to read even the simplest of number sentences.

The types of symbols that children will encounter in quantitative expressions may be classified as quantitative, comparative, operational, and descriptive symbols. (When children are writing statements about geometry, they may also use relational symbols: $\overline{AB} \perp \overline{CD}$; $\overline{EF} \parallel \overline{GH}$.)

When one looks at these symbols, one sees that few if any are new to the language of elementary school mathematics. The point to be made is that the symbolism used in elementary mathematics programs could be made much more meaningful and useful for children.

Examples of Symbols in Algebraic Foundations

Type of Symbol	Examples
Quantitative	$3, 14, \frac{1}{2}, 0.56, 4.3, N, a/b, \pi, \Box$
Comparative	$=, \neq, >, <$
Operational	$+, -, \times, a \cdot b, (a)(b), \div, \sqrt{}, a/b$
Descriptive	$\%, \$, ', '', °, \mathrm{cm}, \mathrm{m}$

Main Ideas of Algebraic Foundations

The main ideas of algebraic foundations are achievement expectations in many elementary programs today. Those expectations include developing familiarity with the nature of equality, inequality, comparisons involving greater than and less than, equivalence, and nonequivalence. However, many classroom elementary mathematics programs do not take advantage of the possibilities for developing firmer foundations for algebra through the arithmetical uses of number sentences in describing and solving problem situations. Number sentences may be open or closed. If closed, they must be analyzed to ascertain whether they are true or false. If open, some type of solution or response is usually required.

Solving number sentences for unknown quantities should involve understandable generalizations rather than rules that have been rotely memorized. Developing understandable generalizations will incorporate the properties of number in operations. These are the same properties used in algebra: the commutative property, associative property, distributive property, identity elements, additive and multiplicative inverses, and inverse operations as they pertain to both addition and multiplication. These ideas are further described in Chapter 9. Developing understandable generalizations for solving for unknowns in number sentences or equations will also involve utilizing procedures similar to those used in solving algebraic expressions: adding or subtracting the same quantitative amount to both of the quantitative expressions that have been described as equal and multiplying or dividing both of the quantitatively equal expressions by the same quantitative amount.

Familiarity with Algebraic Foundations

Familiarity with the main ideas of algebraic foundations is best defined in terms of the performance skills that children can apply to describing problem situations with number sentences or equations and to the skills that they can apply to finding solutions for the unknowns in those expressions. In order to achieve these skill expectations, appropriate symbolism must be introduced and utilized with arithmetical problem situations at all levels. Procedures for solving problems can be meaningfully developed through the use of physical object models for the quantities described in the problems.

Program Scope and Learning Experiences

The scope of the elementary mathematics program described in this chapter is directed toward developing basic mathematical concepts and skills. The task of each classroom teacher is to incorporate into the program at his or her particular level learning opportunities and experiences that include main ideas of the real number system, geometry, and algebraic foundations. The learning experiences should have a breadth and depth in accordance with the scope of the total program and should be appropriate to the maturity and performance level of the individual children in that classroom. This is a difficult professional responsibility and requires teachers to know not only the characteristics of the children in the classroom but also sources and resources for appropriate learning experiences.

Analyzing Existing Programs Chapter 2

The theme of this text, as implied by the title, is that pupil participation in active laboratory-type learning experiences will be more conducive to overall achievement in elementary mathematics than will participation in more passive learning activities. The degree of activeness in learning opportunities involves the processes of learning experiences as well as the amount of time that children spend on various kinds of tasks. In passive learning activities, children listen to explanations, watch demonstrations, and complete pages of exercises or examples. The learning experiences of children in an active program should be quite different from those in a program dominated by teacher explanations and demonstrations and by printed materials.

One great difference between passive and active learning experiences is in the type and amount of materials used and the frequency with which they are handled by children. In passive programs, children primarily utilize reading and writing materials. Instructional aids may be used briefly when introducing or demonstrating an idea, when children are having difficulty with memory or rules to be applied, or to sweeten the taste of mathematics classes. When aids or physical materials are used, they are often viewed as a crutch by the teacher and, thus, dutifully avoided by children. Children's interactions with exploratory manipulative materials are brief and sporadic, while their interactions with printed, stimulus-response, abstract drill, and practice materials are intense and continuous.

An active laboratory approach to instruction requires a broader spectrum of materials and a different style of utilization. The foundation of a laboratory-type program lies in the continuous use of and reference to concrete materials, which serve as physical models for mathematical ideas. Each physical model has the characteristics of the mathematical idea it is being used to introduce and develop. Manipulation of the model serves as a vehicle for the child's early verification procedures. Other instructional aids or materials are used only after children can handle the ideas effectively with models. Practice of ideas occurs with pupil record keeping while using models and other manipulative materials, applications through pupil-made projects, and games involving the ideas to be practiced. Problem and exercise worksheets are used for evaluative purposes. Mathematics books and other descriptive explanatory materials are used as reference and resource aids.

Instruction is highly individualized in an active laboratory approach, with learning experiences selected for and directed toward achieving specific objectives with individuals or small groups of children. Teachers of elementary mathematics who wish to use an active laboratory approach must collect, develop, and modify possible learning opportunities dealing with the mathematical content to be introduced and developed and appropriate for the variety of learners in the classroom. *Active Learning Experiences for Teaching Elementary School Mathematics,* a teacher's handbook published in tandem with this text, is intended to help teachers with these tasks.

Teachers as Program Modifiers or Developers

A major underlying premise of this text is that beginning teachers immediately become involved in modifying or developing the classroom elementary mathematics program toward their own beliefs and perspectives and that experienced teachers have been and will continue to be involved in this professional activity. When new teachers accept responsibilities for classroom programs, they find what is called an elementary mathematics program already on the scene. There are generally materials on hand that the teacher is expected to use, experienced teachers in adjacent classrooms or who are teaching at earlier or later age or grade levels may try to explain the details of the program, and some evaluative procedures such as the use of standardized tests will have been established. The existence of that program, however detailed or vague it might be, is accompanied by a variety of expectations on the parts of fellow teachers, administrators, children, parents, and perhaps others in regard to the program and teaching procedures.

The preservice training and the continuing professional education of teachers include study of learning theories, child development, the mathematical content of the elementary program, and suggested methods of teaching that content to children. Therefore, it is not unusual for both beginning teachers and experienced teachers to become dissatisfied with those aspects of the program that conflict with their own beliefs about elementary mathematics, materials to be used in the instructional processes, children and how children learn, or teaching procedures. When dissatisfactions or conflicts occur, teachers are likely to attempt to modify programs.

The experienced teacher has had informal opportunities to analyze or evaluate the elementary mathematics programs in the schools or classrooms where they have taught. The experienced teacher may also have served on a mathematics curriculum committee looking into the possibility of instituting program changes. It would be most unusual for an experienced teacher not to have personally changed in some way either the mathematical content or an instructional approach in a particular classroom. Through their teaching experiences, they have expanded their knowledge and understanding of children and the learning process; the content of elementary mathematics; the nature, extent, and uses of available materials; the possible difficulties that children might encounter; and alternative approaches. As they acquire further knowledge and understanding, teachers will generally attempt to change materials, approaches, and procedures and, perhaps, even the content to be studied by children.

Classroom teachers, both new and experienced, are the planners and presenters of children s learning opportunities or experiences in elementary mathematics programs. One must encourage and applaud their attempts to make improvements that are directed toward helping children learn. It is the responsibility of supervisors, administrators, consultants, and mathematics educators to assist classroom teachers in these endeavors. Such assistance might well begin with a thorough analysis of the existing program.

Reasons for Program Analysis

The process of analyzing the elementary mathematics program should be continuously employed as part of the curriculum evaluation endeavors of schools and school systems. Contemplation of curricular improvements or program changes begins with an analysis of the existing program. In order to gather useful information for making decisions about possible curriculum or program modifications, the process should not be limited to systemwide or school-building efforts but should extend to particular ages or grade levels and to individual classroom programs. A thorough analysis of the program must involve those closest to the instructional program—the teachers who are responsible for delivering learning opportunities or experiences to children. It is the classroom teacher who puts program changes into classroom situations. Outside evaluators, consultants, program supervisors, school system and building administrators, special committees, and other teachers may be involved, but the most pertinent information and most useful insights will come from the classroom teachers of elementary mathematics.

There are several major reasons for suggesting that both beginning and experienced teachers would need or want to analyze the existing elementary mathematics program in the classrooms and schools in which they are teaching. Analysis of the program will at least make the classroom teacher aware of the concepts and skills that should be introduced to a majority of children at a particular level. Analysis of the program will also make teachers aware of the concepts, ideas, and skills that have already been introduced and developed with these children and with the instructional approaches that were used in those endeavors. Teachers can use this information when they are working with children who have not achieved as expected. It will help teachers decide whether the unacquired content and skills should be retaught in the same manner using the same materials or whether different approaches with the same or different content might be more effective. In the same vein, analysis of the program will reveal some information about appropriate directions and learning experiences for the more talented children.

The insights and information acquired in the process of analysis will help teachers to plan, prepare, and present classroom learning experiences that are consistent with total program descriptions and efforts. For example, if one type of material or one approach to a particular topic of content is emphasized at other age or grade levels, that material or approach can be utilized, at least in part, with the children in the concerned teacher's classroom. If materials or approaches that appear to children to be different were employed and the materials and approaches utilized at other levels ignored, some children surely would become sufficiently confused for learning difficulties to arise. The use of only one kind of material or only one instructional approach to particular topics is not being advocated in this text. Quite the contrary is true. It will be suggested that teachers use what they learn from analyzing the program to plan and present active laboratory-type learning experiences in which children use a variety of materials and activities to practice and apply ideas and skills. Nevertheless, if a particular type of material and/or a particular approach is being utilized heavily in other classrooms at other levels, that material and/or approach should at least constitute a part of more varied learning activities or experiences in successive classrooms. If that particular material and/or approach is incorporated into the classroom program, children are less likely to experience confusion and difficulty at the current level or at later levels or to see one topic of content as two or more completely different learning tasks.

Analyzing an existing program involves identifying the components of the program and establishing the roles and interrelationships of those components. Ascertaining the influential characteristics of the program allows those conducting the analysis not only to classify the program in terms of an identifiable category or general type but also to isolate those characteristics that are desirable and those that are undesirable. Each characteristic can be considered in relation to the philosophy of the school system, school, or classroom teacher. In addition, analysis of the program will bring to light the nature of the satisfactions, dissatisfactions, and problems with the program of those responsible for planning and presenting the learning activities and of the parents and others who are interested in school programs and products.

Program Components and Factors

The nature of the components and factors that influence the total school or classroom programs of elementary mathematics are so interrelated that it is difficult to approach them in the same way. However, it is possible to outline the categories of concern to be emphasized in the process and to center thoughts and discussions on one of those categories. As ideas or comments that actually pertain to another category emerge, those thoughts or ideas may be noted or recorded under the appropriate headings. For example, if statements of problems or dissatisfactions with the program emerge during a discussion of components and influential factors of the program, those statements can be recorded for the purposes of follow-up and further consideration. The process of analyzing the program should proceed from gathering information, identifying facts, and ascertaining ideas and feelings about the program to considering interrelationships among the various factors and observations.

Identifying program components and factors may be the most logical initial activity of the analysis process. This information can be easily obtained, and initial consideration of those factors may stimulate lively participation, which leads to a better identification of ideas to be examined in the other analysis tasks. When attempts are being made to identify program components or influential factors, it will be virtually impossible to avoid discussing the extent of their existence, their nature, and their relationships to each other. Program components or influential factors to be considered in the process of analysis should include the mathematical content of the program, the materials used, the personnel involved, the established organization for instruction, the instructional techniques employed, and the evaluation procedures used. School systems, schools, or individual classroom teachers may wish to extend these subcategories to include other components or influential factors.

The approach here will be to list subcategories and to cite several exemplary questions under each. These subcategories and questions may be used to analyze a total school program or a particular classroom program. Those involved in the process of analysis may find it desirable to list other questions in order to gather additional pertinent information.

Mathematical Content

Does the scope of the program include development of familiarity with the main ideas of the real number system, geometry, and algebraic foundations?

Is emphasis placed on helping children acquire the basic concepts and skills of elementary mathematics or on coverage of the content? What are those basic concepts and skills?

Does a scope and sequence chart accompanying a commercially produced program currently in use prescribe and define content to be dealt with at particular age or grade levels? To what extent is the prescription followed?

Has the school or school system developed a curriculum guide for the elementary mathematics program? To what extent is the curriculum guide available or consulted? To what extent does it prescribe or define the content that is to be covered at particular age or grade levels of children?

What mathematical content should be added to the program? At what levels or stages should it be added?

What mathematical content, tasks, or aspects of content should be deleted from the program?

What is the nature of the sequencing of content? Is this sequencing based on children's acquisition of true prerequisites?

Is content sacred to grade or age levels of children? Or, is content adjusted to the maturity and capabilities of potential learners?

Instructional Materials

What printed commercially produced instructional materials are available for use by children? To what extent are these materials appropriate? To what extent are they used? What supplementary printed materials are available?

What printed commercially produced materials are available to assist teachers in planning and presenting learning opportunities for children?

What facilities are available for teachers and other staff to produce instructional materials? Are these facilities limited to reproducing worksheet-type materials?

What physical object models for mathematical ideas are present in the school? To what extent are these models available for use in each classroom?

What pictorial manipulative materials are present in the school? To what extent are they available for use by children and teachers in the classrooms?

Are different types of materials available in sufficient quantities?

Personnel

Who are the professional educators involved in the development and presentation of the program?

What roles do administrators, supervisors, consultants, master teachers, special teachers, and teacher teams or teacher committees play in the program?

Are the responsibilities of the classroom teacher clearly defined or specified?

To what extent do lay committees or groups and parents influence the program?

Do teacher aides or volunteers participate in the program? What is the nature of their participation?

Organization for Instruction

How is the school organized to facilitate instruction in elementary mathematics? Does a departmentalized approach with a special teacher for mathematics exist? Is a team-teaching approach utilized? Do children move from classroom to classroom in interclass groupings by ability levels? Is each classroom teacher responsible for the mathematics instruction of the children in his or her homeroom?

How is each classroom organized to facilitate children's learning in elementary mathematics? Is the total class treated as one instructional unit, with similar assignments, tasks, and expectations for every child? Does some type of intra- or within-class ability grouping exist? Is the program highly individualized, and if so, in what manner?

Are supplementary materials, physical object models, and pictorial manipulatives easily accessible to children?

What organizational arrangements are made to adjust instruction to pupil differences?

Instructional Techniques

What instructional techniques or procedures are suggested by any printed commercially produced materials in use?

What instructional techniques or procedures are suggested by any curriculum guides produced by the school or school system?

What instructional techniques or procedures are advocated by the administrators, consultants, and supervisors of programs in the school system?

What instructional approach dominates each classroom program? Do printed materials dominate the program? Is the approach one in which the teacher shows and tells and children are expected to reproduce similar actions? How are teaching-learning aids and supplementary materials utilized? To what extent are children allowed to assist each other in the learning process?

Evaluation Procedures

How is the total school program evaluated? Have principles and objectives by which the program can be judged been established?

How is each classroom program evaluated? Have principles and objectives by which the program can be judged been established?

Are the programs, both total school and classroom, evaluated on both general objectives for the program and specific objectives for individuals or small groups of children?

What role does the standardized testing program play in the evaluation process? Are criterion-referenced tests used? If so, in what way?

Do skills check lists exist, and if so, how accurate are they and how are they used?

Are children's attitudes toward mathematics and the study of mathematics considered in the evaluation process?

Is each child's achievement evaluated in a manner that will assist teachers in planning and directing future learning opportunities and experiences? Is that evaluation a continuous process?

Contemplating Total Program Modification

Changes suggested by program evaluators are most likely to be directed toward improving children's attitudes toward mathematics and the study of mathematics and toward increasing children's understanding and knowledge of mathematical concepts and skills. The suggested means of attaining these general objectives will be directed toward helping classroom teachers plan, select, conduct, and evaluate learning opportunities and experiences for children. Perhaps the most difficult task in the process of analyzing an existing program is to turn observed or felt problems and expressed dissatisfactions into positive new directions. It is toward these ends that an active laboratory-type approach to elementary mathematics learning and instruction is suggested.

Evaluators of a particular program will probably find that the mathematical content outlined or prescribed for that program is quite similar to the content expectations of most elementary mathematics programs. Their particular concerns and suggestions must be directed at the completeness and appropriateness of content expectations for children. They must determine when specific content topics are introduced and developed, when those specific content topics are related to and used in conjunction with other content topics, and whether the program objective appears to be general coverage of the content topics rather than the achievement and growth of individual children.

Although a variety of instructional materials are utilized in almost all elementary mathematics programs, some programs can be adequately described by simply referring to the single type of instructional materials that prescribe, dominate, and influence content, sequencing of content, and instructional procedures. Classifying a program in terms of an identifiable category or general type based on the dominance of particular materials is important only insofar as the materials and instructional procedures employed are in accord with the prevailing philosophies and influence the attainment of program objectives. A large majority of elementary mathematics programs employ selected pupil textbooks and/or workbooks for each grade level. In some instances, school or teacher dependence on these textbook programs means that coverage of the materials is the major objective, a classroom of children is treated as one instructional unit with the same assignments and achievement expectations for all, and teachers conduct primarily passive learning experiences for children. Some schools and classrooms depend on the use of sequential dittoed or printed worksheets in a similar manner with similar negative results. When recommending changes, program analyzers should not be as concerned with the presence of these printed materials as with dependence on or uses of them. Specific suggestions can be made for the use of these materials in conjunction with active laboratory-type materials and approaches. Teachers' manuals for textbook series can be used as resource books for instructional sequences and activities. Texts can be used by children as reference books after mathematical ideas have been introduced with laboratory-type materials and can be used with workbooks and worksheets as sources of practice exercises and tests.

Contemplating and suggesting program modifications of instructional procedures require consideration of other factors, including the prevailing organization for instruction, the nature and availability of needed instructional materials, and the uses of appropriate evaluation techniques. The belief that children learn best through active participation in learning experiences might give rise to the suggestion that children should see and handle concrete objects and other manipulative materials in active learning experiences. This suggestion implies that children work and study in small groups or as individuals, that sufficient appropriate materials are available and used in directed activities, and that evaluation procedures include teacher observation of children's successes with processes, procedures, and skills involved in the activities. It might be suggested that an organization that attends to small-group or individualized rather than total class instruction should be used to provide for individual pupil characteristics, differences, and difficulties in regard to growth and achievement in elementary mathematics. This implies that learning activities and tasks appropriate to the abilities of individual children will be within the repertoire of the teacher and will be carefully selected for particular children, that the materials necessary for these activities will be readily available to the teacher, and that the evaluation procedures will be as individualized as the instructional procedures. Other suggested modifications pertaining to instructional procedures will also have related implications for change.

Immediate Classroom Concerns

Individual classroom teachers may not want to wait for the suggestions resulting from a process of total program analysis to initiate program changes. Their dissatisfactions or felt problems are immediate and pressing, and their concerns are for specific children. They may feel that the materials, content expectations, and suggested instructional procedures of the existing program are not in agreement with their educational philosophies or are inappropriate for the abilities and interests of their pupils. In such instances, classroom teachers need not and usually do not delay considering and implementing classroom program analysis and modifications.

Program analysis within the classroom is less comprehensive and formal, but more specific, than analysis of the total school program. The specificity focuses on at least two related concerns: concern for the growth and development of selected children and concern for better ways of presenting the generally prescribed content topics for that particular age or grade level. Concerns for the growth and development of selected children may involve attempts to alleviate the problems of children who are having difficulties or attempts to expand or extend learning activities for children who appear to excel. In either case, an analysis of children's understanding and abilities and the selection of appropriate learning experiences is required. A desire for greater pupil achievement may involve a search for alternative materials and instructional procedures. Selecting potentially effective alternatives requires analysis of the mathematical ideas and skills that are both prerequisites to and inherent in the content topic to be undertaken; consideration of the materials that can best be used to help children see, understand, and apply the concepts to be utilized; consideration of the materials that can best be used to allow children to practice applying the skills to be acquired; and consideration of possible learning opportunities and experiences for children.

Classroom teachers are encouraged to direct program modifications toward an active laboratory-type instructional approach. Although these changes should be well planned and deliberate, it is not necessary to plan the complete program before initiating some changes. Some teachers may find that the first logical step is to begin using some laboratory-type learning experiences with their current program, incorporating laboratory activities into the textual program. Others may first use such activities with selected children for specific corrective or developmental purposes. Others may develop a unit of study in a content topic that entirely comprises active laboratory learning experiences and interject that unit into the program. As further units of study are developed, as greater collections or resources of laboratory learning experiences are acquired, more and more of the total classroom program can be modified toward an active laboratory approach.

Characteristics of an Active Laboratory Approach

Either the departmentalized elementary mathematics classroom or the self-contained elementary classroom can be the scene of an active elementary mathematics program. However, certain aspects of planning, provision, management, and operation must be considered.

Use of Models

Laboratory-type learning experiences are grounded in the use of physical object models for mathematical ideas. Models for whole numbers (chips or counters, ice cream sticks, base-ten blocks), models for common fractions (fraction pies and fraction squares), and models for decimal fractions (base-ten blocks and squared paper) are used to introduce and develop concepts and skills of naming and communicating about numbers; to illustrate problem situations and solutions to problems, including writing number sentences; and to develop meaning of the operations with numbers. Models for geometric entities are used to acquire knowledge and skills pertaining to the nature and characteristics of geometric entities and the relationships that exist within and among those entities. In other words, physical object models are used to help children become familiar with the main ideas of the real number system, geometry, and algebraic foundations.

Individual or Small-Group Activities

Learning experiences in a laboratory-type program are organized as individual or small-group activities. In this manner, learning activities can be better selected for and adjusted to differences in children's maturities, learning characteristics, and ability levels. Individuals and small groups of children are directed toward learning activities that require active participation and toward generating their own problems involving facts, operations, or observations.

Inquiry-Oriented or Problem-Centered Learning Experiences

Introductory and developmental learning experiences in a laboratory approach are inquiry oriented and problem centered. There is a concern for developing major ideas, concepts, and generalizations in a meaningful manner so that children can utilize them in real problem situations rather than merely repeat terms and definitions in a rote manner. This concern goes beyond practicing skills and technical operations via tables and memorized rules with page after page of abstract materials. Inquiry-oriented and problem-centered learning experiences that are used to introduce or develop ideas, concepts, and generalizations as well as to establish facts and operations involve data or information collection, data organization, and a search for patterns on the parts of children. Record keeping of observed phenomena associated with the use of physical object models is a crucial aspect of the program.

Sequencing Experiences

Learning experiences in a laboratory-type program are sequenced so that the practice of skills or ideas is built on, related to, and comes after the introduction and development of major ideas, concepts, and generalizations. Initial learning activities in a content topic will involve few if any writing and reading tasks, either informative or directive. The acquisition of mathematical knowledge and skills does not depend on previously acquired reading skills. Only after children understand a process involving ideas, concepts, and generalizations and can demonstrate that process or idea through the manipulation of a physical object model are they asked to develop further aspects of the ideas, facts, or skills related to or inherent in a particular content topic. Initial practice activities greatly resemble introductory and developmental learning experiences. Later practice activities may not utilize physical object models but will utilize more abstract pictorial manipulative materials in ways that are meaningful and useful to the child. Even in the later practice stages, the physical object models are available for verification purposes. Many of the later practice activities are in the form of games that children are capable of playing and appear to enjoy.

Printed Materials

A laboratory-type program requires that a significant number of physical object models and pictorial manipulatives be available for use by children. Laboratory-type programs are not dominated by the printed pages of textbooks, workbooks, activity cards, or worksheets. Such materials do not define or delineate the content or prescribe the instructional approaches to that content. Topics of content are not sacred to age or grade level, and a variety of instructional approaches to one content topic are used. When printed pages, textual or worksheet, are used, they are used for purposes of evaluation. Based on the belief that children can only write what they know, such pages are used primarily to ascertain whether children have mastered the concepts and skills necessary to respond correctly to the abstract exercises.

Available Learning Activities

Another requirement for a laboratory-type program is that the teacher have a large collection of laboratory-type learning experiences available. Provision must be made in all content areas for children of different ability levels who may learn best in different ways.

Pupil Evaluation

Evaluation of individual pupil growth or achievement is based on information obtained in several ways. The major purpose of evaluation is to select and direct the future learning experiences of children. The teacher's unobtrusive observations of children in the act of working on laboratory-type learning activities, children's oral responses to questions about their procedures, the verification processes they use when challenged, anecdotal records of their performances, records of the activities in which they have participated well and accurately, check lists of skills acquired, and projects they have made—all contribute to the evaluative effort as significantly as the children's performance on worksheets. Continuous evaluation of pupil performance is a major responsibility of teachers in this type of program. Prior to classroom action, the teacher's role is one of planning, preparing, collecting, and selecting laboratory-type learning experiences appropriate to the varying capabilities of the children in the class. In action, the teacher's role is to direct children to learning activities, guide and question their actions, and evaluate their performances.

An Active Program in Action

If one were to observe a good laboratory-type program in action, one would see individuals or small groups of children engaged in a variety of learning experiences. Depending on the content approach used by the teacher, all of the children might be working on different activities in the same content area at varying levels of difficulty or complexity with a variety of materials, or they might be working in different content areas with an even wider variety of materials. The teacher would be moving around the room questioning, guiding, or directing children in their activities. At first glance, the class might seem very disorganized and nonstructured, but longer, more careful observation will reveal that the classroom program has been well planned, is organized, and is indeed structured for individual achievement.

Chapter 3

Establishing Guiding Principles

Principles are basic beliefs that are held by individuals of all ages in all walks of life. Each of us has accepted beliefs pertaining to the various aspects of our lives, and these beliefs serve as the foundations or bases for our behaviors and actions. Beliefs about society, government, religion, family life, and other cultural considerations help us to make decisions or direct actions in most real life situations. In some instances, those beliefs are so strongly held that others, who also hold firm beliefs, cannot convince us to alter either our beliefs or our actions, which we base upon those beliefs. In other instances, beliefs have not been so firmly established and information is sought in different ways so that more intelligent or well-founded decisions can be made and actions performed.

Most adults would like to make their own decisions about potential actions in situations where possibilities have not been circumscribed by the laws of the society. When they are coerced into actions that are contrary to their own beliefs or principles or when they voluntarily or involuntarily perform actions that conflict with their beliefs or principles, they are likely to experience dissatisfaction, disgust, self-accusation, and general unhappiness. Dissonance between beliefs and behaviors or actions creates conflict within the individual. Yet, when we encounter others whose beliefs seem dissimilar or whose actions do not appear to be based on the beliefs that we hold to be true, each of us attempts to alter both their beliefs and their actions.

Presentation of learning opportunities for children and teaching-learning practices and procedures in every elementary mathematics program are influenced by the beliefs about children, elementary mathematics, teaching, and how children learn mathematical ideas held by the adults responsible for the conduct of the program. When the existing elementary mathematics program is being analyzed, beliefs about the components of the program are certain to emerge. These beliefs or principles should be recorded for further consideration. There will not be total agreement or even consensus among the analyzers in regard to all of the expressed beliefs about how the elementary mathematics program should be conducted. However, those beliefs or principles about which there is agreement or consensus can serve as foundations for suggesting or directing curricular modifications.

Uses of Principles

A belief about the nature of learners, content, teachers, or the possible relationships among learners, content, and teachers is an *educational principle* when it is used to guide or to govern the conduct or practices of an educational program. To be more specific, beliefs about children, the content of elementary mathematics, the roles of teachers and other personnel in elementary mathematics programs, the nature of the materials to be used in elementary mathematics programs, the kinds of learning opportunities or experiences that are appropriate for children, the techniques and procedures of instructional practices, the evaluative processes to be used, and any other aspects of the program become the principles of the elementary mathematics program. Once established, these principles can be used to direct and control the actions of the program, and it is against these principles that the total program or segments of the program can be evaluated. When actions or procedures in the program are in conflict with the established principles, either the principles or the actions should be modified.

Any attempt to modify an elementary mathematics program or to redirect the activities or procedures of a program should be based on principles that have been clearly established and stated.

Components and characteristics of the existing program should be considered in relation to the stated principles that are intended to define or govern programmatic efforts. Suggested modifications and current practices should be assessed for consistency with guiding principles. In some instances, it will be necessary to ask why certain components or characteristics of the program exist.

Principles and Program Procedures

Beginning teachers emerge from preservice training programs and enter teaching positions holding certain beliefs about how elementary mathematics should be taught to children and how they should conduct the elementary mathematics class. These beliefs may not be as firmly held as those of more experienced teachers and, thus, may be more susceptible to change. Beginning teachers may find that their set of beliefs or educational principles pertaining to helping children learn mathematics does not fully cover all of the situations that arise in their classrooms. Their beliefs about the conduct of the program may also be considered idealistic by other teachers who have been involved in the school program for some time. While beginning teachers may hold to those idealistic beliefs, they may encounter difficulties and opposition when trying to implement a program in accordance with those principles. Some beginning teachers may even find that their beliefs about conducting elementary mathematics programs are quite conservative in comparison to those of teachers in adjacent rooms who have made curricular modifications in the directions of an active laboratory approach. Some beginning teachers will find that they have not acquired the knowledge and teaching skills needed to conduct a program that is consistent with their beliefs or principles.

It is possible that experienced teachers have forgotten that they once held similar beliefs or that they, too, were once so unfamiliar with certain aspects of the elementary mathematics program. Many experienced teachers have altered their original beliefs or principles. Some beliefs may have been disregarded for so long that for all practical purposes, they are no longer a matter of consideration. Other principles have been established and adhered to. The directions that this development has taken will differ with the professional attitudes of individual teachers. Some teachers have been conducting one type of elementary mathematics program for so long that they no longer give much thought to the beliefs or principles that govern the program. Other principles or beliefs that are professed may be simply ignored in classroom practices.

When printed materials have been followed to the extent that those materials are the program, the principles and accompanying practices—or the principles implied by the instructional practices—become the guiding beliefs of the program. The program of instructional procedures is merely implemented in accord with the materials. Teachers may be dissatisfied with many aspects or components of the program, but they may continue to conduct that program while expressing those dissatisfactions.

Virtually every piece of professional literature dealing with elementary mathematics, this text included, contains explicit or implied principles to be applied to the instructional program. Obviously, the authors are attempting to convince readers to adopt their stated or implied beliefs and to guide or conduct elementary mathematics programs in accordance with those beliefs. Other materials dealing with elementary classroom organizations and programs also stress the importance of the personal and professional beliefs and values of classroom teachers. It is interesting to attempt to select or determine the principles being expounded in the professional literature and to debate the acceptability of those beliefs.

Ideally, teaching practices in every elementary mathematics classroom program should be guided in some manner by basic beliefs or principles about children and how they learn mathematical ideas that are held by a responsible teacher. The mathematics teacher in a self-contained classroom seeking to initiate an active laboratory-type program must develop individual beliefs or guiding educational principles and prospective practices consistent with those beliefs. While those beliefs may be similar to beliefs held by teachers who use other approaches, the techniques and practices applied may be quite different.

Statements of Principles for an Active Program

The following statements of beliefs are examples of educational principles that might be used to guide or to govern the teaching-learning activities of an active laboratory-type elementary mathematics program. Readers should consider these statements in relation to their own beliefs with the intention of accepting, modifying, or rejecting the statements as guiding educational principles. Some readers may want to include other statements of beliefs in their personal lists. However, care should be taken to make certain that accepted statements of educational principles are consistent in approach and do not contradict each other. Care also should be taken to keep personal lists of beliefs reasonably short. An analysis of statements on such a list may reveal that some of the beliefs are inherent or subsumed in broader statements and, thus, are not needed for either guidance, governance, or evaluation.

Some readers may wish to cite authoritative references to support their beliefs. While this endeavor may be more scholarly in approach, and while it may provide support in argumentative situations, it is not a prerequisite for future conduct of the elementary mathematics program. Other planners, developers, or presenters of elementary mathematics programs may want to classify or categorize statements of guiding principles as to whether they apply to the mathematics content of the elementary program, the nature of children in the program, the ways in which children learn elementary mathematics, the nature of the materials to be used in the program, instructional procedures that are to be utilized, or other categories. Categorization of guiding or governing principles may facilitate evaluation of the program, but striving to cite beliefs in pre-established categories also may deter program planning and development because efforts will be directed toward listing and perfecting principles rather than toward program improvement.

Perhaps the best approach for classroom teachers is to establish a few major beliefs and to consider the implications of those principles for the planning and presentation of learning experiences in the elementary mathematics program. Consider the following as guiding educational principles in regard to an active laboratory-type approach and how instructional practices and learning experiences for children might differ in other approaches. The list is intentionally short in order that a brief discussion of each belief will allow readers to expand certain ideas and develop others. However, commitment to these few guiding principles may be sufficient for initial program modifications toward an active elementary mathematics program.

Children differ in their intellectual abilities, their performance abilities, their interests, their rates of learning, and the ways in which they best learn.

This statement could, of course, comprise five distinct beliefs. However, the crux of the statement is that each child as an individual differs from other children in many ways and that those differences should be taken into account. Whether considered an adage or an axiom, all educators concerned with the elementary school have nodded at one time or another to the saying "Begin instruction at the level of the child, or where each child is." However, the child is not merely at the same age, at the same grade level, or in the same classroom as other children. Each child is a composite of individual characteristics: physical, emotional, and intellectual. Each child is attempting to develop or acquire a set or structure of mathematical ideas, concepts, and skills. The extent and the nature of that development is an individual matter for each child. Attempts by teachers to impose one piece of a structure—either their own or that of a textbook—of mathematical ideas, concepts, and skills on an entire classroom cannot be expected to be successful. Significant numbers of the children in that group will not be ready for the ideas being presented. Other children may already have acquired the ideas, perhaps in other manners, and may be disinterested or confused.

This belief is at the center of all efforts at "individualized instruction." Of course, all learning may be considered individualized. Each child either learns or does not learn what is intended when content or skills are presented. In many instances the child is blamed for not acquiring concepts or achieving skills when a teacher has presented that content to a classroom of children with a single approach or technique, especially if that technique has been appropriate or successful in previous circumstances. One may question the degree to which the earlier procedure was actually successful. All classroom teachers of elementary mathematics have met or will meet children who "had that or knew that" at an earlier age or grade level. For some reason, the injection did not take effect. The concepts and skills were not incorporated into the individual structures of mathematical ideas that the children were building.

Adjusting instruction, learning opportunities, and experiences to pupil differences is a major principle of instruction in an active laboratory-type elementary mathematics program. Content, concepts, and skills are not sacred to particular ages or grade levels. Bits of content are not dealt with only once or twice in the program at a designated level. Instead, the intellectual and performance abilities of children are continuously observed so that specific achievement objectives can be established for each child. Selected learning experiences and opportunities can then be directed toward the attainment of those specific objectives. The prevailing idea is to help each child acquire the concepts and skills of elementary mathematics regardless of his or her current age or grade level. This idea applies not only to children who are having or have had difficulties, but also to those children who are making what may be called normal progress and to those who are acquiring concepts and skills more rapidly.

The contradictions or inconsistencies between this principle pertaining to differences in children and the instructional practices employed in a textbook-oriented approach in which an entire classroom of children proceeds to cover successive pages simultaneously should be evident. Some elementary mathematics programs that are highly influenced by printed materials do provide for children's differing rates of learning. Children go through the same materials at differing rates of speed. However, these materials and this approach to instruction pay little attention to pupil differences in interests and to the ways in which they best learn. The materials generally utilize approaches in which there is one way and only one way for children to become familiar with an idea or to become proficient at a skill. Children are to learn in whatever way is favored by the authors of those materials. Interests of children are either ignored or simulated by authors. In many instances, the problems, illustrations, or ways of practicing ideas are presented in terms of what the adult authors think children's interests ought to be. There is very little variety in the physical object materials that are used to illustrate or demonstrate an idea and few ways to practice ideas and skills in childlike manners.

It would be extremely difficult to utilize all children's environmental or out-of-school interests when introducing, developing, or practicing elementary mathematical concepts and skills. Sometimes problems that deal with the interests of some children can be utilized, but those problems and those interests will not be shared by all children. In an active laboratory approach to elementary mathematics programs, efforts are made to use materials and learning experiences of such a variety that greater numbers of children are attracted to the instructional activities. Concepts and skills can be introduced, developed, and practiced with materials and learning experiences that are realistic, meaningful, and useful to children. At the very least, materials, approaches, and learning experiences should not be distasteful to children nor lead them to develop unfavorable attitudes toward mathematics or toward the study of mathematics. At best, the materials, approaches, and learning experiences should be fun for children. In an active laboratory-type elementary mathematics program, using physical object models and pictorial manipulative materials in a variety of ways to introduce, develop, practice, and apply concepts and skills is an attempt to stimulate interests, and provide opportunities for children to learn in different ways.

Major concepts or ideas of elementary mathematics can and should be introduced early in the school program.

The major concepts or ideas of elementary mathematics are not synonymous with facts, rules, definitions, operations, or the skills associated with them. The computational operations of addition, subtraction, multiplication, and division with whole numbers, common fractions, and decimal fractions are not the major concepts of the elementary mathematics programs. The computational operations are performance skills, which are to be applied in accordance with or in relation to major concepts or ideas. A major concept or idea is a content theme that persists throughout the program. That content theme or idea appears again and again in the program, and the idea is consistent at all levels of complexity. A major concept, idea, or content theme of those parts of the program aimed at developing familiarity with the main ideas of the real number system would pervade all subsets of the set of real numbers and would be consistent at all levels of complexity within any one subset.

Consider, for example, the idea "There are many names for the same number." This idea persists throughout the study of the real number system. A great many skill-development activities are directed toward helping children rename numbers of different types in different ways. In the early school years, children are expected to rename nonnegative integers (counting numbers) used to describe quantities of a small size. Later they are expected to name and rename quantities of a larger size using the units of the base-ten, positional value, system of numeration. They will also learn to use computational operations to rename expressed quantities. At some points in the program, they are expected to replace common fractions with equivalent fractions, to rename common fractions as decimal fractions and vice versa, to utilize percentage statements, and to use the new names in computational operations to solve problems. While different facts, rules, and skills may be utilized in the renaming processes, the content theme or idea remains the same: "There are many names for the same number." Other statements, definitions, and illustrations of major concepts and ideas within main content areas are cited in later chapters.

Introducing a major idea early in the school program does not imply that children will be able to apply either the idea or the skills associated with the idea at that level of complexity to problems at higher levels of complexity or with different types of numbers or exercises. To *introduce* means to begin an initial acquaintance with the concept or idea. That initial acquaintance may be quite elementary, so elementary that the child does not even acquire all of the skills associated with or related to the idea at that level of complexity. The child who learns how to rename a quantity of five objects (5 and 0, 4 and 1, 3 and 2, and the correlates to these), may have an idea about how to rename another quantity (for example, eight objects) but may not be able to find all of the names. What is established in the introduction is the idea of what is happening: numbers are being renamed in one way. At later times, other ways will be examined and the idea or concept will eventually be extended from "there are several names for the same number" to "there are an infinite number of names for the same number."

Several implications for classroom elementary mathematics programs can be derived from acceptance of this principle. The notion of developing or organizing the program around major concepts, ideas, or content themes is expanded in later discussions of a spiral curriculum plan and specific content areas. The practices of introducing major ideas earlier in the program without expecting children to completely master the concept or associated skills and of building basic skills, development topics, and exercises around major content themes are also explained in more detail. In order to introduce major concepts or ideas earlier, major content themes must be identified. Performance objectives for children and the related skill-development activities and exercises must be thought of in terms of how they relate to the major content themes rather than as isolated or unique means to an end. If performance objectives and skills—the tasks children are expected to undertake—are analyzed to determine the true performance prerequisites for those tasks, teachers may find that certain skill development activities that are related to major content themes may be introduced much earlier in the mathematics program. A sound foundation of interrelated ideas and skills can be established earlier and, thus, better serve each child in future learning opportunities or experiences.

Consider a child in the early years of school working on tasks that appear to be directed toward the acquisition of skills related to the ideas of base ten and the positional value in the system of numeration we use. The child may be given the task of making arrays, in which she is to lay out a certain number of chips in each row, to make a certain number of rows, and to determine the total number of chips. This activity is generally associated with establishing the multiplication facts. The child generates numerals by rolling two numeral cubes. One numeral will tell how many chips to put in each row, and the other numeral will tell how many rows to make. Determining the total number of chips in the array will require only that the child be able to rearrange the chips into groups of ten, describe the number of groups of ten, and state how many single chips are left over. When the child is able to do this, she may be asked to record her findings or observations in a chart similar to Figure 3.1. While it appears that the child is working on establishing the multiplication facts, she is really dealing with base ten and positional value. The only true prerequisites for the task are an understanding of the numerals on the cubes and an ability to count ten chips. While the child is performing the task, she is also being introduced to the major ideas of zero as a factor in multiplication, the identity element (1 row of *n* chips or *n* rows of 1 chip has a total of *n* chips) of multiplication, and the commutative property as it pertains to multiplication (2 rows of 3 chips has the same total number of chips as 3 rows of 2 chips). The terms *multiplication, arrays, times, identity element,* and *commutative property* need not and probably should not be mentioned at this point in the child's studies. The child is merely being introduced to the ideas.

Figure 3.1

How many rows?	How many in each row?	Total	
		Tens	Ones

Children control when and what they learn.

Every child has both input and output mechanisms. The input mechanisms allow the child to observe and to gather information; the output mechanisms allow the child to communicate, to question, and to demonstrate performance capabilities. The senses of sight, hearing, smell, taste, and touch serve as means of observing phenomena or gathering information, the first steps in learning. Each child controls when and what he or she learns by first deciding whether or not to participate and second by being able to accept, reject, or hold in abeyance any of the aspects of the elementary mathematics program that confront him or her. We cannot force children to hear, see, or feel what we want them to hear, see, or feel in order to acquire information. We can present stimuli or opportunities, but the child controls the input mechanisms. One should remember that as adults we often fake attention without really allowing input. Children are quick to acquire this talent. In a like manner, each child controls his or her own output mechanisms. Desire to participate precedes actual communication, questioning, or performance, and true abilities can be disguised or hidden.

Children are likely to accept what they see, understand, and are able to associate with previously acquired information, knowledge, or skills. Ideas, facts, rules, operations, or generalizations that cannot be seen, understood, or associated with previously acquired information are not likely to be accepted for input. They are likely to be rejected immediately, or the child might keep them in limbo while attempting to associate them with other knowledge or to commit them to memory without meaning or understanding in order that they might be regurgitated or repeated when called for by a stimulus. Poorly understood or weakly associated ideas, facts, rules, operations, or generalizations are likely to be rejected or forgotten when they serve no useful purpose or when the stimulus for recall is absent for a period of time.

Children also control and support their own learning by reinforcing themselves with their own feedback. Reinforcement as a principle or important aspect of the learning process has been rather thoroughly dealt with in professional research and literature. Discourses on the timing, nature, and extent of reinforcement given by teachers or printed materials to children for correct and incorrect responses to stimuli or for proper and appropriate behaviors or performances are not difficult to find. Reinforcement given to children by teachers or materials is effective only if that reinforcement or feedback is valued by the individual child. Each child controls the importance of reinforcement or feedback. The child either accepts it or rejects it. In addition, individual children give themselves feedback about their own performance. They commend themselves when they know that they have responded correctly or performed well, and they fault themselves when they know they have not done well.

Each child also controls the when and what of learning by generating, selecting, and directing the potential learning experiences or opportunities in which he or she will participate. In potential learning situations, active voluntary participation on the part of a child is likely to be more achievement oriented than enforced or imposed passive participation.

One implication of this belief for elementary mathematics programs is that teachers should attempt to present the kinds of learning opportunities or experiences, tasks, and exercises that will maximize acceptance and minimize rejection by children. Experienced teachers are well aware of the kinds of instructional activities, procedures, and tasks that turn children off. Dull, tedious paper-and-pencil exercises; exercises that children believe are intended only to keep them busy because they know that they are already proficient at the tasks; assignments in which the ideas to be applied are not clearly understood; expectations of performance that are beyond or below the capabilities of children; tasks or assignments that test the endurance of children; and directed learning experiences in which the children are to participate by passively listening and following directions—all are procedures that are not likely to be appreciated or accepted by children. Efforts must be made to provide learning opportunities and experiences utilizing a variety of materials and approaches that are motivating and attractive, not dull and distasteful. Accurate information about the performance capabilities of children must be at hand in order that new learnings (ideas, facts, rules, generalizations, and skills) can be associated with or built on old learnings. Consistency in the general nature of the uses of materials and types of learning experiences must exist within the variety of learning experiences that are available. Learning experiences must be such that children's passive participation is almost impossible and active participation can hardly be avoided. Learning experiences for each child should be selected so that success in the experience is highly possible and should include the potential for pupil self-reinforcement or feedback.

Children in the elementary school learn best by actively working with realistic problems and real objects in concrete situations.

A supplementary statement of belief or principle is that there is a physical object model for virtually every mathematical idea dealt with in the elementary school program. Children in the elementary school are at a level of intellectual development where real learning best occurs when they handle, manipulate, and observe phenomena while working with concrete objects. Having children manipulate real objects that are appropriate models for mathematical ideas and seeing what occurs is the avenue for developing understanding of oral and printed communication abstractions. Realistic problem situations can be structured with physical object models. These problems will be meaningful because they can be seen, understood, handled, and solved. The process of handling or manipulating a model will not only help children understand the situation but will also allow them to see how the problem can be solved. In this sense, a problem is not merely a series of printed words or symbols containing quantitative information and requiring a solution. A problem or a problem situation can be communicated to children by other means, which include utilization of a physical object model and simple oral directions and questions pertaining to the nature of the problem situation and the need for a solution.

A problem is real for children when its nature can be seen and understood and when the situation is within the general out-of-school or environmental experience of children. Using a physical object model to structure a problem presents the problem in a visually real manner. Using gamelike activities to introduce and develop concepts, facts, operations, and skills allows the teacher to approach the solution of problems at a level appropriate to the social and intellectual development of children. Problem situations can also be made real for children through the construction of pupil-made projects and through the use of childlike games in which a series of problems must be solved in the act of constructing or playing. Pictorial manipulative materials can be used with the physical object model at the introductory and developmental levels and alone when children have acquired an understanding of the ideas represented by the models.

Active participation or work with real problems requires that children handle the models and seek the solutions by manipulating the pieces of the model in the gamelike introductory and developmental activities, that they are the builders in the construction of projects, and that they are players in the games. Under this principle, the phrase "children learn by doing" does not refer to paper-and-pencil exercises or to imitating actions and operations that have been demonstrated by others.

The communication skills of listening, speaking, reading, and writing about mathematical ideas can be developed through active involvement of children in the uses of physical object models in realistic problem situations. Communication skills cannot be well developed in a content vacuum. There must be something to talk, read, and write about. Initially, when a new mathematical concept or skill is being introduced or developed, the communication will be between child and child or teacher and child in a strictly oral (listening and speaking) manner. The first forms of reading and writing will include only the simple quantitative, comparative, and operational symbols that children have been using orally. These printed symbols will be associated with the physical object models and their manipulations. Later, printed words and phrases will be added in an effort to help children read and comprehend the language of mathematics. The operations of one-to-one matching and counting and the fundamental computational operations of addition, subtraction, multiplication, and division—which are used to find solutions to problems—can all be developed with concrete models in realistic problem situations.

The implications of this principle are crucial to the development of an active elementary mathematics program and apply to the acquisition and uses of materials as well as the planning and presentation of learning experiences. Physical object models that display the main ideas of the real number system and of geometry must be acquired and made available for use by children in the classroom. Children must be allowed, even directed, to use those materials in appropriate learning experiences. To ensure active participation, those learning experiences must be planned and presented as individual or small-group activities. The teacher must know the performance capabilities of all the children in order to direct individual children toward suitable introductory, developmental, or practice learning activities. And, to adjust instructional activities to the differing ability levels of children, to provide the desired scope of the program, the teacher will have to collect a wide range of potential learning experiences extending both below and above the conventional content for a particular grade level. These experiences will have to be categorized by topic and purpose for future selection and use by the teacher and children.

A spiral plan of curriculum development is an effective way of organizing the curriculum of the elementary mathematics program.

The purpose of stating this principle is to stress the need to consider both reorganization of content and approaches to content when program modifications are directed toward an active laboratory-type mathematics program. In a spiral plan of elementary mathematics curriculum, the content to be undertaken is not a series of fragmented bits and pieces dealing with isolated skills. In fragmented programs, the major objective appears to be coverage of content or materials rather than increasing children's proficiency or power in using mathematical concepts and skills in problem situations. In such programs, content is separated into many small areas, and within each area, content is subdivided into discrete steps or difficulty levels. The small steps or difficulty levels, each involving either a new step or a new rule, are arranged in a linear or hierarchical order, and one step is studied at a time, with other bits of content interjected between the steps. For example, the process of addition of whole numbers may be considered one content area. After the facts have been introduced, the types of examples or exercises worked at one time might be as fragmented as the following:

Add:	3	2	6	13	20	30	20	23	11
	2	4	7	4	6	40	10	34	32
	4	7	6		1		50		24
	26	15	54	56	300	234	405	237	316
	7	39	65	76	400	143	203	922	427
	563	268	987						
	290	374	654						

. . . and on and on to more and larger addends.

In a spiral plan of elementary mathematics, the major ideas or concepts within broader content areas are spirally developed, not merely the separate difficulty levels within the numeration system or within the computational operations with the subsets of the set of real numbers. Skill development is associated with the major concepts or ideas of each content area. The ideas and skills of one content area are studied in relationship to one another. When possible and appropriate, relationships *between* content areas are emphasized and the skills from one content area are used in other areas. Mathematics is approached as an interrelated structure rather than as a collection of isolated and unrelated concepts and skills. Each child must spend sufficient time when studying or working in one content area to gain proficiency in the application of concepts and skills to immediate problem situations and to prepare for further study of that content area.

A spirally planned program has a continuity in its emphasis on major ideas and the skills associated with those major ideas in an ordered, structured manner. Study of a major mathematical idea is not completed at any one time; the same idea arises and is utilized at different times with increasing degrees of difficulty and with additional skills and applications. At each new instance, the idea and its previous applications can be reviewed as preparation for further development.

The implications of this principle for an active elementary mathematics program pertain primarily to program organization. The content of elementary mathematics can be reorganized into a smaller number of main content areas without reducing the basic concepts and skills to be developed in the program. In each of those content areas, one can identify major concepts, ideas, or content themes that persist and are consistent throughout that area. The skills associated with each of the major ideas can be ascertained and arranged in a logical, sequential manner. Then learning experiences directed toward the introduction and development of the major ideas and the associated skills can be identified and arranged in a logical, sequential manner. Learning experiences directed toward the introduction and development of the major ideas and the skills associated with them can be combined into units of work and study. Each unit would be of sufficient duration to allow a child working on that unit to become more powerful in applying the major idea and its related skills. Materials and instructional approaches within one content area should be consistent from one unit of study to the next. The program plan should aim at thoroughness and pupil achievement through participation in learning experiences that truly relate and integrate major ideas. If that plan can be put into effect, each child will have greater opportunities to develop his or her own interrelated structure of mathematical ideas.

Verification procedures should be an integral part of problem solving at all levels.

Children should be encouraged to become responsible for the correctness of their own work, both in the processes they employ and the responses or answers they obtain. In a laboratory-type elementary mathematics program, children are often engaged in gathering and recording quantitative information, including number values, facts, and solutions derived from manipulating models for mathematical ideas. Some of the recorded information will consist of computational operations as they are developed from problem situations. Children enjoy knowing that they are employing proper procedures and that they have arrived at correct responses. In a true active laboratory-type elementary mathematics program, children can and should know when they are using correct procedures because those procedures are associated with the manipulation and handling of physical object model referents. They can also be certain of the correctness of their responses because verification procedures can be incorporated into the program at a very early stage.

    The verification procedures of a laboratory-type approach to elementary mathematics do not depend on the teacher or some other adult for authoritative support or for checking responses. The verification procedures are employed by children at levels appropriate to their performance capabilities. The role of the teacher in this aspect of the program is to assure children that the responsibility is theirs, to question children's procedures and responses in order to get them to show or "prove" that they are correct, and to encourage and support children's use of verification procedures as a means of providing their own feedback and self-reinforcement. Of course, teachers will want to and should observe children at work and look at the written records and exercises that children complete. But these observations are not for the purpose of checking or correcting responses and marking red X's on incorrect answers. It is, first of all, a check on whether the child is working on a given task. Second, it demonstrates interest in the child's endeavors. It is also a check to make sure that the child is using correct processes and verification procedures, an evaluation-of-progress technique.

The first type of verification procedure that children should employ for any mathematical idea or operation being introduced or developed involves the use and manipulation of a physical object model. A child simply shows that he or she is correct by demonstrating with the model. The only communication associated with this procedure would be verbal, with the teacher questioning and the child responding while the model is being manipulated. As children acquire other skills, they are expected to use more abstract procedures. Some early verification procedures employ a simpler operation than the one being used. For example, counting might be used to verify simple multiplication exercises and subtraction to verify simple division exercises. Sometimes the properties of number as they apply to addition and multiplication may be used to verify those kinds of computational exercises. The associative property of addition might be used to verify sums; the commutative, associative, or distributive property might be used to verify products. Eventually, when children begin to understand the relationships between the computational operations, they may use inverse operations to verify answers. They will use addition to verify differences arrived at in subtraction exercises, subtraction to verify the sums of addition, multiplication to verify quotients, and division to verify products. When children become familiar with the sizes of numbers and the operations, they might use estimation to decide if a response is reasonable. The use and manipulation of physical object models is the first form of verification, but the other processes cannot be introduced or developed in a true or consistent hierarchy.

The implication of this principle for elementary mathematics programs is that verification procedures should be an integral part of the program. Children should be expected to verify all of their responses or at least all of the responses about which they are uncertain. Checking or verifying answers is not a sometimes assignment; on the other hand, tasks or assignments should not take twice the time or effort because checking or verification is a part of that task.

The preceding six statements of educational principles are cited because they have important implications for an active laboratory-type elementary mathematics program. Additional principles and their implications might have been listed; others are stated in later sections of this text. However, these few principles serve to emphasize the point that attempts to modify an elementary mathematics program should be based on established principles. Individual teachers' reactions to these beliefs and their implications can indicate commitment to an active laboratory approach in elementary mathematics, and teacher commitment is the prime prerequisite to program modification.

Program Organization   *Chapter 4*

When existing elementary mathematics programs are studied in order to direct future program modifications, the program's organization comes under close scrutiny. Organizational aspects of the program include all physical arrangements involving the use of space and grouping of children, the assignment of topics of content to particular age or grade levels, designation of materials to be used, guiding principles, and policies or decisions that are made at the school or district level in efforts to facilitate program operation. Organizational aspects also include consideration of these factors as they pertain to individual classrooms. At all levels, decisions and actions involving program organization are made in an effort to facilitate either conduct of the program or pupil growth in the direction of achievement goals.

Policies or decisions having widespread impact on program organization generally are made at the school district or building level. These policies or decisions are communicated to classroom teachers through curriculum guides, selection of basic textual materials, budget allotments, directives about evaluative procedures (including testing dates and tests to be used), and procedures for grouping children for instruction. When content is referred to, statements usually pertain to minimums, but specifics may be given. At the school district or building level, concerns about pupil achievement are commonly directed toward comparisons of means or averages of the children at various grade levels with national norms. Decisions and policies made at the school district or building level may seem restrictive to individual classroom teachers, but they are usually quite general and do not greatly confine classroom instructional procedures or materials that are selected to facilitate individual pupil achievement.

How the program thrives in the classroom depends primarily on the organization of the program at the classroom level. Responsibility for the elementary mathematics program—its organization and its conduct—at the classroom level lies with individual classroom teachers. Developing an active classroom program in which all children are provided with appropriate opportunities to learn requires organizational arrangements that facilitate the attainment of the desired attributes of the total program. Teachers must see that the scope of the classroom program is consistent with the scope of the total program: learning experiences must be planned to help children attain familiarity with the main ideas of the real number system, geometry, and algebraic foundations and acquire the skills that are associated with those main ideas. Teachers must attempt to organize the program so that the dissatisfactions with preceding or existing programs are likely to be remedied. Most importantly, teachers must organize the program so that the established guiding educational principles are evident in all characteristics of the classroom program arrangements.

Reorganization of Content

The need to modify the content organization or structure in elementary mathematics programs is based on dissatisfactions with the organization, structure, selection and arrangements of content used previously and the belief that a better organization is possible. Teachers are often dissatisfied with content organizations in elementary mathematics programs that are dominated by textual or printed materials. Because much of the material presented in such program organizations is inappropriate for many children, they tend to develop feelings of rejection or dejection. As can be seen from the content organizations of pupil textbooks and workbooks and the accompanying scope and sequence charts, content is often fragmented. In most instances, students spend most of their time and effort on developing computational skills in an isolated manner and not on the major mathematical ideas that could and should be used to relate and integrate major ideas and skills. Sequencing of both ideas or concepts and skills is often based on *false prerequisites*—concepts and performance skills that really are not necessary for children to begin the study of new ideas and skills. Some programs are organized or arranged in manners that appear to make coverage of materials rather than individual pupil achievement the major program objective. Most certainly, the greatest teacher dissatisfaction with elementary mathematics programs stems from a high percentage of pupil casualties. ("They just aren't interested. They won't work. They aren't ready for this material.") Behind or underlying each of these dissatisfactions is the belief that there must be a better way to organize or arrange the content of elementary mathematics to achieve the primary objective of the program—individual pupil achievement.

Major Content Areas

Elementary mathematics curriculum planners and developers at the school district, school building, and individual classroom levels can and ought to organize or reorganize the content structure, arrangement, and presentation into major areas, which can be dealt with both separately and in an integrated manner. At the core of the organization are the basic concepts and skills of elementary mathematics—the concepts and skills that are required to solve immediate or current problem situations or that are true prerequisites for the introduction, development, and acquisition of other concepts and skills that will, in turn, be applied to solutions of problem situations. In actuality, the designation of a concept or skill as basic is not an *either-or* consideration, *either* it is a current requirement *or* it is a prerequisite for future development. In a spiral plan of curriculum development, basic concepts and skills that are current requirements are also the prerequisites for later introduction and development of concepts and skills at a higher level of complexity and with an expanded applicability.

Organizing or reorganizing the content structure and arrangement into major content areas is intended to minimize the fragmentation of concepts and skills into isolated, unrelated ideas, facts, and rules. Organizing or arranging the content of elementary mathematics into major areas also allows for the logical, sequential introduction and development of concepts and skills that help children to acquire an integrated structure of mathematical ideas. Equally important is the possiblity of providing opportunities for each child to achieve greater proficiency with the basic skills inherent in each of the areas.

A major content area in elementary mathematics may be defined as a segment of concepts and skills that are logically related and associated with a broad general objective or goal. For example, one general goal or purpose of elementary mathematics programs is to help children learn to communicate effectively about number or quantity. Therefore, content that is directed toward introducing, developing, and practicing the concepts and skills associated with communicating about quantities described by the elements of the real number system can be collected into a major content area. Each major content area has a set of content themes or main mathematical ideas that are consistent throughout the area regardless of the level of complexity. Associated with each content theme or mathematical idea is a logical sequence of performance-skill expectations. When woven together, the threads of the content themes or main ideas and their associated performance skills become a content area. Within each content area is a set of vocabulary or communication skills (listening, speaking, reading, and writing) that are basic to that content topic or area. Defining a major content area in this manner reduces the number of content topics that might have been dealt with separately. It does not, however, reduce the scope—the breadth and depth of concepts and performance skills—of the program. This definition also allows the program planner or organizer to think of concepts and skills to be introduced and developed in relation to other ideas and skills and to arrange content topics or tasks into more logical sequential learning opportunities for children.

Reorganizing the content of conventional elementary mathematics programs into major content areas is neither a simple nor an easy task. The following designations of major content areas were derived from (1) actively working with children who were studying elementary mathematics, (2) working with classroom teachers and school administrators who were attempting to modify and improve the programs for which they were responsible, (3) analyzing the content of existing elementary mathematics programs, and (4) attempting to develop an active laboratory-type approach to elementary mathematics instruction. Those efforts have led the author to organize and arrange the content of elementary mathematics into five major areas: numeration and notation; operations on collections of objects; operations on number using numerals; geometry; and measurement. Each of these major areas has a broad or general goal or purpose; each has a set of main mathematical ideas or content themes, which persist and are consistent throughout the area; each main idea can be associated with a logical sequence of performance skills to be achieved by children; and each major area has some particular vocabulary (oral and/or written) that must be introduced, developed, and practiced so that children may learn to communicate effectively in that area. Although Part Two of this text deals more extensively with the five designated content areas, a brief description of the nature of each area is presented here.

Numeration and Notation

In most elementary mathematics programs, a great deal of time and effort is spent helping children learn to describe quantities (numbers) with numerals. Children are expected to acquire the communication skills of listening, speaking, reading, and writing about the quantities or amounts described by the elements of the set of real numbers. At one time or another, children encounter the nonnegative integers, the negative integers, the rational numbers (in the forms of common fractions, decimal fractions, and percentages), and perhaps some irrational numbers. At each encounter, children are expected to acquire further performance skills in meaningfully describing quantitative situations. The communication skills expected in each of the subsets of the set of real numbers are not unrelated; they can and should be associated with the main mathematical ideas about naming or describing number in quantitative situations. While working on the communication skills associated with the content themes, children will also be developing skills in the operations of comparing: matching in one-to-one correspondence, ordering, and counting quantities or numbers. Some of these operations will involve the concepts of base and positional value in a system of numeration. The symbolism and vocabulary employed will include names for numbers (numerals), both oral and written, and the comparative symbols $=$, $\neq$, $>$, and $<$. Since the content of this area deals primarily with naming numbers and using a set of signs or symbols to record or describe numbers, the content area is called *numeration and notation*.

Operations on Collections of Objects

This content area does not appear in many existing elementary mathematics programs as a distinct content area. Instead, some activities or exercises involving the manipulation of objects may be used to introduce specific types of problems or to attempt to develop understanding of the regrouping ("carrying" and "borrowing") that is necessary in the fundamental operations of addition, subtraction, multiplication, and division. It would appear that each time objects are pictured or suggested for use, the purpose is unique. Yet, when those purposes are analyzed, two distinct purposes can be seen for them. Performing operations on collections of objects can and should be used as the basis for understanding the fundamental computational operations. Perhaps more important, performing operations on collections of objects that are physical models for numbers will help children acquire an understanding of problem situations and the similarity of problems regardless of the types of numerals involved. A major purpose of including operations on collections of objects as a major content area is to help children improve their problem-solving capabilities. The content themes or main ideas of this area encompass the nature of problem situations, the operations that can be performed on collections of objects, and the relationships among those operations. When problems are structured with physical object models, it is obvious that all problems encountered in the elementary mathematics program are either (1) problems that involve combining two or more quantities or collections; (2) problems that involve comparing two quantities or collections; or (3) problems that involve the separation of one quantity or collection. When problems are structured with physical object models, the problems can be solved by manipulating the objects. The fundamental computational operations are technical skills that can be utilized to solve problems if the problem solver knows how to perform the operation and knows when to use it. The physical operations of combining and separating are inverse—or opposite—operations; therefore, the fundamental computational operations used to solve problems of combining or separating are inverse operations. The operations that children learn to perform in this content area are primarily physical manipulations of the models. They will utilize the concept of base when they exchange several small units for one large unit of quantity or exchange one large unit for small units. Performance skills to be acquired include classifying problems as combining, comparing, or separating and communicating about the numbers involved in the problem. Other than the terms used to classify problems (*combine, compare, separate*), there is no vocabulary or symbolism peculiar to this area. Children will continue to use the vocabulary and symbolism necessary to describe orally quantities or numbers, printed or written numerals, and comparative symbols. The terms, signs, and symbols particular to the four fundamental operations may or may not be introduced after children understand the processes of combining, comparing, and separating; they are not necessary for the development of the major ideas or the performance skills involved in performing operations on collections of objects.

Operations on Numbers Using Numerals

Using numerals to perform operations on number must be considered a major content area of the elementary mathematics program. A great deal of time and effort is directed toward helping children learn to add, subtract, multiply, and divide with whole numbers, common fractions, and decimal fractions, and some time may be spent on the operations with positive and negative integers. Many laypersons and educators consider these operations to be the basics of elementary mathematics programs. Children are expected to master the facts and the algorithms of the operations and to apply those performance skills to the solution of problems. The themes or main ideas that persist and that are consistent throughout this content area are neither the facts nor the operations. It is true that the basic facts of addition with whole numbers also are the basic facts of addition with common fractions and decimal fractions, and the same is true for the basic facts of subtraction and multiplication. Nevertheless, the facts and their applications are performance skills to be mastered. The main ideas of this content area are (1) generalizations about the computational operations, such as "only like size units of numeration can be added or subtracted" and "addition and subtraction are inverse operations" and (2) the properties of number (commutative, associative, and distributive properties; identity elements; additive inverse; and multiplicative inverse) as they apply to the operations of addition and multiplication. The operations that children perform in this area are the computational operations of addition, subtraction, multiplication, and division with whole numbers, common fractions, and decimal fractions. Children's understanding of the facts, rules of regrouping, and complete algorithms are developed as they keep records of the manipulations they perform as they operate on collections of objects. The vocabulary and symbolism of the content area are those pertaining to the operations. They include the quantitative, comparative, operational, and descriptive symbols used in quantitative expressions, number sentences, and equations. It is in this content area that algebraic foundations are introduced, developed, and practiced.

Geometry

The content area of geometry does not occupy as much time and effort in the elementary mathematics program as do the other major areas, but the ideas and skills of geometry should be introduced in the early years and developed throughout the program. The geometry of the elementary program is not similar to or a miniproduction of the geometry in secondary programs, where there are axioms, theorems, and formal proofs. The general purposes of geometry in the elementary program are to develop informally ideas of geometric entities and their relationships to each other so that children can apply these ideas in problem situations. Concepts and skills are introduced and developed with physical object models for geometric entities, laying the foundations for more formal study of the area.

The content themes or main ideas of the area pertain to the relationships that may exist between or within geometric entities: congruence, similarity, symmetry, perpendicularity, and parallelism. Initially, the formal terms used to name these relationships are not part of the vocabulary of the program. Instead, the relationships are described in the words of children. The vocabulary and symbolism of the area are primarily oral and involve naming and describing the entities of geometry and the relationships that exist between them. The operations to be performed are basically physical manipulation and construction of geometric models. The skills to be acquired by children are those of identifying, naming, comparing, classifying, and constructing models of the entities of geometry. Some attention may be given to drawings and to designs that employ geometric concepts. Solving problems involving measurements of geometric configurations or models may be utilized in this content area as well as in the content areas of operations on number and measurement. Later, when the formulation of relationships or the development of formulas is the primary instructional concern, activities will more closely resemble traditional geometry.

Measurement

Designating measurement as a major content area of the elementary mathematics program may be questioned by some teachers and curriculum developers because the acts of measuring can be considered merely as applications of the concepts and skills of numeration and notation. Problems involving measurements require the same fundamental computational operations as other problems. However, one dissatisfaction with existing programs communicated by laypersons and teachers of higher levels is that children are not acquiring the concepts and skills of measurement. Apparently, those ideas are not being introduced and developed in an effective manner. Special attention to the activities of measuring and to the concepts and skills of measurement is needed to help children achieve these everyday skills. The general goals of measurement as a content area are obvious. Content themes that persist and that are consistent throughout various types of measurement involve the general nature of measurement and the acts of measuring and include the following ideas:

All measurement is comparison in which one quantity is compared to another quantity.

Numerals derived from measurements are approximate. They are not exact numbers.

Standard units are utilized in order to do a better job of measuring and to communicate about measurements.

Precision of measurements depends on the instrument used and how accurately it is used.

Ideas about comparisons, standard units, approximateness of measurements, precision, accuracy, and estimations of measures pertain to all types of measurement. It does not matter what system of measurement is being used; whether the measures be of distance, amount of surface, volume or capacity, or weight; or whether the measurements are made in a direct or an indirect manner.

The performance skills to be acquired in this content area are the skills of measuring. The operations performed in the processes of acquiring these skills are the physical acts of measuring. Children will use crude measuring instruments and standard tools and devices, utilize the concept of base in measuring and in naming measures in several ways, and solve problems involving measured quantities by employing computational operations. The particular vocabulary and symbolism of the content area deals with naming, describing, and comparing units of measurement and the things that are to be measured.

Procedures for Reorganizing Content

Organizing the content into these five major areas is not intended to isolate or fragment bits of content. The intent is to make possible a more thorough analysis of the content of the program so that concerted efforts can be made to plan and develop appropriate sequential learning experiences for children. When the content is organized into these areas and the content of each area is well known by the adults who are responsible for the conduct of the program, it is much easier to provide learning opportunities that emphasize and utilize the relationships that exist between mathematical ideas and that integrate and correlate concepts and skills from the various content areas and from other academic fields.

Planners of elementary mathematics programs may wish to designate additional major content areas. They might ask specific questions, such as, "Why not include problem solving or graphing as major content areas?" When such suggestions are made, the nature of that content topic and the concepts and skills related to it should be analyzed: Where would those concepts and skills best fit into the total program? Should that particular set of concepts and skills be designated as a major content area? In the approach presented here, problem solving is intended to be an integral part of each content area. New ideas and skills are introduced and developed with structured problems and practiced in childlike problem situations. *Graphing* is a form of notation, a way of representing quantities or numbers in various classifications or a way of pictorially presenting relationships between quantities and categories. Children should be helped to interpret data presented in this manner, to read graphs, and to construct graphs that present mathematical information pictorially. However, it might be better to cover the concepts and skills of graphs and graphing in an integrated manner when children are dealing with the basic concepts of numeration and notation, operations on number, and measurement rather than to attempt to integrate the concepts and skills from those content areas into an area dealing primarily with graphing. The designation of these five major content areas is consistent with the definition of the scope of the program presented in this text. Within the delineated content areas, it is possible for children to develop familiarity with the main ideas of the real number system, geometry, and algebraic foundations.

Initial attempts on the part of classroom teachers and others to reorganize the content of the elementary mathematics program may be greatly simplified if the printed materials at hand are utilized. Content organization would be extremely difficult without reference to the existing program and materials. Initial efforts might pursue the following course:

1. Designate major content areas on which there is consensus.
2. Peruse the printed materials of the existing program. Assign topics of content to the major areas. Study curriculum guides, teachers' manuals, pupils' textbooks and workbooks, and supplementary materials.
3. Put aside for later consideration topics of content that do not "fit naturally" into the designated major content areas.
4. Analyze evaluative instruments that are a part of the program, including standardized tests, for content achievement expectations for children. Consider concepts, ideas, and skill expectations that are not already a part of the program for inclusion in one of the major content areas.
5. Consider logical sequences of concept and skill development. Use a variety of printed instructional materials that range across age and grade levels as references and resources.
6. Identify general purposes or goals, content themes, skills to be developed, and vocabulary and symbolism particular to the established major content areas.
7. Ascertain the need for additional major content areas and for content areas developed from the topics that did not fit naturally into the established areas.
8. Identify possible and important relationships between content concepts and skills. Look for ways to integrate and correlate concepts and skills from different major areas.

9. Determine which portions of the concepts and skills within each content area could be dealt with in one sequence of learning experiences or in one time span with individual or small groups of children.
10. Consider deletions, additions, extensions, and modifications of the content in each of the major areas.

In all their efforts, the planners and organizers should remember that the major purpose of reorganizing the content of the elementary mathematics program is to facilitate pupil learning and not to ease the management or discipline problems of the classroom teacher.

Toward a Spiral Curriculum Plan

In the past several decades, a great deal of discussion at professional conferences and in professional literature has been directed at the use of a spiral plan of curriculum development in elementary mathematics. Unfortunately, the discussions of this suggestion have not contributed greatly to a better understanding of a spiral plan on the part of classroom teachers or to the implementation of a spiral plan in instructional materials or procedures. Implementation of such a plan has been left largely to the commercial producers of instructional materials, and although advertised as such, the products do not satisfy the suggested program plan. The elements of a spiral program plan are difficult to incorporate into salable forms of texts and workbooks.

Nature of a Spiral Plan

The major elements of a spiral plan of elementary mathematics curriculum development are content themes or main ideas (content organized in degrees of complexity around the main ideas), time intervals, and appropriate opportunities for children to acquire concepts and skills. The intent of a spiral plan is to help children begin to develop and understand an integrated structure of mathematical ideas while they are gaining power in the use of mathematical concepts and skills. In a spiral plan, the same content theme arises at many times in the program. Each time the topic reappears in the program skills and concepts are further developed, the learner becomes more powerful in putting the concepts to use in problem situations, and relationships to other ideas or topics are extended.

In a spiral curriculum plan, main ideas are introduced at an early level in ways that do not require formal definitions or verbalization. Children's common experiences with quantitative situations are described in their own language, and they do and see in an intuitive manner with real objects. Enough time is spent at the early stages for children to become familiar with an idea in its simplest form in order for them to use the idea in a simple childlike fashion. Time spent on the idea or topic must be sufficient for each child to become more adept at using the idea or simple skill. Only then will other ideas or topics be introduced or developed. Regardless of the age or grade level at which an idea or topic is first introduced, that introduction should be informal in approach, based on common experiences, and at an intuitive level.

During the time interval when other ideas or topics are covered, children will be required to use the ideas or skills previously introduced or developed. These supporting activities must be provided. A spiral program plan returns repeatedly to the main idea and its associated concepts and skills, using units or topics of study that focus on that content theme and its concepts and skills. The time intervals between returns to one content theme or area are spent working on other topics that are appropriate to the characteristics of the learner. Each time a content theme or area is brought back for further development, there is an increase in the complexity of the concepts and skills. However, extension of the concepts and skills are deliberately related to and built on previous understanding and uses of them. As a main idea, content theme, or content area is repeatedly brought back into primary focus, the study and development of the concepts and skills becomes more formal and more precise. Each encounter with the topic or idea requires enough contact time for children to acquire more power in the use of the skills associated with the topic. The boredom of pure review and reiteration must be avoided.

Dealing with the same concepts and associated skills at varying levels of complexity at intervals in the program does not imply single approaches to any of the topics. A variety of approaches, learning experiences, and ways of practicing—all at the same general level of difficulty—can be utilized each time the content topic is reintroduced.

A spiral plan does not merely arrange a single skill topic, such as multiplication of whole numbers, into segments of difficulty levels and approach one segment at various times in the program. That approach could be extremely fragmented because it would focus on the sequential development of the separate skill topics in a step-by-step manner. The result would be a linear approach to separate skills.

A true spiral plan develops themes of unity and interdependence of mathematical ideas, stressing relationships within and among mathematical ideas. Content themes define content areas to be developed. The content themes or main ideas are the consistent topics that are spirally developed throughout the program. Concepts and performance skills associated with those themes are the apparent teaching-learning topics, because the major underlying theme or idea is not visible in practice exercises. The cursory observer may not see the themes or main ideas that define the content area and direct the program activities.

The preceding statements do not refer specifically to the individuality of pupils—their differences in backgrounds, capabilities, and learning styles. Any plan for a spirally developed elementary mathematics program must consider the uniqueness of the learner and the implied individualization of learning opportunities. The following discussions attempt to present a model of a spiral plan of curriculum development in elementary mathematics appropriate for adaptation to individualized instruction.

Model of a Spiral Plan

The most comprehensive facets of a spiral plan are the major content areas of the program. The content areas are defined by themes or major ideas, which are consistent throughout the area as it is developed in the elementary mathematics program. The major ideas are spirally developed throughout the program through attention to associated concepts and performance skills. The greater the number of main ideas, the broader the content area will be. Figure 4.1 is intended to illustrate how main ideas are woven together into a major content area. The illustration does not attempt to picture the concepts and performance skills that are associated with each of the main ideas or content themes.

Figure 4.1 *Weaving Main Ideas into a Major Content Area*

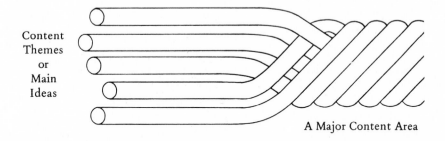

Content
Themes
or
Main
Ideas

A Major Content Area

In Figure 4.2 the major content areas are indicated by varying lines connecting similar geometric figures. Each major content area is composed of strands of main ideas, as was pictured in Figure 4.1. Associated with each content theme or main idea are statements of pupil-performance objectives. These objectives apply to applications of concepts, generalizations, facts, rules, patterns, and relationships that indicate some degree of pupil understanding of the idea. The skills to be acquired in relation to each main idea have a general sequential order based on actual prerequisites. The number of performance objectives in any one major content area depends on the number of main ideas in that area and the nature of the skills associated with each main idea. Sets of performance objectives intersect as the main ideas and skills of one major content area are related through use and applicability to the main ideas and skills of another area. These intersections may be viewed as relationships between major content area and main ideas.

In Figure 4.2 performance objectives in each content area are indicated by small letters (a, b, c, d, . . .). It should be remembered that each content theme will have particular performance objectives. Figure 4.2 is merely illustrative, it does not try to picture the number of performance objectives or the amount or nature of the relationships within and between content areas.

Single geometric configurations in Figure 4.2 represent subsets of the performance objectives incorporated into a unit of study.

Figure 4.2 *Spiral Plan of Curriculum in Elementary Mathematics*

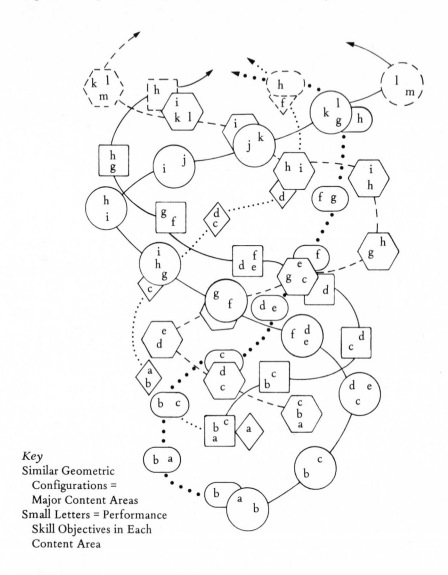

Key
Similar Geometric
    Configurations =
    Major Content Areas
Small Letters = Performance
    Skill Objectives in Each
    Content Area

In that particular unit of study, learning opportunities, experiences, and activities are selected and presented that have high potential for allowing pupils to achieve the objectives. Intersections of performance skill objectives within one content area are shown by having the same small letter appearing in sequential configurations. Some of the children who undertake those learning experiences will not achieve all of the performance skills for one unit of study. When the topic or main idea is reintroduced at a later time, new learnings will be related to and built on previous learnings, and some of the skills learned earlier will once again be related to material under study.

Intersections or overlays of the geometric configurations in Figure 4.2 are intended to portray relationships between major content areas in the nature of foundations or prerequisites, concepts and skills used in problem solving, and perhaps common units of study or learning experiences that have performance skill objectives in two major content areas.

Spiral Development of Main Ideas

Several examples of how main ideas might be spirally developed may be given to expand the illustration of a spiral plan and to assist in program planning. One of the main ideas from the major content area of numeration and notation is that there are many names for the same number. One of the major ideas from the area of operations on numbers using numerals is the identity element of multiplication ($1 \times n = n$ and $n \times 1 = n$, when 1 is a factor in a multiplication exercise, the product is the other factor). Content topics in which these ideas are the major themes appear at various times in the elementary mathematics program. At each occurrence of the theme or main idea in the program, concepts and performance skills are introduced and developed. In existing programs, that theme often is not referred to as the basic mathematical idea underlying the topic; and children's practice of performance skills using rules of operations to obtain correct answers often overshadows the main idea or theme.

In the following examples, some of the more notable occasions at which each idea appears in the elementary mathematics program are given. Others could probably be included. While examining the examples, consider the performance skills and operations required of children.

There are many names for the same number.

Topic	*Example*
Developing number names; counting	*Two* and one more is *three*

Grouping, different ways of describing one small quantity	*Five is two and three, four and one*
Basic facts	$4 + 3 = 7$ $8 - 2 = 6$ $4 \times 9 = 36$
Base ten; positional value	$\underline{\ 2\ }$ tens $\underline{\ 3\ }$ ones $= \underline{\ 23\ }$
Fraction names for whole numbers	$\dfrac{2}{2}, \dfrac{3}{3}, \dfrac{4}{4}, \dfrac{5}{5}, \ldots$ $\dfrac{4}{2}, \dfrac{6}{3}, \dfrac{8}{4}, \dfrac{10}{5}, \ldots$
Equivalent fractions	$\dfrac{1}{2} = \dfrac{2}{4}$ $\dfrac{1}{3} = \dfrac{2}{6}$ $\dfrac{3}{4} = \dfrac{9}{12}$
Computational operations	4 groups of $24 = \square$ $\begin{array}{r} 24 \\ \times\ 4 \\ \hline 96 \end{array}$ $\begin{array}{l} 4 \times 4 = 16 \\ 4 \times 20 = 80 \\ 4 \times 24 = 96 \end{array}$
Converting common fractions to decimal fractions	$1/3 = 0.\overline{3}$ $1/4 = 0.25$ $1/6 = 0.1\overline{6}$
Common fractions, decimal fractions, percentage equivalents	$1/2 = 0.50$ and $0.50 = 50\%$ $3/4 = 0.75$ and $0.75 = 75\%$
Equations	$11 + 4 = \square$ $3x - 7 = 5$ $x^2 - 2xy + y^2 =$ $(x - y)(x - y)$

When 1 is a factor, the product is equal to the other factor: the identity element of multiplication, $n \times 1 = n$ and $1 \times n = n$.

Topic	*Example*
Counting; group recognition	"One group, with three in the group." * * *

1 as a factor in the multiplication facts	1 row, 5 in the row　$* * * * *$ 5 rows, 1 in a row

```
* * * * *
    *
    *
    *
    *
    *
```

The identity element used in the multiplication operation

$$1 \times 13 = 13, \; 13 \times 1 = 13$$

$$
\begin{array}{r}
325 \\
\times \quad 11 \\
\hline
326 \\
3260
\end{array}
\quad
\begin{array}{l}
= 1 \times 326 \\
= 10 \times 326
\end{array}
$$

Equivalent fractions

$$\frac{1}{2} \times \frac{1}{1} = \frac{1}{2}$$

$$\frac{1}{2} \times \frac{2}{2} = \frac{2}{4}$$

$$\frac{1}{2} = \frac{2}{4}$$

Division with common fractions

$$2/3 \div 1/4 = \square$$

$$\frac{2/3}{1/4} \times 1 = \square$$

$$\frac{2/3}{1/4} \times \frac{4}{4} = \frac{2/3 \times 4}{1}$$

$$\frac{2/3 \times 4}{1} = 2/3 \times 4$$

Division with decimal fractions

$$6.4\overline{)8.54}$$

$$\frac{8.54}{6.4} \times 1 = \square$$

$$\frac{8.54}{64} \times \frac{10}{10} = \frac{85.4}{64}$$

$$\frac{85.4}{64} = 64\overline{)85.4}$$

Moving toward a spiral plan of curriculum development in elementary mathematics requires both reorganization of content and organization for effective learning opportunities for children. The plan calls for designating major content areas; ascertaining the content themes or main ideas in each content area; collating the concepts, content topics, and performance skills associated with each content theme into a logical sequence; and developing potential units of content to be studied by children. Organizing for effective learning opportunities for children implies that the potential units or topics of content can be dealt with effectively within the established guiding principles of the program. For example, if provision is to be made for pupil differences, consideration must be given to the types of materials used, varieties in approaches, types of appropriate learning experiences, and evaluative procedures that might be used to assess individual progress. Planning must also involve setting the scene in which the content is to appear and the program is to function with children as the primary participants. The classroom, its physical features and atmosphere, is a most important organizational aspect in developing an active elementary mathematics program.

Classroom Features

The modern self-contained classroom needs very little more than the physical facilities it already has to make it suitable for an active laboratory approach in elementary mathematics. The task is to make better use of what does exist. Ideally, physical requirements include storage space available to children for materials that are not in immediate use, open shelf or table space for materials that are being used, and movable desks or tables to serve as work spaces for small groups. Display spaces on bulletin boards or shelves for the projects made by children are also desirable.

Of course, the self-contained classroom should not be devoted totally to mathematics for the same reasons that it should not be a reading-language arts room, a science room, or an art room. Plans and arrangements for utilizing space and classroom facilities must take into account all aspects of the comprehensive academic elementary program of a self-contained classroom. Each area of study requires storage space for materials that are not being used currently and open shelf space to make the materials that are currently being used available to children. Some teachers designate shelf or table spaces along the walls for each of the areas and centralize the materials for elementary mathematics in one of these areas. These areas should be more than display centers prepared by teachers. With some ingenuity, the elementary mathematics space can be arranged to make materials available for use at other areas in the room, to stir the interests of children in mathematical topics, and to display some of the children's products.

Space Utilization

It would be most desirable if all of the models and the manipulative materials to be utilized in all of the content areas of the elementary mathematics program were open-shelved by category or assignment so that they would be available to all of the children all of the time. If that were possible, children could review or repeat previous learning experiences as they desired, explore new and different ideas and materials, and work in small groups in different content areas at the same time. When that type of open shelf space is not available or when the instructional program is built around a unit-of-study plan in which all children work on the same content area at different levels, open shelf space must be found for the necessary materials. Open shelf space allows children to be responsible for obtaining materials when they are needed and for returning materials to their proper space when they are no longer needed or when the work period is finished. Materials on open shelves must be stored neatly if children are to serve themselves. The open shelf space available in the room should be scrutinized carefully by the teacher not only in terms of amount of open space but also in regard to current usage. Materials that are not being used or that are seldom used might better be stored elsewhere. Some classroom teachers who complain about lack of open shelf space may find that they are not using available shelves appropriately.

Storage of materials that are not being used currently or that are used infrequently is another problem. No one ever has enough closets or cabinets. Storage in faraway closets or in materials or learning centers means that the materials are never on hand when they are needed on the spur of the moment. Planning for the use of materials never seems to be complete. Some teachers prefer to box materials by categories, label the boxes, and leave the boxes in the room so that the materials can be found quickly.

What must remain available at all times are work spaces for children on open or clear table or desk tops, on the floor, and on some counter or cabinet tops. Ideally, small tables seating no more than five children would best serve the learning activities of an active laboratory approach in elementary mathematics. Laboratory-type learning experiences are designed for individuals and small groups of children. Table tops allow children to spread out and use the physical object models for mathematical ideas and pictorial manipulative materials in introductory and developmental activities and in games. However, flat-topped, movable individual pupil desks can be arranged to serve as table tops of varying sizes. Being able to make table tops of varying sizes is an advantage in providing for different group sizes. The only disadvantage is that the desks can be nudged apart and allow the materials to become disarranged or to fall on the floor. Some teachers prevent this occurrence by taping the legs of the desks together and leaving them grouped for several days at a time.

Some of the learning activities and games of an active laboratory program are better conducted in open floor space with the children sitting on the floor. This is especially true of those activities and games that require larger spaces for spreading out the materials. It is also true of those activities in which materials might topple and fall: building a "Tower of Twos" (intended to help children learn to count by twos and to introduce even numbers) with dominoes or building a "Tower a Meter High" (intended to help children develop ideas about centimeters and height of a meter) with graduated centimeter rods. It is not so much the noise of objects toppling from table tops that suggests use of floor space as the need for a solid base in order to accommodate the task.

Some of the activities of an active laboratory approach require construction of pupil projects. Easily cleaned counter space is needed for measuring, cutting, pasting, and other construction tasks. The same type of space is needed for similar activities in other areas of study and that space should not remain cluttered with previous construction activities or with incomplete projects from one session to another. Projects should be selected that can be completed in one work period or that can be easily stored for later continuation. Otherwise, the space will be continually unavailable when children seek to work on special projects.

Almost all elementary classroom teachers use wall space to display children's work. Quite often that space is completely covered with exhibits from areas other than mathematics. Pupil work in mathematics is seldom displayed, and in programs that are dominated by printed materials that may be the right decision. Worksheets or workbook pages completed by children do not make interesting or attractive displays. However, in an active mathematics program, interesting and attractive pupil projects are constructed, and every reason for displaying work in other areas applies to displaying the work of mathematics. Wall space may also be utilized to make certain kinds of materials that are to be continuously used available. For example, multiple-use record-keeping sheets such as the one pictured in Figure 4.3 should be constantly available for children. Simple cup hooks can be mounted on the wall, holes punched in the tops of the sheets, and the sheets hung on the hooks where they can be readily obtained. The walls of the self-contained classroom should be considered as much a part of the domain of the elementary mathematics program as they are of the other subject areas.

The same may be said of bulletin boards and other display areas. Bulletin boards can serve as more than display surfaces or spaces to be decorated by the classroom teacher. Bulletin boards can be active in their design, encouraging children to initiate learning activities. "Working" bulletin boards can be designed so as to be a part of the materials of instruction. Such a bulletin board might be directed toward a content area of elementary mathematics. Some information or examples can be displayed along with some directions or questions to be answered. The working bulletin board in Figure 4.4 is directed toward initiating activities in a combination of geometry and measurement learning experiences. The pockets or envelopes stapled to the board contain activity cards. The activities are classified according to the materials that are to be used. In each pocket, the activity cards are numbered in a logical sequence. Children can take cards from any pocket and initiate the activity on their own.

Figure 4.3

Activities and Instructional Materials

The learning experiences and activities in any elementary mathematics program might be classified as introductory, developmental, practice, and evaluative. There is no distinct dividing line among them in the conduct of the classroom program. A child who is participating in what was thought to be an introductory activity might in fact be developing the meaning of or practicing the idea that was to be introduced. A child who is participating

Figure 4.4 *A Working Bulletin Board*

in what was considered to be a developmental activity might still be acquiring introductory ideas or might be practicing the application of the ideas. However, the child who is working on a learning experience that has been classified as practice could hardly be acquiring introductory ideas or developing the meaning of those ideas.

The materials for activities or learning experiences that generally are classified as practice are primarily abstract. The child who is working with abstract or printed materials, no matter what the abstraction is printed on, is practicing something. However, that something may not be what was intended as the practice activity. For example, if a child is given the task of finding sums when the stimuli of two one-digit addends are given (supposedly practicing the addition facts), the child practices whatever it is he does to arrive at the sums. Regardless of how the stimuli are generated (by rolling two numeral cubes, by drawing two numeral cards, by spinning a spinner, by addition flash cards, or by exercises on a worksheet), if the child counts on his fingers, he is practicing counting.

If the nature of evaluation is as comprehensive as it should be in active laboratory-type elementary mathematics programs, all learning activities or experiences can be classified as evaluative. The teacher can evaluate pupil performance and progress by observing students engaged in introductory, developmental, and practice exercises. The teacher can also evaluate pupil perfor-mance by reviewing the projects or products that a pupil has completed. In a comprehensive evaluation approach, evaluation is not based primarily on checking a student's responses on work-sheets, assignments, and tests. However, tasks on worksheets, written assignments, and tests cannot be considered introductory, developmental, or practice learning experiences or activities. Those tasks are strictly evaluative. All of them require writing, and children can only write what they know. When children are told to complete a printed worksheet, a written assignment, or a test, the teacher is only finding out what they know, the teacher is evaluating.

The nature of instructional materials to be used in an active laboratory approach to elementary mathematics is closely related to the intent of the learning experience. If the intent of the activity is to introduce a mathematical idea, concept, or skill, the basic materials will be physical object models for that idea. A few pictorial manipulative materials might be used, but they would not dominate the activity. If the intent of the activity is to further develop an idea, concept, or skill that has already been introduced, the basic materials would be physical object models and pictorial manipulatives. Some paper-and-pencil recording procedures may be used in the later developmental stages. An activity primarily intended for practice would employ pictorial manipulatives. Practice follows understanding. Physical objects might be used and should always be available for verification purposes. As previously stated, worksheets or dittoed pages of exercises, other written assignments, and tests are evaluative devices only.

The basic instructional materials needed to conduct an active elementary mathematics program are physical object models for the mathematical ideas of each of the major content areas and pictorial manipulative materials to supplement the models. A physical object model is concrete. It can be seen and touched. In its concreteness, it has the characteristics of the abstract idea that it represents. The pieces of a good model are movable and can be manipulated easily by children. In essence, a good model possesses or illustrates the properties involved in the idea. The pieces of the model are simple, regular, and consistent with the idea and do not detract attention from the idea being emphasized. Pictorial manipulatives also represent a mathematical idea but are more abstract in nature. Pieces of pictorial manipulatives may be pictures of a model, diagrams or drawings of an idea, or merely pieces of some material that have words or numerals (abstractions) on them. Such pieces are more manipulative than they are pictorial. Examples and lists of physical object models and pictorial manipulative materials are given in Chapters 7 through 11, which deal with the major content areas. Those chapters suggest various uses of those materials. Additional information about mathematical models and pictorial manipulatives is given in Appendix A.

Other types of instructional materials are also of value in moving toward an active elementary mathematics program. Various kinds of pupil record-keeping sheets and various kinds of teacher record-keeping devices are a necessity. The materials commonly found in existing programs can be put to good use. The teacher's manual and the student's textbook can serve as resource and guide books for the teacher. The student's textbook can serve as a reference book for children after ideas and skills have been introduced and developed. Selected pages or parts of workbooks and worksheets can serve as evaluative instruments, and other supplementary materials (additional texts or nonfiction books, for example) can be used to broaden children's mathematical understandings and interests.

Organizing for Instruction

Effective learning opportunities or experiences take place in a classroom atmosphere that exudes interest in and enthusiasm for the concepts and skills to be learned and the ways in which those concepts and skills are presented. Children's interests in and enthusiasm for the study of elementary mathematics are the product of past experiences with the subject. If past experiences have been dull, if the attitudes of peers and parents toward the study of mathematics are unfavorable, or if the child perceives that the teacher views mathematics with little enthusiasm, that child is not likely to show great interest in or enthusiasm for learning mathematics.

Roles and Responsibilities

Establishing a classroom atmosphere that helps children learn the concepts and skills of elementary mathematics is the responsibility of the classroom teacher. The principles and procedures of an active laboratory approach to elementary mathematics programs are directed toward creating and maintaining high interest and enthusiasm on the part of children. The level of interest and enthusiasm displayed by the teacher will have a direct effect on that of the children in the classroom.

The role of the teacher in an active elementary mathematics program is not to direct children through pages of printed materials nor to "show and tell" about concepts and skills. The active teacher is a planner, selecter, presenter, and director of high-involvement learning experiences for children. Those roles include providing the necessary materials and the appropriate activities for using the materials in helping individual children develop a sound and related structure of mathematical ideas. To initiate the activities of individuals or small groups of children, the teacher provides the materials and starts the children with simple questions, suggestions, rules, or directions. The teacher does not "show and tell" the children how to do it. When the activities are in process, the teacher questions and guides with such comments and questions as, "What are you doing?" "Why did you do that?" "Are you sure that's right?" "Show me." "I don't believe that." A reasonable rule to attempt to follow is to try not to answer children's questions about facts, rules, generalizations, or concepts with anything other than questions or suggestions that will lead children to their own correct responses. Such comments and questions do not preclude complimenting children when they are performing well.

In an active elementary mathematics program, the roles of children are not to sit and listen, follow rules of operations, and mimic the performances of a demonstrator. The "active" aspect of the program pertains primarily to the nature of children's involvement in the learning experiences. They are to be actively engaged in laboratory-type learning activities. Their responsibilities are extended from merely completing written assignments as accurately as possible to assuming responsibility for their own behaviors, respecting the rights of others, and helping to maintain the appearance of the room. In the ideal classroom, children will be actively participating in some learning activity, they will try not to distract others, and they will obtain materials from and return materials to their proper places. They will also assist and learn from each other. In the conduct of the program, the teacher will be able to observe which of the learning opportunities are of interest to children. Those that are not of interest may be either poorly selected (wrong children, wrong materials, wrong time) or may need modification.

Most elementary mathematics classes have a specific time allotment. If a definite period of time is scheduled for mathematics activities, brief pre- and post-time periods can be used by children and teacher to arrange the materials and furniture for the sessions and to rearrange the room afterward. If no definite period of time is scheduled for mathematics class, some work spaces must be established for mathematics activities. Since the teacher may be the lone adult in the situation, children must take part of the responsibility for maintaining order and organization in the arrangement of materials and work spaces. Frequent "pow-wows" or talk sessions between teacher and the class about organization, ongoing activities, and other possibilities may help to evaluate past actions and to direct and encourage future actions.

Organizational Approaches

Initiating Activities

One way to begin changing an existing program is to incorporate a few introductory and developmental learning activities and a few gamelike practice activities into a textbook-oriented program. These activities should be related to the current topic of study. Not all of the children in the class need to participate in the activities at one time. While most of the class is engaged with some common worksheet or textbook assignment, the teacher can select a small group to introduce the laboratory-type activity.

Perhaps those having the most difficulty or the most disruptive should be selected to work on an introductory or developmental activity using a physical object model. If the activity is a game for practice, children who understand the idea should be selected. The teacher needs to teach the activity only to one small group. At least one of the participants in that group will understand the activity well enough to teach it to others who have not participated and, thus, new "teachers" are made. More and more laboratory-type activities can be incorporated as the teacher acquires the resources and as the children adapt to the new atmosphere.

Unit Planning

Another organizational approach is to utilize a unit plan of instruction. By looking ahead in the program, the teacher can select one major area of content that will be studied soon. The printed materials generally used in the program will indicate the level of complexity that is common to the particular age or grade level involved. Analyzing those content suggestions will help the teacher to determine what performance skills children are expected to acquire, some of the materials that might be used, the nature of the prerequisites that children need to deal with this level of content, and the content that is likely to follow. With these ideas in mind, the teacher can begin to collect appropriate laboratory-type learning activities and materials for that one content area. A large collection of laboratory learning activities can be considered a resource unit. A teaching unit, or unit of instruction, is a set of activities that are selected and presented because they are appropriate to the ability levels of children and pertinent to the specific goals held for those children.

Because individual children have different needs, the activities selected for any one unit of instruction will vary in terms of difficulty, purpose, materials to be used, and the processes, concepts, and skills to be developed. Any activity may appear in several different units of instruction as those units are spaced throughout the program. A particular activity may reappear for a variety of reasons:

1. Some children could use the activity at their particular level of development.
2. Some children may need the activity to review the ideas in preparation for further development.

3. The activity might be useful for further development or practice, particularly if another simple aspect or rule is added.
4. The activity might be a high-interest activity needed for stimulation.
5. The physical object materials in the activity might become less and less necessary for children to handle the concepts and skills.
6. Children may request it because they like it.

One way of operating is for the teacher to plan and select a number and variety of learning experiences from a resource unit or major area of content. All children would be working at different levels in the same major area to acquire different concepts and skills. Don't flood the classroom with a multitude of activity opportunities; that may lead only to confusion and chaos! In a class of 30 children, 9 or 10 appropriate activities would be sufficient. That may seem like a large number of activities, but some of them may be identical and others will be very similar, differing only in the nature of the materials that are utilized. For the children to be actively engaged in the learning opportunities, they must work in small groups. The activities are made available to children at various places or interest centers in the room (table tops and desk tops). Particular children are directed to specific activities. The first request of the teacher may be for the children to investigate the materials to be used, "What's there?" Poster notices, question cards, pictures, or displays of materials might also call attention to the activity possibilities. If the teacher desires, children can be free to select their own activity (a rule of thumb might be that no more than 4 children can settle at one working space). As the teacher moves about the room to guide, to question, and to record children's endeavors, the need for certain children to work on selected activities will become apparent. Those children can then be guided in that direction.

New and different learning experiences are added as particular activities become less interesting to the children or are no longer needed in a particular unit of study. It will not be unusual for children to request an activity that was previously available or to suggest other possibilities. In most instances, that request should be honored if the activity fits with the general purpose of the content area or the specific purposes of the unit. Children may be requesting that activity because they have not yet had an opportunity to do it; because they know they do not know the ideas, concepts, and skills inherent in the activity; because they want to review the ideas and skills; because they want to teach the activity to some of their peers; or for other reasons. In reality, all previously available activities should remain available but out of sight to be brought back if needed at a later time. There should be a consistency in both the materials and in the nature of activities within one major content area and the units of instruction pertaining to that content area.

Teachers of an active laboratory-type elementary mathematics program will be continuously planning and preparing future units of study. As resources of activities are expanded and as experience with conducting the instructional units is gained, the time and effort needed to plan and prepare new units will decrease. There is a great deal of professional satisfaction and pleasure in planning and preparing learning activities and in watching children learn through them. The magnitude of the total task or program should not be overwhelming. One unit of instruction can be planned and prepared at a time, and the security of the existing program is ever present until the new unit of instruction is ready.

The transition from one unit of instruction to another becomes smoother with organized resources and experience. Resources of potential activities can be organized in several ways, but the suggestion here is to organize them by major content area and by topics within that content area. Keeping a separate index of potential learning experiences categorized by purposes would be very helpful. The resources of a unit of instruction are never worn out—they can be used again and again.

In actual classroom operation, units of instruction will take different lengths of time. Every child cannot be expected to participate in every available activity. The unit should continue at least until every child is more powerful with the concepts and skills of the main ideas in the major content area and should be discontinued (to be brought back later with similar activities) while pupil interest and activity are still high. When a teacher determines that a new instructional unit should be initiated, opportunities in that area can be phased in gradually or a whole new group of learning activities can be made available at one time. Teachers should keep records of the extent and nature of children's participation in the learning opportunities or activities of each instructional unit. These records will be very useful in guiding and directing learning experiences in future instructional units in the spiral plan of curriculum and will indicate to the teacher which children can assist in teaching other children.

The teacher using an active laboratory approach will find that less time is spent on the drudgeries of conventional mathematics programs: repeating assignments, preparing dittoed worksheets, and grading papers. More time is spent in the professional activities of planning, developing, directing, and evaluating. The teacher's time will be spent in those professionally self-satisfying activities of circulating among children, informally communicating, guiding, and questioning, which brings the teacher closer to the children and helps them to learn.

In all of the considerations of the organization of the elementary mathematics program, the most important elements are the children in the program. Organizational efforts must be directed toward facilitating individual achievement, not merely toward ease of management.

Selecting Learning Experiences *Chapter 5*

Planning, selecting, and providing learning experiences to suit the individual characteristics of children is one of the most important responsibilities of the teacher of elementary mathematics. The teacher's initial task is to provide opportunities for children to learn. The act of teaching has occurred when a person acquires ideas and skills because learning opportunities have been made available and because that person interacts with the materials, with the person responsible for directing the activity, and with other people who are involved. When potential learners have not acquired new ideas or skills or have not increased their powers or abilities to apply concepts and skills to problem situations, nothing has been learned and, therefore, nothing has been taught. Teaching implies learning. When the potential learners do not achieve the goals of the activity, the attempt to teach has failed. It is true that the potential learners might acquire other information, ideas, or skills than those intended as objectives of the learning experience that has been presented. These acquisitions are sometimes called *incidental learnings*; they are likely to occur in almost any learning opportunity. However, when incidental learnings are the only results of an intended learning experience, the intended learning experience has been inappropriately planned, selected, or presented. In an active elementary mathematics program, the classroom teacher attempts to provide learning opportunities for children that meet the general objectives of the total program and that help individual children acquire the basic concepts and skills associated with specific individualized goals.

Characteristics of a Laboratory Approach

The learning opportunities presented to children in an elementary mathematics laboratory approach will be much different from those used in a program dominated by printed materials. One great difference is in the type and amount of the concrete and manipulative materials and the frequency with which they are handled by children. In programs that depend heavily on printed materials, children primarily utilize reading and writing materials. Other more concrete instructional aids may be used briefly to introduce or to demonstrate an idea, in corrective procedures to assist children who are having difficulty, or occasionally to add to the appeal of mathematics classes. When manipulative aids or physical materials are used in such programs, they often are viewed as crutches by the teacher and, thus, are dutifully avoided by the children. Children's interactions with exploratory manipulative materials are brief and sporadic, while their interactions with printed, stimulus-response, drill, and practice materials are intense and continuous.

An active laboratory approach to elementary mathematics requires a broader spectrum of materials and a different style of utilization or learning experiences. Active laboratory-type learning experiences are

1. grounded in the use of physical object models for mathematical ideas.
2. organized as individual or small group activities.
3. inquiry oriented and problem centered.
4. concerned with developing major ideas or generalizations (not merely with practicing skills or technical operations).
5. not dominated by the printed pages of textbooks, workbooks, activity cards, or worksheets.
6. based on data collection, data organization, and a search for patterns, facts, and/or generalizations in the organized information.

7. sequenced so that the practice of skills or ideas is built on, related to, and comes after the introduction and development of major ideas and generalizations.
8. extended to the practice of facts, operations, and skills in ways that are meaningful and useful to the learner.

In regard to every major idea, basic concept, and skill to be learned by children, the general sequence of types of learning experiences in an active laboratory-type program proceeds from introduction to development to practice with applications. Different kinds of learning opportunities or experiences can be associated with each stage in the sequence.

Activities

Within this category of learning experiences there are three sub-classifications: exploratory activities, introductory activities, and developmental activities (see Figure 5.1). The purpose of each type of activity is implied by the term used to name it. The common element in all three types of activities is the use of physical object models for mathematical ideas. The importance of these activities or learning experiences lies in the development of foundations of understanding of the basic concepts and skills of the elementary mathematics program. Such learning experiences, with the exception of exploratory activities, are inquiry oriented or problem centered, and the problems are modeled by physical objects.

Figure 5.1 *Types of Activities*

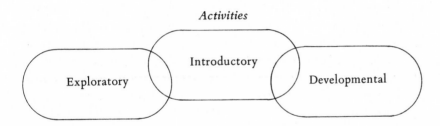

Exploratory Activities

Exploratory activities generally are intended merely to allow children to become familiar with the physical object materials and the physical characteristics of the materials. The materials are physical models that will be utilized in later introductory and developmental activities. Children may acquire some ideas about the relationships of the pieces of the objects in the model, but most often the acquisition of those ideas is not the primary purpose of the exploratory activity. However, some activities that appear to be exploratory in nature may, in fact, ask children to ascertain relationships between the object pieces of the physical model or to use the pieces of the model in ways such that mathematical ideas are actually being introduced. There is no clear dividing line between the three types of activities. Because one cannot tell exactly what ideas children are acquiring or developing when they are working with the materials of an activity, the types intersect.

The teacher can, however, set the scene for the activity with the materials and the directions that are given to the participants. The evaluative observer of the activity can tell if the activity participants are utilizing the materials in the expected manner. An exploratory activity is initiated by presenting the materials. The teacher usually asks a single, simple question or gives a direction in a manner that is both understandable and encouraging to the participants. The question or suggestion must be open-ended so that different children can explore the materials in different ways.

For example, suppose that graduated centimeter rods (see Figure 5.2) are to play an important part in later activities. The classroom teacher wants certain children to become familiar with the physical characteristics of the rods. An exploratory activity can be initiated with those selected children by simply presenting them with the rods, assigning them a work space, and giving the simple oral direction "Build something."

The children can build any structure they wish and, in fact, will probably build many structures. It is expected that through their explorations with the rods the children will become familiar with the physical characteristics of color, length, and size relationships of the rods. Similar kinds of exploratory activities can be initiated with little cubes, plastic squares, base-ten blocks, attribute blocks, parquetry blocks, pegboard pegs and string,

Figure 5.2 *Graduated Centimeter Rods*

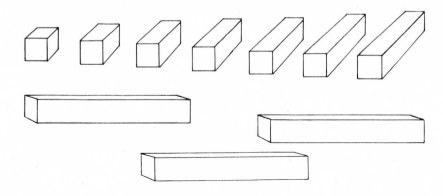

pieces of rope, geometric solids, or any other materials that are used as physical object models for mathematical ideas.

Introductory Activities

Introductory activities are designed and intended to introduce children to mathematical ideas, concepts, and skills. The materials may be both physical object models and pictorial manipulatives, but the pictorial manipulatives are used only to generate mathematical aspects, such as numerals or types of geometric entities randomly. The intent of introductory activities is to allow children to see and handle mathematical ideas in a pre-mathematical or intuitive way. Introductory activities are inquiry oriented or problem centered; the activity is task-specific in that there are questions to be answered. Each introductory activity is initiated with simple statements, questions, or problems communicated to the potential participants in an understandable manner, usually orally. The individual or small group of participants is given the physical object materials and, if necessary, the pictorial manipulatives. After the materials have been examined and perhaps discussed, the directions or questions to be answered are given briefly. The initiator of the activity, perhaps the teacher, or a child participating in the activity is left to do things with the objects, applying the idea that is being introduced in following directions, answering the questions, or solving the problem. The child's communication is by doing and showing to the observer-questioner and to the other participants in the activity and by listening and talking.

For example, suppose that a small group of children is given a set of poker chips or counters and a numeral cube with the digits 0, 1, 2, 3, 4, and 5 on the six faces of the cube. After examining the materials, the small group is told to take turns and given the following directions: "What you roll is what you get—make stacks of ten." The primary purpose of this activity is to introduce the concept of base ten. A prerequisite for the activity is that children can associate quantity (number) with the printed numerals—in other words, they can read the numerals —and this skill will be reviewed and practiced in the activity. Another prerequisite is that the participants can count objects to ten or can match the chips or counters in one-to-one fashion with their fingers. A skill to be introduced is naming numbers in terms of _____ tens and _____ ones. The decade number names may also be introduced: "*Two* tens and *three* ones are *twenty-three*."

In the process of the activity, each participant takes turns rolling the numeral cube and taking the number of chips described by the top numeral on the cube. The child is not allowed to put chips in a stack until at least ten have been obtained. Circulating among the members of the group, the teacher observes the stacking process and asks various children how many chips they have. Each child is expected to respond either by saying, for example, "*two* stacks of ten and *three* ones" or by giving the decade name "*twenty-three*." Regardless of the response, the teacher might ask, "Do you know another name for that many?" The activity continues until all of the chips or counters in the original group have been taken by the children. One may add the rule or direction that as each child completes his or her turn, the child must tell the other participants how many chips or counters he or she has.

This particular activity may be extended to a developmental activity pertaining to base ten and an introductory activity for the idea of positional or place value by using a record-keeping sheet such as the one pictured in Figure 5.3. However, a record-keeping sheet should not be used until the teacher-observer-evaluator has determined that the children are quite familiar with the process of the introductory activity. After each turn, the child enters on the record-keeping sheet the total number of chips or counters he or she has.

Figure 5.3

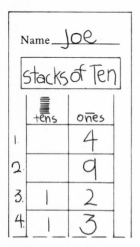

This particular activity might be considered by some teachers and children to be a game. The children will be very interested in who has "won" the most chips. However, since the primary purposes of the activities are to introduce and develop ideas, the activity is basically introductory or developmental. In any case, tenuous discussions about the classification of a particular learning experience are not of great importance.

Developmental Activities

Developmental activities are intended to extend the elementary understandings that have been introduced through children's participation in earlier activities. Developmental activities are initiated only after processes are generally understood and the children have acquired the basic idea and have demonstrated their understanding with performance. Developmental activities demand a greater degree of concentration and rigor. In many instances, they incorporate practice of the basic concepts, ideas, or skills involved in the activity. In most developmental activities, some form of written record is kept by the participants. The materials to be used include physical object models, pictorial manipulatives, and some type of writing materials. The objects and pictorial manipulatives are used in much the same manner as they are in introductory activities. Developmental activities are also intended to guide children to greater use of written or printed mathematical symbolism. Developmental activities are inquiry oriented and problem centered and include specific tasks or problems that require solutions. The processes of the solution and/or the results of the processes must be recorded. Developmental activities may be initiated with either oral or written statements, questions, or problems depending on the verbal capabilities of the participants. Participants are given the physical objects, the pictorial manipulatives, and the recording materials necessary for the conduct of the activity. The materials and their uses are discussed, communications needed to initiate the activity are given, and one of the participants attempts to demonstrate the correct procedure. Participants in the activity are then left to continue the activity. It should take no longer than a few minutes for the classroom teacher to help participants begin an introductory or a developmental activity.

If extensive time is needed or if confusion reigns, the activity is probably inappropriate. The children's communication is by doing and showing, listening and talking to other participants, and writing. When the teacher-observer-evaluator returns to the group, he or she observes the action, questions or makes suggestions to the participants, briefly peruses the written records of some of the participants, and then moves off to another group of children. The teacher stops only long enough to make certain that the activity is proceeding as planned.

Consider the developmental activity in which two children are extending ideas about comparing common fractions and utilizing the comparative symbols =, >, and <. They have previously participated in an introductory activity called "Challenge," and observations of their participation in that activity indicated that they seemed to understand the basic idea of comparing unit-fraction pieces from a physical object model; for example, fraction pies or disks. In that activity, the pieces of the fraction disks were laid out on a work space to make pies with same size or identical pieces making up each pie. Each participant was given a unit-fraction numeral cube with the fractions 1/2, 1/3, 1/4, 1/5, 1/8, and 1/10 on the six faces of the cube. The children rolled their numeral cubes simultaneously and each child picked up the fraction piece named by the numeral on the top of his or her cube. Then they compared the sizes of the pieces that they picked up.

In this developmental activity their understanding of the main idea that two numbers can be compared and the specific idea that two fraction numbers can be compared are extended to describing that comparison in both oral and written form. The children lay out the model on the table, and each child takes a record-keeping sheet and a fraction numeral cube. The cubes may be the same ones used in the introductory activity, or they may have both unit fraction and multipart fraction numerals on the faces of the cube. Again, the participants roll their cubes simultaneously, pick up the pieces named by the fractions they rolled, and make the comparison. Oral descriptions of the comparison are made, and each child records the results of the comparison.

Notice that on the individual record-keeping sheets in Figure 5.4 each child wrote his or her name in the first column. Thus, when the fractions were not equal in size, two different ways of describ-

Figure 5.4

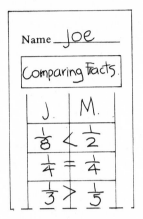
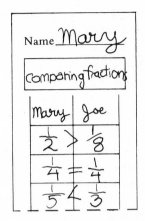

ing each of the comparisons were presented, but both describe the same situation.

Communication Skills

One of the major purposes of those learning experiences generally classified as activities is to introduce and develop communication skills in the language of mathematics. One might start with the premise that communication skills are not developed best in a vacuum of content or as a self-structured field in which oral sound symbols are merely exchanged for printed symbols. To study language or communication skills as a separate field is to deal with meaningless abstractions. Children must communicate about something they can see and do for that communication to be meaningful. Yet, it is not uncommon to find children in elementary mathematics classes who are saying, reading, and writing communication symbols in the area of mathematics much as if they were repeating nonsense symbols. In some instances, this style of communication is due to the fact that the children are working only with symbols. In other instances, there seems to be no association between what they manipulate or work with and the arithmetical symbols they appear to be very proficient in handling. Apparently, the children have been working with real things at one time and with the symbolism of mathematics at another, so that what is real is not mathematics.

The development of communication skills in elementary mathematics is closely related to the idea of the spiral development of mathematical ideas. In early stages, or at the level of introduction of ideas, the communication pattern may be as simple as doing something with physical object models and showing that action to others. Later, the child learns to communicate with sound symbols about the idea. At first a child uses his own words. Through listening, hearing words used by others to name or to describe actions, the child begins to use the common oral language of elementary mathematics. Those words and the meanings of those words are entered into his listening vocabulary by teachers and others using the terms and phrases in real, concrete, meaningful situations. With encouragement, the child begins to use those words in telling other people his ideas and describing what is happening or in asking questions.

When children have acquired the oral capabilities to describe situations, the written symbols for the oral sounds are presented and children learn to name those printed symbols and to associate those symbols with an idea. In the early stages of developing a mathematical idea, those symbols are not words, but the short quantitative, comparative, and operational symbols. Children cannot discover these symbols, they must be shown them by someone who knows. Finally, after children can read and understand these printed symbols, they are ready to begin to learn to draw or write the symbols. The activities of a laboratory approach to elementary mathematics allow children to acquire meaningful listening, speaking, reading, and writing communication skills.

Projects

Applicative Purposes

Projects are the products of children's investigations, designs, and constructions. Each project is directed toward a special task, which will result in a pupil-made product. The task or assignment calls for personal initiative, effort, and application on the part of the pupil. The importance of pupil-made projects as learning experiences lies in the applications of mathematical ideas necessary to complete the projects. Other purposes include making mathematics an integral and important part of the total elementary school program, developing the psychomotor skills of children, and developing pupil pride and self-satisfaction in a personal or individual piece of quality work. Other areas of the elementary school program provide sources or ideas for projects that students can construct. It is not unusual for classroom teachers to provide opportunities for children to plan and construct projects or products related to the ideas being introduced and developed in, for example, the areas of reading-language arts, science, social studies, and art. Many of those projects involve the application of mathematical ideas and skills. In many instances, the possibilities of integrating and applying mathematical ideas and skills in these endeavors are ignored or underplayed, and the opportunities to integrate, apply, and practice mathematical ideas and skills are lost. Such projects can be initiated either in the classes directed toward those areas of study or specifically in the mathematics class.

One of the general goals of the elementary school program is to help children develop and improve their psychomotor skills. When they construct projects, children use a variety of tools in drawing, cutting, pasting, measuring, and assembling pieces and in other physical movements. These physical actions help children develop muscular control and hand-eye coordination. Children generally enjoy making things, and the physical presence of something that they are personally responsible for, something on which they have done their best and which is appreciated by their peers and teachers, is a cause of pride and self-satisfaction. When a child's project is acceptable to the child and to others, that child is likely to develop more favorable attitudes toward mathematics, the study of mathematics, and school in general.

Completed worksheets, workpages, record-keeping sheets, and other written practice or evaluative materials should not be considered pupil projects. However, recordings, scripts, and other pupil efforts in oral or written prose that describe or give directions for a learning experience and that are intended to communicate ideas to others may be considered mathematical projects. Children who participate in such activities are developing and applying communication skills in the language of mathematics.

The purposes of utilizing pupil-made projects as learning experiences relate to cognitive, affective, and psychomotor domains. The development and application of mathematical ideas and skills and the development and utilization of communication skills are cognitive in nature. Opportunities to acquire pride and self-satisfaction and to develop more favorable attitudes are affective in nature. Actual involvement in the physical movements necessary to construct a project are related to the development of psychomotor skills and coordination. The skills to be developed and applied in project learning experiences are mathematical, linguistic, and physical.

Characteristics of Projects

Use of Materials

Learning experiences that might be classified as projects have definitive characteristics. Each project results in a pupil-made product. Most importantly, the production or construction involves the application or utilization of at least one mathematical idea or skill. The production or construction requires materials other than the physical object models and pictorial materials that are used in introductory and developmental activities and the printed or written materials that are employed in practice-evaluative experiences. In those projects where the product is linguistic in nature, the necessary materials may be recording devices and/or writing or printing tools and equipment and materials on which to write or print. For other projects, the materials are basically construction materials and tools, but writing or printing materials may also be needed. Appendix A suggests some instructional aids that children might construct, which would be considered pupil-made projects. Materials that might be used in the construction of each aid are listed.

Pupil Effort

A project-type learning experience requires intense, concentrated physical effort as well as intellectual effort. The resulting product is a material thing. It can be seen, handled, and referred to by other children and by the classroom teacher. The product is a real exhibit of both a mathematical idea and a learning experience. It is also a real exhibit of the child's prowess as a producer. The mathematical idea that was utilized or that is displayed by the product may or may not be immediately evident to the unknowing observer. Since projects are intended to be displayed or made available to other people, one characteristic of projects is a high standard of expectations on the parts of both the producer and the adult supervisor of the learning experience. Children cannot derive pride or self-satisfaction from a product that is not well done, that does not convey the intended idea, or that is not suitable for its intended use. For example, if the proposed product is to be a model of a cube made from one sheet of construction paper, the result must look like a cube and be identifiable as a cube by people who know the characteristics of a cube. Anything less than that should not be accepted as a finished product by either the child producer or the classroom teacher. The attributes and shortcomings of the unacceptable product should be determined in a comfortable way, the characteristics of the desired product should be reviewed, and another attempt should be made by the child.

Extent of Difficulty

The complexities of possible projects vary greatly, and the selection of a project learning experience for or by a child depends on a number of factors. Primary among these considerations is the child's understanding and ability with the mathematical ideas or skills that are to be applied in the construction of the product. The child's capability and familiarity with the materials and tools that are to be used in the construction must also be considered. For some projects, safety factors are involved. Some projects in the major content area of numeration and notation are so simple that they require only drawing or cut-and-paste materials and only the most elementary of number concepts or ideas. For example, a child at kindergarten level may be asked to make a number poster "All About Five." The child's concepts of number need only extend to five; the arithmetical skill to be applied need not extend beyond an ability to count up to five objects. The child might have the ability to read and write the numerals 0, 1, 2, 3, 4, 5, but that is not necessary for a project that does not require the pictures to be labeled by the child. Any labeling on the poster can be added by the teacher. The teacher can cut as many of the materials beforehand as is deemed necessary. Gummed labels or pictures might also be used. After the materials are presented, the directions may be as simple as telling the child: "Put five objects into each group. Then paste the objects in rows in different ways to put five

Figure 5.5

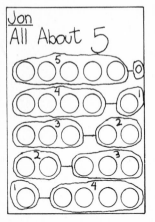

Figure 5.6

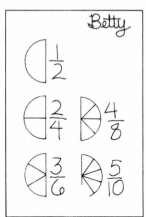

objects in two groups." (This project should be preceded by an introductory activity employing the same idea and utilizing physical objects.) The resulting product may look like Figure 5.5. The same general idea may appear at a more complex level later in the school program. A child may be given the poster paper and circular shapes and asked to make a poster about one-half. The project requires the child to fold and cut the circular shapes to make a poster showing equivalent fractions. The product may be more extensive than that shown in Figure 5.6 depending on the child's capabilities.

Projects may range from the simplicity of number posters to graphs, maps, simple teaching and learning aids, and models for mathematical ideas. More complex projects could include scale drawings, three-dimensional geometric constructions, scale models, doll houses, and other usable items. Projects can be utilized as learning experiences in each of the five major content areas and can be associated with each of the main ideas or content themes. However, projects are also a medium for correlating or integrating the concepts and skills from two or more content areas. A project that is directed toward the application of concepts and skills in numeration and notation, for example, might also employ ideas and skills from the areas of geometry and measurement. The degree of correlation or integration of ideas and skills from different content areas affects the complexity of a project.

Use of Tools

When contemplating possible projects as learning experiences, a classroom teacher must make certain that the children can safely use whatever tools will be required for the production or construction of the product. Projects allow children to learn to use common tools or devices properly and practically. Appropriate construction or production materials, sufficient work space, and the necessary tools in sufficient number must be provided so that children do not lose interest in the project because they have to wait for materials, space, or tools. The length of time needed for a child to complete a project is an important matter. If it takes so long that the child loses interest or the time available for introducing and developing other important ideas is drastically diminished, the project is probably inappropriate. Very complex and compelling projects should be divided into segments that can be considered evaluative units or periods of success and satisfaction.

Communicating Directions

Communications from the classroom teacher to children to initiate a project may take a variety of forms. Oral suggestions and directions are probably the most effective approach for very young children and for others who have not acquired reading skills. Other projects can be initiated with very simple written suggestions, questions, or directions. In some instances, the teacher may wish to prepare a set of written directions for assembling a product. These will be much like the directions that appear in commercial products that are assembled by the purchaser. Such an approach can help children learn to read and follow directions.

Interest in other projects may be stimulated by presenting a completed model or product and suggesting that children make one like it. For example, the teacher may make a sign that says, "Make a Pinwheel," construct several pinwheels with different numbers of vanes, and mount those pinwheels on the sign (see Figure 5.7). Construction materials and tools would be available near the sign. Children would not be allowed to detach the pinwheels from the sign; their major task is to figure out how the pinwheels were made. To make the project more interesting, the teacher may allow children to enter a pinwheel contest. The contest may have several categories depending on the number of vanes on the pinwheels that children make. Of course, the best pinwheels are those that turn well in the least wind. In the absence of wind, have children move their pinwheels through the air by moving their arms or by walking. Providing templates of a large square, a large equilateral triangle, and a large hexagon, along with the other construction materials, may help children figure out how the pinwheels were made.

When a child completes a project, the child might well be allowed to show the product to the other children in the class and to discuss how it was made and how it can be used. The teacher's questions can guide the discussion toward the mathematical ideas and skills that were employed in producing or constructing the project. Care should be taken not to overexplain or to explain in a show-and-tell manner that would discourage other children from attempting the project. The purposes of the discussion and questioning should be to give the producer a feeling of accomplishment and satisfaction and to motivate others. The child producer might also be given the option to take the product home.

Figure 5.7

Games

Place and Purpose

Games are not without purpose in active elementary mathematics programs. As with any planned learning experiences in the program, games are used either to introduce new ideas, to further develop or expand ideas or skills, or to practice ideas or skills. Most elementary mathematics games are directed toward the practice of ideas, facts, and operations. Through games children can practice the concepts and skills they are expected to master. The specific purposes of a particular game need not be expressly clear to the children who are playing it, although they will certainly become aware of the skills that are needed to play the game well. However, teachers or supervisors must be aware of the mathematical ideas, skills, and abilities required in the game because these are directly related to the reason for allowing or encouraging children to play a game. Through informal comments, questions, and suggestions, the teacher or supervisor can help children increase skills and abilities and apply them in the game situations. (*Note*: Games are one type of learning experience in which teacher aides and volunteer classroom helpers can supervise the action.) When a particular child is not doing well in a game because she lacks understanding or skills, the teacher may suggest other learning activities that will increase the child's skills and abilities and will help her play the game better.

Naturally, children will at times want to play games merely for fun, utilizing skills that they appear to have mastered. While they will not be developing or practicing ideas, playing games for fun should not be denied completely. Such participation can have a favorable effect on children's attitudes toward mathematics, the study of mathematics, and the application of mathematical ideas and can influence social behavior in a positive manner. On the other hand, children should not be allowed to play games indefinitely at which they are adept.

The teacher should encourage children to play games that are appropriate to their educational needs. To do this, a teacher must have a firm belief that children can learn (acquire concepts, ideas, and skills) in gaming situations. The teacher or supervisor can suggest that students try new games, can help pupils to expand the games they are playing into new games with more complex rules, and can introduce new games by becoming a player and inviting children to join the action. The supervising adult cannot introduce each game to each child, but a few children can be taught how to play a game, and these children in turn can teach other children the rudiments of the game.

Puzzles and trick problems should not be construed as games. While they may be of value in introducing, developing, or practicing mathematical ideas and can be utilized in active elementary mathematics programs, they are more in the nature of individualized activities and do not satisfy the criteria for children's games in elementary mathematics.

Educators do not all agree on the exact nature of a game suitable for use by children in their study of elementary mathematics. It may be said that existing lists of criteria have been more stifling to the use of games than they have been conducive. Not all educators or psychologists would agree with the suggested characteristics of a good elementary mathematics game that are presented here. Some may even disagree with the thought that games are a worthwhile educational experience and would suggest that the activity of the game hinders achievement of learning objectives. Teachers in elementary classrooms and supervisors of elementary learning experiences should not make up their minds about the educational value of games without actively trying purposeful games and evaluating outcomes.

Characteristics of Appropriate Games

Good games, which might be used to help children learn elementary mathematical ideas, have certain characteristics. The value of a game depends on the purpose(s) of the game and the extent to which it serves that purpose. The characteristics of an elementary mathematics game that is most likely to achieve its stated purpose(s) may be described as follows:

1. *The game must involve the use of at least one basic mathematical idea, and preferably the use of several related ideas.* The game will not be purposeful unless the players are being introduced to, developing, or practicing mathematical ideas or skills. In some instances, individual players will participate for similar

reasons because the players will have similar abilities or needs. But in other instances, individual players will participate for different reasons, and not all players in one game will be at the same level of development in regard to the basic mathematical concepts and skills involved. For example, the game may be an introduction to the basic ideas for a new player, another player may have a general notion about the basic ideas and is further developing them, while a third player could have developed the ideas to the extent that he or she is playing the game for practice.

2. *The game should have basic rules for play that entail behavioral obligations as well as how proper plays in the game are made.* Learning how to take turns in playing, sharing, being partners, and developing respect for the playing rights of others may be as important for some children as the development of mathematical ideas. Initial playing rules should be very simple and very clear to the players. Rules of the game should provide for every contingency for the playing actions of the players. The playing rules of games may be spirally developed, just as mathematical ideas are spirally developed. Rules are sometimes better learned by example than they are learned through verbal descriptions. One good procedure is for children to take several turns just to practice the playing rules before the game really begins. Another good procedure is for the adult supervisor (teacher) or a child who knows how to play to participate for a few minutes or turns until the group knows how to play the game. The seat can then be relinquished to another child. When players in a game agree that a rule should be changed or that a rule should be added, that change should be made by the group. A rule change may also be suggested by the teacher or other supervising adult.

3. *The game must require the participation of more than one child.* A child might use the materials of a game and actually follow the rules laid out for a game in an individual activity, but such solitary efforts are not gamelike in other ways. What one calls such an endeavor is not important, but in the categorizations used here, individual efforts of this type are called activities. Some games may be more effective with two players. Others require more than two players either for the game action to proceed according to the rules or for attainment of the game's purposes. The size of the group playing the game is best determined by the extent of continuous participation on the part of individual players and by the guiding adult's knowledge of the behavior patterns of the children. If children are obviously losing

interest between turns to play, the game is either not fun to play or there are too many players in the game.

4. *The game should be regarded as fun by the children—they should want to play the game.* When a game is not fun or the players do not enjoy it, it is not likely to achieve its purposes. At the very least, playing the game should not make the child unhappy. Losing a single game can cause momentary unhappiness, but this should quickly fade with the beginning of a new game. Children's attitudes toward games are greatly influenced by the attitudes and visible enthusiasm or lack of enthusiasm of the adult present. Children will not regard as fun those games that require skills and abilities far beyond their own levels of attainment, and some children will look on some games as beneath them. It is the responsibility of the guiding adult to help children find games that are both fun and challenging—appropriate to their general mathematical development. This task is more difficult when the idea of using games is first introduced to children; it becomes easier as more and more games are added to the children's repertoire and as rule changes for the games are made.

5. *Children's activities in the game should require constant participation, as a player during their own turn and as an observer-checker while others are playing.* In many game situations, the variations or possibilities for a successful play change with each succeeding play. Each player in the game should be aware of the possibilities as they occur rather than waiting for his or her turn and then surveying the opportunities. Play in a game is greatly delayed when players are not continuously aware of the changes in possibilities for play, and when delays occur player interest in the game wanes. Children playing an elementary mathematics game should be encouraged to keep up with the progress of the game. Some short delays at a player's turn are inevitable because that person must search for a successful play. In addition, players should constantly observe and check the correctness of the plays made by other participants. It is quite possible that a player can learn as much from the play of others as from his or her own plays. In all games, incorrect plays are not allowed. In some games, incorrect plays are merely taken back and a new play is allowed; in other games incorrect plays are penalized in some manner. Each player's participation as an observer-checker of the moves of other participants not only maintains the fairness of the game but also increases the attention given to the mathematical ideas incorporated into the game.

6. *The game should be competitive. There should be a winner and/or a loser.* Some educators and psychologists feel that competition is to be avoided, but in reality, competition is natural for children as well as for adults. It is only when the positive reinforcement for winning or the negative reinforcement for losing overshadows other aspects of the game situation or when the emphasis on winning is overly great that competition is inappropriate. In other words, the nature of the follow-up action should not greatly influence the nature of the game situation. Players should want to win and should try to avoid losing, not for the following reinforcement, but for the fun and spirit of the game. Competition is most appropriate among players who have similar skills and abilities. At times it is quite difficult for the supervising adult to select players for a particular game who are comparable in the attainment of the mathematical ideas and skills required for the game. When games are used as an integral part of the elementary mathematics program, a natural selection of game participants by children will evolve. In many instances, they will seek their own levels and want to play with others who will be good competitors for them. At different times, they will want to play with their friends and will not mind either losing to a friend with better skills or helping a friend learn to play the game better. In some games it is possible for a child to practice computational operations or some other mathematical idea by keeping a record of the scoring.

7. *The element of chance must be present.* Chance implies that each player in the game has equal opportunity to obtain similar playing situations. When the outcome of a game depends only on the skills and abilities of the participants, competition can become fierce and the participants can become very aggressive. When the element of chance is present, the player who is slightly less skilled has a greater possibility of winning than he or she would otherwise have. Children who are slightly dissimilar in skills and abilities can, thus, be participants in the same game, and the spirit of competition can be maintained. The presence of the chance element also makes the game more exciting for the players. The element of chance is interjected into elementary mathematics games through the drawing or dealing of cards, the drawing of dominoes, the rolling of cubes, or the spinning of a spinner.

8. *Strategies for play should be inherent in the game.* The employment of strategy in a game merely means that plays are planned, conducted, and combined so that the goal of scoring

or winning the game is more likely to be attained. A player's strategies may involve not only planning and playing to increase his or her own opportunities, but also planning and playing to decrease the opportunities of other players or competitors. Strategies of planning and playing involve surveying individual opportunities and observing the competitors' plays. The simplest games may be devoid of any complicated strategy for play and involve only a very simple approach. As games become more complex, the possibilities for employing strategies increase. The strategies should not be explained to children, but it is quite appropriate for the supervising adult to ask an individual player why a particular play was made. In that way, the adult can ascertain whether the player is seeking or utilizing a strategy. When asking the question, the adult is also hinting to the player that there might be some strategy involved in the game. Children should not be expected to employ the strategies unique to a game in their first sessions with that game. However, as children develop and practice the basic mathematical ideas of the game, they should be encouraged to plan and conduct their plays in a strategic manner.

Materials for Games

The basic game materials for the active elementary mathematics program in a self-contained classroom need not be extensive nor go far beyond the physical object models and the pictorial manipulatives that are necessary to conduct the introductory and developmental learning activities. With the addition of various decks of playing cards, sets of dominoes, and several carefully selected commercially produced mathematics games, a large assortment of games can be made available. A large financial expenditure is not necessary. What cannot be purchased can be easily constructed, using the materials that should already be available for pupil-made projects. If possible, several decks of the numeral cards commercially available as children's games, several sets of regular dominoes, and several carefully selected commercially available mathematics games should be purchased. Such purchases are not expensive and would greatly decrease the amount of time and effort needed to prepare materials and would allow more time for the construction of materials that are not available. Such purchases would also allow children to play games with high-quality materials. The key is to purchase or construct only those materials that have a very high potential for a large variety of uses.

The following ideas apply only to whole numbers, but similar kinds of materials and games can be planned or constructed for use with common fractions, decimal fractions, and the major content areas of measurement and geometry. It would not be feasible to give examples here for each of these ideas. There are more than a volume of possibilities. Suggestions for and descriptions of games pertaining to each of the ideas appear in *Active Learning Experiences for Teaching Elementary School Mathematics*.

Numeral cubes and the physical object models for whole numbers, including poker chips, ice cream sticks, and base-ten blocks, can be utilized in games directed toward developing and practicing ideas and skills pertaining to associating numerals with number or quantity; base ten and positional value; acquiring and naming quantities; comparing quantities; the basic facts of addition, subtraction, and multiplication; problem solving; and the computational operations.

Numeral cards, such as those available as children's games (for example, Rook, which is commercially produced by Parker Brothers), can be used in games to develop and practice concepts and skills of associating numerals with number, comparing numerals, place value, order and sequence of numerals, the basic facts, and the computational operations.

Equation or number sentence games (for example, Tuf, which is commercially produced by Avalon-Hill) can be used to develop and practice almost all aspects of algebraic foundations, including the uses of quantitative, operational, and comparative symbols. The cubes that come in many of these games can also be used in other activities or games.

Regular dominoes can be used to develop and practice ideas and skills of counting, matching, comparing, order and sequence, group recognition of number, odd and even numbers, addition, and multiplication.

All of the commercially produced games include rule books, some with a variety of games. While these games might be appropriate in the active elementary mathematics program, an even greater value lies in the adaptability of the materials to variations in the games they suggest and to games and activities that might be created or developed by the classroom teacher, other educators, or children.

Practice-Evaluative Exercises

Practice-evaluative exercises are paper-and-pencil oriented. The learning experiences of introductory and developmental activities, pupil-made projects, and games are also practice-evaluative: children practice concepts, ideas, and skills in the course of these activities, and classroom teachers evaluate children's performances and achievements through observation, oral questioning, and record keeping. This section, however, focuses on practice tasks in the more abstract form of printed materials, which are further removed from concrete situations. The printed exercises or problems seek responses to be derived from memory or from computational operations that children are to perform. Some of the exercises may require the child to discover a pattern in number sequences or results and apply that pattern in making responses. The exercises are to be completed without the aids of physical objects or other materials through the child's recall and application of concepts, facts, rules, and generalizations. The sources of practice-evaluative exercise materials of this type include worksheets, dittoed pages, workbook pages, and pages of exercises copied from textbooks. Anyone who has attended or visited an American school is familiar with the variety of these materials and their uses.

Purposes

In elementary mathematics programs that employ these materials intensively, the reason most often given for their use is practice. However, the materials are also used in an evaluative manner. Evaluations are based on children's responses to the stimuli presented and are carried out checking or correcting the completed works and recording the findings. The degree to which a child responds correctly to the exercises becomes a matter of record. That recorded performance may or may not influence the child's further participation in that type of exercise and may or may not influence new directions in the instructional program. A high degree of success generally will lead the child to more complex exercises of the same type or to another topic of study. A low degree of success may lead the child to more work with the same kind of exercises or to corrective instruction. In some instances when printed exercises dominate the program, the evaluative procedure is based completely on the child's ability to arrive at correct responses. Understanding of the concepts, ideas, and skills is neither required nor tested. In another approach, the child's incorrect responses are analyzed to ascertain whether there is a pattern of misconception or a pattern of misapplication of facts and rules. This analysis is followed up with some type of corrective procedure.

Uses in an Active Approach

In an active elementary mathematics program, paper-and-pencil practice-evaluative experiences are used more sparingly and are used more for evaluation than for practice. The purpose of practice in elementary mathematics programs is to help children perfect or master concepts and skills and their applications. An active laboratory approach offers better ways to practice than printed exercise sheets. Very few printed exercise sheets are designed so that they cause children to reason. Correct responses on a page of exercises do not guarantee that a child understands the concept or skill or even that the intended operation or thinking was performed. The time and place for practice is after a child understands the concepts and operations and is working toward mastery. Pages of printed exercises might be used to help children acquire speed in the application of ideas, facts, and operations after they have demonstrated understanding and basic knowledge through performance in other learning experiences. However, the development of speed in applications can result from activities and games that utilize pictorial manipulative materials and recording sheets. Some teachers, children, and parents feel that some printed exercise materials should be used in order to acquaint children with the "realness" of the future study of mathematics and the testing programs that they will encounter. A sufficient number of exercise "practice" sheets of various types can be used for evaluation in an active laboratory-type elementary mathematics program to achieve these purposes.

After children have demonstrated proficiency with particular concepts, facts, and operations in introductory and developmental activities, pupil-made projects, and games, they can be given a printed sheet of exercises, examples, or problems to determine whether they can apply their knowledge in those abstract situations. This is actually a testing or evaluative procedure. Classroom teachers should not utilize printed pages in this manner until they are reasonably sure that the child will be highly successful in the endeavor. When a misjudgment about readiness is made and the child is not successful, the lack of success should not be stressed. Instead, the cause of the difficulty should be ascertained as either a reading problem or a lack of understanding or skills, and the child should be redirected to appropriate learning experiences. Printed exercises employed in this manner can also be used to acquaint children with the types of examples and stimuli that will appear in future mathematics and testing programs. However, those types of examples and stimuli can be a part of the activities, projects, and games of the active program.

Selecting Learning Experiences

Selecting learning experiences for a classroom of children in an active laboratory-type elementary mathematics program is a truly professional endeavor. Teachers who wish to modify the mathematics program in that direction must collect, develop, and modify possible learning experiences that might be appropriate for the variety of learners and for the mathematical content to be introduced and developed. Fortunately, several trends have made the task less monumental. More and better physical object models for mathematical ideas and associated pictorial materials have appeared on the market. Suggestions for laboratory-type learning experiences are not only appearing in elementary mathematics textbooks but also in published collections of ideas. While not all of the authors or publishers of those materials agree on the nature of a laboratory or active approach to elementary mathematics or on the nature of appropriate learning experiences, these materials can help teachers, schools, and school systems to develop individual collections.

Chapter 6

Evaluation Procedures

Evaluation procedures are associated with every elementary mathematics program, but the extent to which those procedures are an integral part of instructional considerations may differ from school to school and from classroom to classroom. In some instances, the evaluation efforts appear to have very little relationship to the on-going teaching-learning activities. The children in the classroom are the subjects of the evaluation procedures, and tests of one type or another are administered from time to time to ascertain comparative general achievement levels, to find out what children have not achieved or do not know, or to assign a grade to each child. In other instances, testing activities dominate the program of activities and a cyclical process of test-retest-reteach-retest goes on and on with each content topic that is undertaken.

Purposes of Evaluation

More comprehensive evaluation efforts are undertaken in elementary mathematics programs that have extended the purpose of evaluation beyond that of comparing the achievement of one child or group of children to the achievement of others, of finding out what children do not know or cannot do, and of assigning grades.

Individual pupil growth and acquisition of mathematical ideas and performance skills is the major goal of the elementary mathematics program. Individual achievement can be facilitated if evaluation efforts and procedures involve all aspects of the program.

Evaluation of all aspects of an elementary mathematics program is a continuous process of obtaining and using pertinent information and data about the total program and individual pupil performance. The child or children in the program are at the center of evaluation efforts, because their growth and achievement is the major issue, but the function of evaluation is not merely to determine the nature and extent of that growth and achievement. Comprehensive evaluative efforts are directed toward increasing pupil growth and development in mastering or acquiring familiarity with the main ideas of the real number system, geometry, and algebraic foundations. Facilitation implies programmatic adjustments or modifications based on evaluative information.

Evaluation in Teaching

Evaluation is an integral part of teaching. Every classroom teacher observes pupil performances in one way or another to make evaluative judgments. These judgments may pertain to the past achievements and experiences of children, to possible future instructional activities for children, or to the success of a particular activity. In many instances, the classroom teacher's informal evaluative efforts lead to minor program adjustments.

All attempts to modify or to improve an elementary mathematics program are based on the information and data that are obtained from evaluative procedures. Even when minor changes in the content or in instructional procedures are made, those changes are initiated either because of an observation of or a dissatisfaction with what is going on in the program or because some planned or intended instructional activity was found to be inappropriate. Minor changes in single aspects of the program may be initiated without the support of factual information or without a serious analysis of either the total school or classroom program. Modifications or alterations in program content or procedures may be the result of nothing more than observations, attitudes, or feelings on the part of the classroom teacher or a small group of concerned teachers.

Substantial and lasting program modifications or developments result from comprehensive evaluative efforts. Evaluation procedures themselves should be analyzed and evaluated in terms of the contributions they make to program improvement. The purposes of each evaluation activity should be determined, examined, and challenged. The kinds of information and data that are obtained and that could or ought to be gathered should be considered in terms of their possible uses in program modification and improvement.

Assessing the Total Program

Certain evaluative procedures have traditionally been used to assess the efficiency or effectiveness of the total elementary mathematics program in terms of the general skill and proficiency expectations of the field. Evaluative efforts of this sort appear to be global in nature: they are total school or school system efforts, and the achievements of large groups of children are compared to national expectations. In order to make such comparisons, evaluative instruments that have been standardized on a national sample are administered to large groups of children in the program. National general achievement averages for various age and grade levels have been established for these instruments, and proportions of degrees of achievement below and above grade level averages are cited. These instruments are often administered and used to make comparisons without considering local program goals, objectives, and procedures. The instruments compare the capabilities and proficiencies of children in the local program with the norms that have been established by the test producers. In a sense, the procedure is not one of evaluating the total program, but rather of evaluating the program segment by segment because the evaluative instruments are prepared and administered in a level-by-level approach. This kind of evaluation is of greater concern to school administrators, parents, and interested laypersons than it is to the classroom teachers and children who are the active participants in the program. Classroom teachers are interested in the judgments that will be made of their classrooms but recognize the limitations of the testing instrument and the test results in redirecting or improving the instructional program. Most children want to achieve at or above the national average for their age and grade level, but for those who do not do so, the testing experience and the results (if made known to them) may be discouraging and detrimental to future efforts.

Reporting to Parents

Other procedures of evaluation entail the assessment of pupil progress in regard to both program expectations and pupil efforts and participation for the purposes of reporting to parents. The procedures for reporting to parents are generally defined by school or school system policies, but it is the responsibility of the classroom teacher to conduct the individual evaluations that are required, to prepare the evaluation documents or statements, and to do the reporting. The nature of the reporting may vary from merely reporting a letter grade to issuing some form of progress report to conducting a parent-teacher conference or some combination of the three. If reporting to parents is a serious endeavor, if concerned parents are to be given comprehensive information about their child's growth, achievement, progress, and participation, and if parents are expected to help their children attain better participation and greater achievement, the information and data gathered must go beyond that obtained from teacher-made tests and written assignments. Parents are concerned about their child's achievement and participation in the elementary mathematics program and they seek sincerity in the reporting process. Subjective judgments on the part of the teacher are neither valued nor appreciated by parents, and honest reporting requires supporting information and evidence.

Planning an Active Program

Evaluation in an active elementary mathematics program involves the assessment of individual pupil participation and progress for purposes of selecting and directing future learning opportunities and experiences. To achieve these ends, a variety of information and data pertaining to each child is necessary. Possible ways of obtaining and collecting that information are briefly described in the following section. In a well-planned and well-conducted active laboratory-type elementary mathematics program, obtaining and collecting the information and data necessary to assess accurately pupil growth and participation for those children who appear to be progressing normally is not a difficult task. The information and data collected are integral parts of the program efforts. The same materials are used to direct and guide future learning opportunities and experiences. However, normal progression or growth should not be defined as including only those children who are accomplishing the expected tasks of their particular grade level without any great difficulty, often referred to as achieving at grade level.

Normal progression should be planned for and expected of those children whose mathematical understanding and capability are beyond those of the rest of the class, the better-than-average achievers. Normal progression should also be planned for and expected of those children who got a slower start in developing and acquiring mathematical ideas, concepts, and skills and/or who may be slower learners. In these instances, normal growth and progression do not pertain to the development and acquisition of the same mathematical concepts and skills as those being encountered by other children. In this reference, normal progression pertains to continuous growth and development in a logical, sequential manner. For that logical, sequential manner of continuous growth and development to take place, teachers must plan learning experiences for and present learning opportunities to children based on the children's mastery of true prerequisites—concepts and skills that are absolutely necessary for understanding and achieving new or different performance tasks.

Collecting Evaluative Information and Data

The classroom teacher is both the principal gatherer and the principal user of evaluative information pertaining to the elementary mathematics program. Procedures for gathering data are both formal and informal. The amount of formal data and formal evaluative procedures varies from classroom to classroom and from school to school, but almost every school system prescribes and requires some minimum amount of standardized testing and formal evaluative procedures, including reporting to parents. Quite often teachers prepare and utilize their own testing devices as a part of the formal evaluative procedures. In other instances, tests that are prepared as a part of the adopted textual materials or workbook pages are used as formal data-gathering instruments to ascertain the extent of individual pupil achievement. More informal evaluative information will also be utilized by teachers to evaluate pupil achievement and progress and perhaps to direct future learning activities. Some classroom teachers make little or no effort to organize or to individualize the informal information that they receive every day, relying on memory, feelings, and most recent observations to evaluate pupil performances and to plan or present future learning opportunities. Other teachers organize and individualize informally obtained pertinent information in order to utilize that information in total program evaluation, assessment of pupil growth and development, and program planning. Efforts at program modification and program development can benefit from a great variety of evaluative information and data.

Standardized Tests

Standardized tests are tests of general mathematical ability and contain items dealing with concepts, skills, and abilities that are believed to be necessary achievement goals of the elementary mathematics program. The tests use a general level approach (primary, intermediate, and upper grades), and tests at each level contain a majority of items that are taken from the content prescribed for the age and grade level being tested. Other items pertain to content—concepts and skills—that is generally thought to be below or above that level. The items are carefully selected in an attempt to discriminate between the better, average, and poorer achievers at each level. Prior to their commercial distribution, the tests are administered to samples of children, and raw score results are used to establish norms and grade-level equivalents of achievement for each raw score. Thus when tests are administered to a school or classroom, each child's grade-level-equivalent score allows a comparison with a national norm derived from the samples, and the mean or average score of a group of children allows a comparison with a national average. A child's grade-level-equivalent score does not reveal any specific information about his or her mathematical abilities, nor does it indicate that the child can perform the mathematical tasks commonly associated with that grade level.

Textual Tests

Textual tests are tests that are prepared by the publishers of
textual materials that are adopted for use by school systems.
They may be a part of the textbook or may appear in separate
packets to be administered after completion of a particular segment of content by individual children or by groups of children.
The test items deal specifically with the concepts or skills of the
particular unit or segment of content, and thus the results can
be used by the classroom teacher to assess the extent to which
children have achieved or remembered the content that was
covered. Workbook pages or worksheets could be used in much
the same manner. Such tests might be used to evaluate instructional procedures, but more often the results and evaluation
refer only to the achievements of children.

Teacher-Made Tests

Teacher-made tests serve much the same purpose as textual tests.
In the absence of textual tests, teachers often construct their own
testing devices to determine how well the children in a particular
classroom have assimilated the material that was dealt with in the
most recent topic of study. In constructing these tests, teachers
can include the types of items they believe to be most pertinent,
using items that may not have been included on a test prepared
only for the content appearing in the textual materials. Teachers
who are conducting active laboratory-type elementary mathematics programs may use short teacher-made tests to assure themselves, children, and parents that the children can apply their
skills on abstract materials. For example, after a small group of
children has been participating in developmental and practice
activities involving the addition of two- and three-digit numerals,
the teacher may allow them to attempt a test similar to the
following without letting them use the physical object models,
pictorial manipulatives, and record-keeping sheets that were
involved in the activities.

$$
\begin{array}{ccccccccc}
73 & 49 & 84 & 62 & 50 & 48 & 350 & 411 & 267 \\
+44 & +23 & +36 & 30 & 29 & 37 & 264 & 133 & 108 \\
& & & +23 & +18 & +51 & +123 & +228 & +\,92 \\
\end{array}
$$

In the developmental and practice activities, children acquired amounts and determined totals. The amounts to be acquired were generated by rolling numeral cubes, drawing numeral cards, spinning a spinner, or in some other random manner. The amounts to be acquired were represented by ice cream sticks and bundles of ten ice cream sticks, base-ten blocks, play money (only ones, tens, and hundreds), or poker chips with values of 1, 10, and 100 associated with the colors white, red, and blue. One rule permeated the activities—a participant was not allowed to have more than nine of any one kind of the model or pictorial manipulative. Initially, only the pictorial manipulatives and physical object models were used, and totals were named orally. When children could handle that task, they were asked to keep a record of each play they made. At each turn they were to record how much they started with, how much they acquired, and the new total. That type of record keeping was extended to recording the exchanges that were made of 10 smaller units for 1 larger unit. When teachers observe the children performing well at this level, they might suggest that one or more of the children might try the "test" of addition examples without using the objects. After all, the records kept by the children were addition examples.

Anecdotal Information

Anecdotal information that is collected and utilized to evaluate the growth and progress of individual children in acquiring and using mathematical ideas and skills and to direct and guide future learning experiences may take many forms. Generally, *anecdotes* are short narratives of particular incidents or occurrences of an interesting or pertinent nature. Teachers' comments that describe some important aspect of a child's actions or performance are, indeed, a part of the information that should be collected, but for reasons of time and detail required, other records and items should be included in the data or information bank. The task is to gather those bits and pieces of information from the operation of the program that will assist the teacher in making decisions about individual pupil participation and achievement and to supplement those items with purposefully designed recording devices.

The use of an active laboratory-type elementary mathematics program implies and requires modifications or extensions of the procedures commonly used to assess and to record pupil progress and participation in learning experiences. A variety of record-keeping techniques can and should be employed. These records will be valuable for assessing and reporting pupil progress, for communicating to parents, and for selecting future learning activities.

Pupil Folders

The information that is gathered should be collected and organized in individual packets or folders for each child. The packet or folder should be easily accessible to both the teacher and the child because both will want to contribute materials to the collection. These materials may include teacher's comments, anecdotes based on observations, and prescriptions as well as examples of work that are indicative of the pupil's performance. Lists of activities and games in which the child participated, record-keeping sheets from those activities and games, pupil projects, worksheets of practice exercises, skills charts or check lists, special assignments, teacher records from "checking out" sessions conducted with the child, and other materials can be included. Efforts should be made to select materials with a positive performance orientation. Very few if any materials showing a lack of success or having a negative connotation should be included. To avoid bulk and difficulty in handling, an individual student's folder or packet can be partially cleared out from time to time. Materials that are removed can be given to the child, referred or sent home to parents, or used by the teacher.

Participation Charts

If a unit or topic approach is used in the presentation of learning opportunities or experiences in the program, a rather simple device can be used to record individual pupil participation in those activities. In a unit or topic approach, all of the children in a classroom will be working on or studying the same major content area at the same time, but perhaps on the development of different ideas or skills or at different difficulty levels. A variety of learning experiences is made available, and each individual selects or is guided to the activities that are most appropriate in terms of his or her ability, performance, and learning characteristics. To record notable participation, performance, or accomplishment, a large chart containing the names or pictures of the available learning experiences can be prepared and posted in the classroom (Figure 6.1). Under each name or picture, space

Figure 6.1 *Sample Participation Chart*

Numeration and Notation

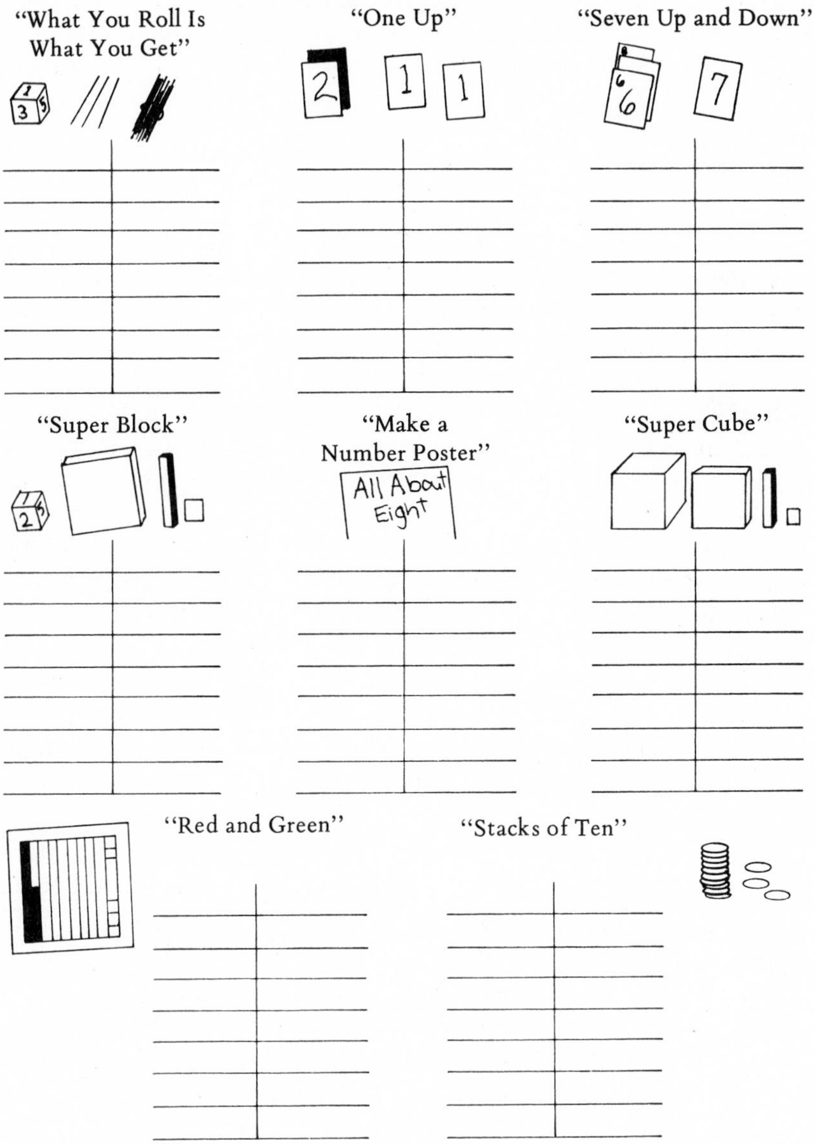
"What You Roll Is What You Get"
"One Up"
"Seven Up and Down"
"Super Block"
"Make a Number Poster"
All About Eight
"Super Cube"
"Red and Green"
"Stacks of Ten"

is left to enter the names of children who have participated in the learning activity and have demonstrated acceptable performance. A similar check list can be prepared for insertion into each child's packet or folder. When the unit or topic of study

Figure 6.2

	Mult. Facts		Name Ralph W.	
Date	Activity		Date	Activity
1/8	arrays (f<5)		1/17	compare products
1/9	arrays (f<5)		1/18	for balance (3×4=4×3, etc)
1/10	leads in boxes		1/19	arrays (f>5)
1/11	cover up		1/22	arrays (f>5)
1/12	check on X facts (f<5)		1/23	cover rects. w/sqs.
1/15	arrays (f<5)		1/24	make big sqs. w/
1/16	arrays (f>5)			little sqs.

has been completed, the large classroom chart can be retained by the teacher for future use and/or the information from the chart can be copied on other recording devices. As each new unit or topic is introduced, a new chart is prepared.

The teacher may also keep individual daily records of each child's participation in learning experiences. These records should be separate sheets or file cards for each child (Figure 6.2). They may be kept in a separate booklet, filing folder or case, or even in each child's folder or packet. The daily notations should be very brief. Only the date and a few brief words, perhaps names for the activities, should be used to indicate the nature of the learning experiences for each daily notation. The notations may be made either prior to the execution of the learning experience or upon its completion. The teacher may want to indicate the child's success in the learning experience. When such daily notations are made, a quick review of any child's record will indicate the past sequence of learning activities. Consideration of these activities should be helpful in selecting possible future learning opportunities.

Instead of or in addition to daily records, the teacher may wish to keep a record of activities in which the child has successfully participated (Figure 6.3). Successful participation implies that the child has achieved the purposes of the activity. Making notations about the same activity day after day may be tedious or

Figure 6.3

Geom.   Name Ralph W.

Activity	Date comp.	Activity	Date comp.
Rectangles w/rope	2/4	geom. dominoes match	2/20
Draw rects. to scale	2/6	geom. dominoes ≅, ∽	2/21
Triangles w/rope	2/7	classify blocks	2/22
Draw △ to scale	2/11	Diff. by "one"	2/23
≅ ⑤ on peg bd.	2/13		
∽ ⑤ on peg bd.	2/15		
Draw ≅ & ∽ ⑤	2/18		

Figure 6.4

Name _____

Numeration and Notation
_____ _____
_____ _____
_____ _____
_____ _____

Operations on Numerals
_____ _____
_____ _____
_____ _____
_____ _____

Operations on Collections
_____ _____
_____ _____

Measurement
_____ _____
_____ _____
_____ _____

Geometry _____ _____ _____

needlessly repetitious. On this type of activity record, a notation of a learning experience is made only once. If desirable, a date may be used to indicate when success or completion of the learning activity has been achieved. One way of preparing the activity record for each child is to list the major content areas or categories of the program, leaving spaces under each category to enter the names of the learning experiences and the dates of successful completion (Figure 6.4).

Figure 6.5

Fraction Numbers

	K	1	2	3	4	5	6	7	8
1. Recognizes half of a region	I	M							
2. Separates sets into halves	I	M							
3. Recognizes one-fourth of a region, set	−	I	M						
4. Identifies 1/3, 3/4, 2/3 of a region, set	−	−	I	M					
5. Writes fractions less than 1 in form *a/b*	−	−	I	I	M				
6. Identifies numerators, denominators	−	−	−	−	M				
7. Orders fractional numbers	−	−	−	I	I	M			
8. Names many fractions for number	−	−	−	−	I	M			
9. Writes mixed numerals as fractions	−	−	I	I	I	M			
10. Writes fractions as mixed numerals	−	−	I	I	I	M			
11. Identifies, names equivalent fractions	−	−	−	I	I	M			
12. Adds fractions less than 1 with like denominators	−	−	−	I	I	M			

Levels: −   Not dealt with
　　　　I   Introduced
　　　　M   Mastered
　　　　□   Continuation in review and use

Achievement Charts

Some teachers may prefer to record pupil achievement only in terms of goals or subgoals in the elementary mathematics program that the child has reached. To do so, teachers can develop an achievement record that includes a list of the mathematical ideas and skills that pupils are to master. Ideally, an individual list for each child would be developed, but more commonly a master list for a class or a group of pupils is used. Such lists are often quite lengthy because skills and ideas are fragmented into difficulty levels or steps in learning and because the lists are often used over long periods of time, perhaps years. Under ideal circumstances, an idea or skill is checked off when a child achieves or masters the idea or skill. However, in some situations the use of these check lists has degenerated to the point that the idea or skill is checked when the teacher has "covered" the material in the classroom, indicating only that the child has been exposed. The chart shown in Figure 6.5 is taken from a skills check list used by one school system.

Achievement lists of this type have many variations in form and in substance. One variation includes the use of a box beside ☐ each citation of an idea or skill on the list in which a teacher may indicate the level of a pupil's familiarity with the idea or skill. An empty box would indicate that, so far as the teacher knows, the child has not encountered the idea or skill. One ◩ diagonal drawn through the box would show that the pupil has ◩ been introduced to the idea or skill; another diagonal in the box ⊠ would be drawn when the pupil has spent some time developing ⊠ the idea or skill; and a midline would be drawn to indicate that the idea or skill has been mastered. For example, a small part of the chart or list might look like this:

Addition

Meaning of combining	⊠
Easier basic facts	⊠
Middle basic facts	⊠
Harder basic facts	◩

The chart shows that the child understands the meaning of addition, has mastered the easier basic facts, has spent some time on the middle basic facts, and has been introduced to the harder basic facts of addition.

Figure 6.6

Other forms of skills check records may be prepared for and utilized by teachers in "checking-out" sessions with individual children. A checking-out session may be an informal or impromptu session that takes place when a child appears to have achieved a degree of mastery during the process of a learning experience. For example, a child may have been playing a game involving the use of the easier addition facts, the facts with addends up to five. The teacher observes that the child appears to know these facts and says, "Let me check you out." By using two numeral cubes with the digits 0, 1, 2, 3, 4, and 5 on the six faces of each cube and a record sheet similar to the one pictured in Figure 6.6, the teacher tells the child to say the sums as soon as the numerals are seen. The teacher rolls the cubes, picks them up before the child can begin counting, and notes how well the child does in quickly responding with the correct sums. A *c* entered in the chart indicates that the child counted to get the sum. An *x* indicates that the child responded quickly with the correct sum, and a *o* indicates that the child responded with an incorrect sum or did not give a response.

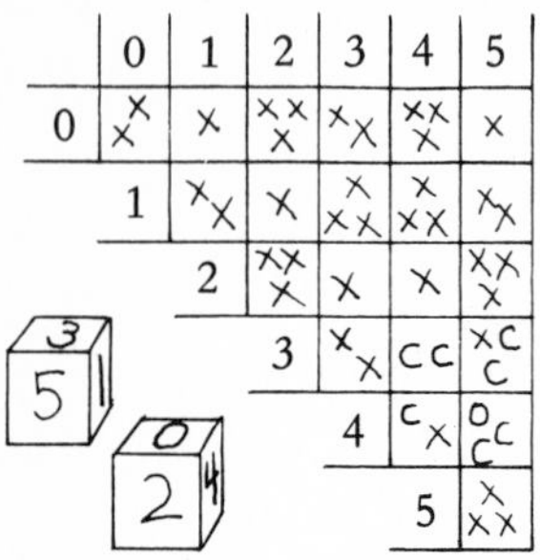

Unfortunately, some information and data do not indicate or include reminders of how the ideas, concepts, or skills were attained; the possible familiarities with materials; or the types of learning experiences that would be useful in selecting and guiding future content and approaches. Informative data should always be gathered for the dual purposes of evaluating pupil growth and development and directing and guiding future or potential learning opportunities.

Analytical and Diagnostic Procedures

Analysis

More intensive *analytical and diagnostic procedures* are needed for those children who appear to have a continuing variety of difficulties in understanding and applying concepts and ideas and/or in achieving and applying skills. A distinction can be made between procedures of analysis and procedures of diagnosis. *Analysis* as an action may be regarded as an examination of something to distinguish its components, either separately or in relation to the whole. A statement of analysis describes the situation as it exists. Classroom teachers of elementary mathematics use informal procedures of analysis virtually every day in observing the operation of the learning activities and the difficulties or successes of individual children. Minor problems or difficulties may be alleviated immediately with simple modifications or suggestions. More intense problems or difficulties require further study, perhaps even diagnosis. Some analytical procedures involve paper-and-pencil testing and can be conducted with groups of children. The instruments used may contain items dealing with a variety of content topics or may deal with one specific topic. Commercially produced tests referred to as "diagnostic" are more often only analytical; an item analysis of the results will only reveal the general areas of successes and difficulties, the errors that are being made, and sometimes an error pattern of a child that is being tested.

In most instances when an error pattern is determined in an item analysis, those errors are only symptoms of a more deep-rooted deficiency. Some hypotheses can be formulated as to how the child is arriving at his or her responses, but the analysis does not and will not indicate the real causes of difficulty or the reasons why the child is responding incorrectly. For example, the following computations reveal a pattern of errors.

$$
\begin{array}{r} 56 \\ + 78 \\ \hline 1214 \end{array}
\qquad
\begin{array}{r} 57 \\ + 25 \\ \hline 612 \end{array}
\qquad
\begin{array}{r} 72 \\ -46 \\ \hline 34 \end{array}
\qquad
\begin{array}{r} 63 \\ -17 \\ \hline 54 \end{array}
$$

$$
\begin{array}{r} 34 \\ \times\ 3 \\ \hline 912 \end{array}
\qquad
\begin{array}{r} 26 \\ \times\ 4 \\ \hline 824 \end{array}
\qquad
\begin{array}{r} 36 \\ \times 24 \\ \hline 144 \\ 72 \\ \hline 216 \end{array}
\qquad
\begin{array}{r} 72 \\ \times 16 \\ \hline 432 \\ 72 \\ \hline 504 \end{array}
$$

Each of these error patterns might be corrected, for the time being, by a rote, mechanically applied rule or procedure, but they are singly and collectively symptoms of an underlying misconception or deficiency. At least two hypotheses are tenable. The child performer lacks understanding of the meaning of numerals, the uses of base ten, and positional value in the system of numeration that we use; or, the child performer lacks understanding of the nature of the operations and their uses.

Diagnosis

The term *diagnosis* refers to the act or process of finding out what serious difficulty a person may be having and the *causes* of that difficulty by examination and careful study of the observable symptoms. The same term also refers to the opinions resulting from each investigation. To the teacher of elementary mathematics, diagnosis is an important professional responsibility directed at ascertaining the conceptual causes of the persistent difficulties of certain children. A diagnosis is a professional opinion as to the cause or causes of those difficulties.

Only a very small percentage of children in any elementary mathematics program require professional examination and study to the extent that it can be truly called diagnosis. Those few children exhibit symptoms of a puzzling and persistent nature, difficulties that are found among many ideas and skills to be developed in the elementary mathematics program and that suggest one or more possible underlying causes of the cumulative difficulties. These few children include neither the slow learner who is making slow but steady progress in the learning of mathematical ideas and skills nor the average or above average pupil who currently may be displaying difficulty. Both types of children require special attention from the teacher in analyzing, planning, guiding, and providing appropriate learning experiences, but not diagnosis. The complexities of the normal act of teaching and learning and the complexities of true diagnosis are such that the act of diagnosis, extensive as it is, should be reserved for those children who truly need it.

Techniques

The major techniques to be employed in the act of diagnosis are individual interviews—questions and comments—with the child client. Such interviews should involve the use of physical object models for mathematical ideas, which can be used by the child in responding to questions or directions. Questions and directions should be aimed at ascertaining the child's understanding of an idea and his or her abilities to perform skills within the content area being considered. Observation of the child's attempts to respond will allow the teacher to make decisions about the child's understanding and capabilities. If cleverly conducted within the confines of the classroom and within the context of the elementary mathematics program, the diagnostic procedures need not place any special stress on the client. Such activities hardly would be noticed in an active laboratory-type program.

Prerequisite Concepts and Skills

One of the major concerns of any diagnostic procedure involves ascertaining whether the child has acquired true prerequisites, those understandings and skills that are absolutely necessary for the content in which the difficulties are appearing. Consider the chart in Figure 6.7. Developing problem-solving capabilities may be construed as the major objective of the elementary mathematics program. A child's inability to solve problems may

Figure 6.7

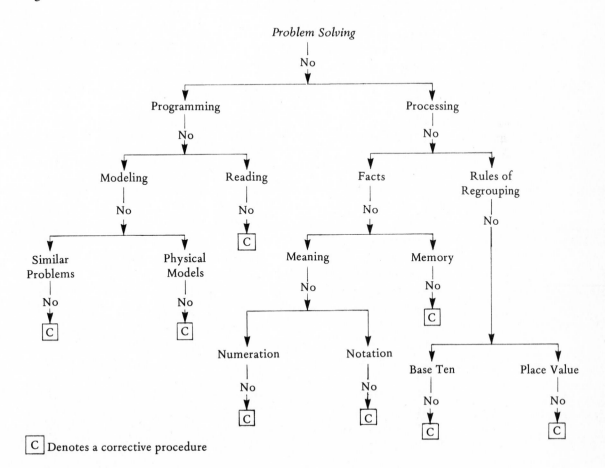

[C] Denotes a corrective procedure

be due to inadequacies in being able to program or in being able to process. *Programming* involves deciding what to do, deciding what technical skill or operation may be applied, to solve the problem. *Processing* involves applying the technical skill or performing the operation or operations. Use this example of a diagnostic flow chart to follow the decisions that must be made. If a child cannot program, it is probably because he or she cannot model the problem or cannot read (comprehend) the problem. If a child cannot model a problem, it is either because he or she does not recognize it in terms of a simpler, analogous problem or because the child cannot structure it with a physical object model. Each decision-making step leads to further decision-making steps or to a corrective procedure. The bottom line of any diagnostic protocol or procedure should imply, indicate, or lead the diagnostician to a deficiency or disability for which there are known treatments. The bottom line implies or suggests a corrective procedure. The corrective procedure must allow the child client to establish understanding of a major idea or skill in elementary mathematics, one that is a true prerequisite of the ideas and skills that have not been mastered previously. The proper application of or participation in the corrective procedure should allow the child client to progress successfully at a normal rate through an appropriate sequence of learning experiences. (*Note*: the chart may be turned upside down and read as a suggested parallel development of ideas and skills leading to programming and processing and to problem solving, a sequence of learning experiences.)

Corrective Procedures

Good *corrective procedures* are no more and no less than excellent teaching procedures or learning experiences: procedures and experiences that are known to help children develop and understand ideas or that may provide good practice. If possible, corrective procedures should be unlike those experiences that created or perpetuated the difficulty or misunderstanding. Corrective procedures should be conducted with intensity, continuity, and over sufficient time that the child has every opportunity to concentrate on and overcome the difficulty. That effort must be viewed as the focus of the child's mathematics program. Children cannot be expected to continue with other agonizing or antagonizing efforts in a regular mathematics class and to overcome the difficulty as an outside effort. The corrective procedure must not endanger the species—it must not harm the child in any way—and this danger may or may not be alleviated by allowing the disabled child to be assisted by peers who are not experiencing a similar difficulty.

When classroom teachers accept their role as diagnosticians, they will (1) appreciate the act of diagnosis for what it truly is; (2) utilize diagnostic procedures that search for the roots of problems; (3) learn to arrive at valid diagnostic opinions; (4) support the validity of their diagnoses by prescriptive, corrective procedures that are successful; and (5) provide corrective procedures that are as rich and full and exciting for children as the initial teaching-learning situation should have been. In regard to elementary mathematics and children, preventative medicine is good practice. Providing initially appropriate learning experiences for all children at all levels will create fewer and fewer casualties.

Using Evaluative Information

Continuous evaluation of an active laboratory-type elementary mathematics program is highly desirable and valuable. The value of evaluative efforts lies not in the processes or materials that are used to gather the information nor in the information that is gathered, but in how that information is used to improve the program of learning opportunities for children. All aspects of the laboratory approach should be considered in the evaluative process.

Classroom Operation

The organization of the classroom operation must be analyzed to determine what is working, what is not working, and what is needed in terms of physical facilities, handling of materials, methods of presenting learning opportunities, use of work spaces, and students' acceptance of responsibility. Management may be a problem, but discipline should not be. When pupil discipline appears to be a problem, it would be a good idea to look closely at the available learning experiences, the arrangement and use of work spaces, and the clusters of children who are working together. The teacher should attempt to determine whether the collections of learning experiences (introductory and developmental activities, projects, and games) available to children at any one time, whether they are units of content in specific areas or whether they are learning experiences from several content areas, provide appropriate opportunities for the growth and development of all children. Information garnered from visual observations of the classroom in action may be sufficient to decide whether or not physical facilities, work spaces, and instructional materials are being utilized to their greatest potentials and whether or not children are accepting responsibility for their behavior as students in a laboratory approach. However, observational techniques alone will not supply the comprehensive information necessary to make evaluative judgments about the breadth and depth of learning opportunities that are needed at any one time. For this purpose, information about individual children is required, and pupil records of all types should be used. Those materials may include records of children's participation in the various learning activities, progress charts indicating individual levels of development, skill charts or check lists, assignments, projects, recording sheets from activities and games, and anecdotal comments as well as the more traditional testing devices.

Learning Activities

Each of the selected learning experiences that are made available to children should be viewed and reviewed in terms of the pupil interest it generates, the appropriateness of the materials that are associated with it, the record-keeping devices that might be useful, the possibilities for extending it to a more complex or difficult learning experience, its appropriateness for a particular content area or topic, its suitability as either a small-group or individual activity, and most important of all, its effectiveness in achieving its intended purposes. Learning experiences that are inappropriate for children in the program for one reason or another at any one time may be quite suitable at another time. It must be remembered that mere participation of children in a learning experience is not the major objective. The participation must lead to acquisition or further development of the concepts and skills inherent in the learning opportunity. The primary method of evaluating the appropriateness or effectiveness of a learning experience in an active laboratory-type elementary mathematics program is by teacher observation of children participating in the activity. Therefore, the purposes of the learning experience or activity and proper student actions and behaviors must be clear to the observer. When things are not proceeding smoothly, something is likely to be wrong with the learning experience. It is not difficult to ascertain by observation when a learning opportunity or experience is beyond the capabilities of the participants. In those instances, procedures or progress in the activity will stall, halt, or degenerate into confusion. Before discarding the learning experience or offering an alternative, the teacher-observer should make sure that the questions or directions used to initiate the learning experience were clearly understood by the participants. Quite often, a brief participation in the learning experience by the teacher-observer will alleviate the initial difficulty. A brief participation period may also serve as a questioning session in which the teacher-observer finds out how well the participants are acquiring and developing concepts and skills. Pupil products and record-keeping sheets derived from learning experiences should also be used to evaluate the effectiveness of the experiences. However, if the teacher-observer is actively participating in the program, neither the product nor the record-keeping sheet will be completed before a difficulty is spotted and direction or redirection can be provided for potential learners. Information obtained from checking-out sessions with individuals or small groups of children conducted during or after specific learning experiences may also be used to direct or redirect these children to continuation of the same activity, to other learning experiences with the same purposes, or to new experiences with different goals or purposes. Analysis and evaluation by the teacher-observer of particular learning experiences and of children's participation in each learning experience is continuous; the major purpose of that continuous evaluation is to direct and redirect children to appropriate learning opportunities.

Achievement

School administrators, interested laypersons, parents of children in the program, and classroom teachers all exhibit concern over how children in the program compare to national, state, and local averages in regard to achievement. For that reason, most schools and school systems administer standardized achievement tests to all children. School administrators and laypersons are primarily concerned with the general comparisons that can be made from the results of the local testing program and the national norms that have been established by the test producers. Satisfaction with the total elementary mathematics program generally depends on whether or not the achievement of the population of children in the local program is equal to or greater than that of the sample of children used by the test producers to establish "normal" growth and achievement at various grade levels. Parents are more specifically concerned with the status of their children. Classroom teachers may be concerned with the comparisons that might be made with their total class and are often fearful that standardized test results might be used to evaluate their effectiveness as a teacher, particularly if the average achievement test scores and the descriptive statistics that are derived from groups of scores are limited to making and disseminating these comparative generalities in accordance with the established school system policies. The tests can be studied to ascertain what concepts and skills are to be tested, and that information may be used in early program-planning stages. But even if an analysis of items missed by children is conducted, the data and information obtained from standardized testing procedures contribute little to the processes of program modification and improvement.

In an active laboratory-type elementary mathematics program, the evaluation of pupil achievement or progress in the development of mathematical concepts and skills goes beyond the use of tests and written assignments. Children's performances on tests of general ability are not true indicators of progress in regard to growth in specific areas. Their completion of written assignments does not guarantee that the learning purpose of the assignment was achieved, that the child did his or her own work, or that the expected processes, ideas, and skills were applied. Evaluation of individual achievement and progress in an active laboratory approach can be much more specific and comprehensive in terms of mathematical ideas and skills that have been attained, learning experiences that have been completed, special problems that are to be worked on, or the directions that a child's work is or should be taking. Evaluation of each child's progress can be individualized. The information and data used in the individualized evaluations is the same as that used to guide and direct each child in the program. Observations of performance in the learning experiences, anecdotal notes and written comments, pupil projects or products, records of participation in activities, record-keeping sheets from activities and games, and even skills charts or check lists can provide the information that is needed. The information and data concerning the nature and extent of each child's work and progress can be kept in an individual folder. If an indication of performances on worksheets and tests is required by the school system or desired by parents, a minimum of these can also be retained in the same folder. Whether or not the information packet follows the child from room to room or from teacher to teacher is a matter for individual teachers and schools to decide, but such information should be extremely helpful in directing and guiding each child's future learning endeavors.

Reporting Pupil Progress

Many teachers are perplexed or troubled by the necessity of assigning grades to children, reporting grades to parents, or discussing a child's progress in a conference with parents. If grades must be assigned, the teacher's dilemma is whether to assign the grades in relation to an expected "norm" or whether to assign grades in regard to an individual's growth, performance, and effort. That dilemma cannot be resolved here. However, objective reporting to parents depends on the same information that is used to guide children into future learning experiences. The documentation in the child's individual record can be used to present a true and honest picture, and that data and information can be related or compared to class, school, and national expectations.

Strategies for Teaching in the Major Content Areas

Organizing the elementary mathematics program into major content areas offers several advantages for those who are concerned about program planning or development. Program planning, modification, and development activities have but one major purpose—to improve the learning opportunities for children, to increase the potential for and possibilities of individual achievement. Appropriate learning experiences can be more deliberately selected and presented when main content themes and attainable goals have been clearly defined in terms of concepts and skills.

Within a major content area, main ideas or content themes can be more easily identified so that the program activities emphasize those major ideas. The main ideas or themes are the consistent and supporting strands of the program, the basic mathematical ideas. Performance objectives for children can be related to these basic ideas or themes. Identification of and concentration on the necessary concepts and skills to be achieved can become a better organized and more effective professional effort. Identifying the major ideas or themes and the performance skills to be developed in a major area of content allows the program planner, developer, and presenter (the classroom teacher) to select appropriate and necessary instructional materials and procedures more effectively.

When the program is thought of in terms of major content

areas, strategies can be established for presenting learning opportunities that are interrelated and consistent throughout a major area. Instructional provisions for pupils with different characteristics may be better planned and presented. The teaching goal is to come as close as possible to individualized instruction.

One possibility is to use a unit of content in which a wide range and variety of learning opportunities, all within the domain of one major content area and consistent in approach, are made available to children. Children can work or study as individuals or in small groups to achieve different objectives within the same major content area. In one content unit, children can be working at different levels, on different ideas or skills, using different materials, or several individuals or small groups may be working at similar levels to achieve the same ideas or skills using different procedures and materials. Within this variety, a consistency in instructional approach within a content area is still attainable. In this text, consistency lies in the attributes of an active laboratory-type approach to elementary mathematics, in which children can communicate with and help each other and feelings of unity or belonging to the group can be maintained.

Another possibility, when teachers feel capable of managing such an instructional organization, is to allow children to work in different content areas on learning experiences that have been properly selected and sequenced according to the main ideas and skills that have been identified in each of the major content areas. This general procedure requires more comprehensive knowledge and understanding of the total elementary mathematics program on the part of the teacher as well as a wider range of planning and preparation.

Within a major content area, there are similarities in the procedures of learning experiences across the hierarchy of skills, difficulty levels, or types of real numbers involved. For example, similar procedures can be used to help children learn to associate numerals with numbers, compare numbers, and order numbers with whole numbers, common fractions, and decimal fractions. These similarities can enhance the learning process. There are also similarities in the materials and procedures of learning experiences between the major content areas. For example, the physical models that are used to help children name and compare numbers are also used to help children learn the computational operations.

Reorganizing the elementary mathematics program into major areas of content for purposes of instruction requires teachers to evaluate pupils' understanding and attainment of concepts and skills. Techniques of evaluation in an active program include the informalities of observing, collecting artifacts, and recording each student's participation as well as the formalities of checking and testing skills.

Organizing the content of elementary mathematics into major areas does not imply that the main ideas or skills of the areas are disjoint or unrelated. The main ideas and skills in one area not only may be related to those of other areas, but also may be prerequisites to the further development of ideas and skills in other areas. The organization merely provides a framework for program development. Within that framework, content themes can be identified, general purposes or objectives of the content area can be defined, specific skills to be developed at various times can be determined, instructional materials can be specified and acquired, general procedures for instruction (strategies for teaching) can be planned, and specific learning experiences (activities, projects, and games) can be collected and selected.

It would be impossible in this text to present or describe the wide variety of learning experiences that are necessary and possible in an active laboratory-type elementary mathematics program. Therefore, only a few possibilities that illustrate the suggested strategies or procedures are presented in each of the content area chapters. Even the accompanying volume, *Active Learning Experiences for Teaching Elementary School Mathematics*, could not exhaust the possibilities, and classroom teachers are encouraged to expand on the suggestions. Some other possible sources of laboratory learning activities are cited in Appendix B. Potential users of these materials are urged to examine carefully both the materials and the procedures for using them to see that they are compatible and consistent with their own philosophies and strategies of elementary mathematics instruction.

Numeration and Notation

This major content area might well be called "Communicating About Number" because its content and goals are directed primarily toward helping children acquire the communication skills necessary to describe quantity or number. The general goal of developing familiarity with the real number system demands that children learn to communicate effectively about quantity or number. The communication modes, styles, and skills that children acquire must be such that meaning and ideas are received from and delivered to others.

Communication involves the use of symbols that are exchanged between receivers and senders and implies that the receiver and sender have mutual meanings for those symbols. Mutual meanings for symbols or ideas does not mean merely associating one symbol with another. For example, it is possible that a child who can associate the verbal term "ten" with the printed sign *10* or even with the printed word *ten* may not understand that the symbols name or describe a definite quantity or number. The child may be able only to exchange one symbol for another. If the child understands the meaning of the symbols, he or she will be able to associate the symbols with a concrete or visual representation of quantity. Unfortunately, in many primary or early elementary mathematics programs, instructional efforts appear to help children relate oral sounds to printed symbols without real meaning.

The reader may want to try the following activity. Ask a small group of adults or children to close their eyes and picture something in their minds for each word that is said. Then say such words as *"dog," "house," "cat," "tree,"* followed by the word *"twenty-three."* Then ask the group what they visualized when they heard the words. Almost all of the group will have visualized objects or pictures of real objects for the words *dog, house, cat,* and *tree*, and almost all of the group will have visualized the sign *23* when the word *"twenty-three"* was said. Is this because the members of the group have learned merely to exchange verbal and printed symbols in their learning experiences with number? Is this reaction due to the lack of real understanding of the term *twenty-three*, that the term names or describes a quantity of objects just as the other terms name or describe objects, and that the term *twenty-three* names or describes the number of objects in a particular way—as two groups of ten and three singles? One would hope that children in the primary and early intermediate grades as well as teachers of elementary mathematics, those who have been meaningfully studying numeration and notation, would have visualized two stacks of ten chips and three single chips, two bundles of ten sticks and three single sticks, or 2 ten rods and 3 one cubes from the base-ten block model when they heard the term *twenty-three*. The reader may want to ask another small group of adults or children to visualize something when they are shown the printed words *dog, house, cat, tree*, followed by the printed sign *23*. What would you expect the group to visualize?

Understanding the meaning of the symbols used in numeration and notation of quantity implies that the unit size is known (what is or how large is one object?) and that a reasonable idea of the magnitude of the amount named can at least be visualized. In the numeration and notation tasks of the elementary mathematics program, this implication applies to whole-number, common-fraction, and decimal-fraction numerals or names at the very least.

Importance of the Area

The ideas and skills of communicating about number are perhaps the most important abilities to be developed in the elementary mathematics program. The ability to exchange information with others about amounts or quantities of things is necessary for full participation in the day-to-day in-school and out-of-school activities of both children and adults. The meanings of number names, numerals, are also prerequisites for the computational operations, whether they are to be performed with paper and pencil or with a calculator. Knowing when the result of a computational operation is reasonable and being able to interpret the response or result in order to apply it in a practical situation are functions of understanding the numerals involved, the nature of the problem, and the nature of the operation that was performed. For example, the child who comprehends the numerals involved in the addition exercises in the margin and who knows something about the use of base ten in the system of numeration used, will recognize that the results or responses are not reasonable. When a child is asked or expected to work with numerals in a computational operation, whether it be at the introduction-of-facts level or at some more difficult level, and the child does not understand the numerals involved, the child's reasoning and understanding cannot play a part in developing the computational operation. Because of the child's lack of understanding, the procedure is limited to the rote recall of facts and rules and their mechanistic application.

$$\begin{array}{r} 56 \\ + 75 \\ \hline 1211 \end{array} \qquad \begin{array}{r} 74 \\ + 48 \\ \hline 1112 \end{array}$$

Communication Skills

The total elementary school program attempts to help children develop and expand two major forms of communication skills— oral and written. We expect children to acquire the oral communication skills of listening and speaking and the written communication skills of reading and writing. The author of this text has taken some license in using the terms *numeration* and *notation* to encompass these communication skills in regard to number. In general, this major content area includes the ideas and skills that other volumes and textbooks include under such headings as *sets and numbers, numbers and numerals,* and myriad other topic descriptions. Specifically, this major content area is directed toward helping children acquire the communication skills of listening, speaking, reading, and writing about numbers. In the processes of acquiring and using those skills in meaningful manners, basic concepts and ideas about number and the system of numeration that is used must also be introduced to, developed with, and understood by the learning child.

The general sequence of development, although it may not be noticeable within the oral context or within the written context, is from listening to speaking to reading to writing. We cannot expect children to speak what they have not heard, to read what they cannot speak, or to write what they cannot read. In actual practice, the development of the oral communication skills of listening and speaking about number of quantity, of using oral number names, will occur almost simultaneously. Children cannot, however, be expected to discover oral number names; they must hear those names in a meaningful context in reference to a number or quantity of objects, preferably a good model for number. It is suggested that oral communication skills be well developed before children are expected to read numerals and that the reading of numerals precede the writing of numerals as performance skills.

General Sequencing

The general goal of elementary mathematics programs pertaining to developing familiarity with the real number system suggests that its attainment will involve, in some type of sequence, the subsets of the set of real numbers. As aspects of each subset of the set of real numbers are introduced and developed, particular attention must be given to the special symbols, both verbal and written, that are used to communicate about those kinds of numbers. Particular attention is given to developing the listening vocabulary, the speaking vocabulary, the reading vocabulary, and the writing vocabulary in regard to the nonnegative integers, the negative integers, and the rational numbers in both common-fraction and decimal-fraction form. Within each subset of the set of real numbers, there is also a logical sequence of development based on the complexity of the ideas of numeration and notation associated with the numbers to be named. If major ideas or content themes are emphasized, the development and acquisition of communication skills need not be as fragmented or sporadic as they appear to be in conventional programs. For example, if the concept and application of *base ten* as "grouping in collections of ten objects" is properly introduced and emphasized as soon as the number named by the oral name "*ten*" is encountered and before the singular teen names ("*eleven*," "*twelve*," "*thirteen*," . . .), before the decade names ("*twenty*," "*thirty*," "*forty*," . . .), and before written positional value, then all of the concepts, ideas, and skills necessary for children to become familiar with the numbers named by two-digit numerals can be approached and developed as one closely interrelated topic. With the proper temporal introduction and emphasis on base ten, meaning and understanding of the oral names for number can be established in reference to physical object models for number. Knowledge of the meaning and use of the oral number names "*one, two, . . ., nine*" is the only prerequisite. (This does not imply that "*zero*" has not been introduced; only that "*zero*" is not used at this time and is therefore not a prerequisite.) Game-like activities can be arranged in which children obtain small quantities of the one units (chips, sticks, or cubes) from a physical object model for whole numbers. The amount of the ones' units that each child obtains can be determined by rolling a numeral cube with 0, 1, 2, 3, 4, and 5 on its six faces. The one procedural rule for the activity is that when more than nine units are gathered, the units must be collected into a group of "nine and one more" (ten). The unit pieces are not collected into a group until there are more than nine. The skill expectation and performance rule is that each participant must be able to describe orally how many objects he or she has obtained. The first oral descriptions will be in the form of "____ tens and ____." (*Note*: It is not necessary for the child to say "two ones, . . ., five ones, . . ., nine ones" if the terms *one* through *nine* are understood.) Children and teachers may observe that collections or groups of ten objects are counted in the same manner as single objects:

one chip	*two* chips	*three* chips	*four* chips
one ten	*two* tens	*three* tens	*four* tens

and so on. One might even count beyond ten tens.

Names and Models

When children can collect the unit objects from the model into groups of ten and can orally describe the number of collections of ten, indicating that they can count the collections of ten, other ideas and skills can be developed with meaning and under-

Figure 7.1

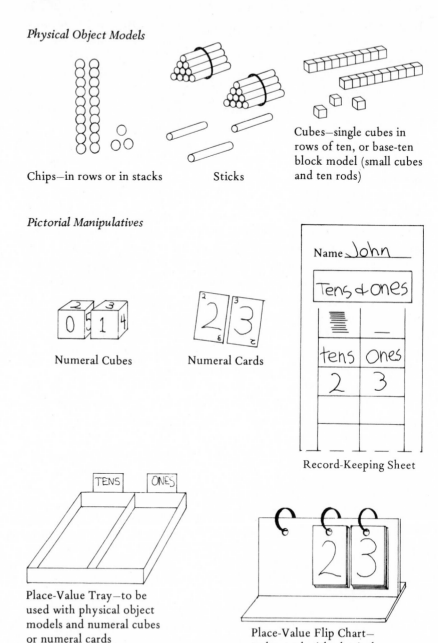

Physical Object Models

Chips—in rows or in stacks   Sticks

Cubes—single cubes in rows of ten, or base-ten block model (small cubes and ten rods)

Pictorial Manipulatives

Numeral Cubes   Numeral Cards

Record-Keeping Sheet

Place-Value Tray—to be used with physical object models and numeral cubes or numeral cards

Place-Value Flip Chart—to be used with physical object models standing. For example, the decade names can be introduced and practiced by showing children the relationship between the beginning sounds of the words:

two tens	twenty
three tens	thirty
four tens	forty
five tens	fifty

Attention may even be given to how the tongue and lips are used to make those beginning sounds much as other oral vocabulary is introduced and developed with young children. Introduction of the decade names may or may not precede the use of the printed digits (0, 1, 2, 3, 4, 5, 6, 7, 8, 9) to describe the number of collections of tens and the number of single objects. Introduction of the use of digits to describe the number of groups of ten objects requires the performance skill of associating the digits with amounts of up to nine objects. Helping children learn to associate meaningfully (read) a two-digit numeral with a quantity of objects will involve the use of physical object models for whole numbers and a variety of pictorial manipulative materials. (See Figure 7.1.)

The same general approach or instructional strategies are used to extend the oral and written vocabularies of children so that they can use numerals to describe larger quantities or whole numbers. A similar approach may be utilized to develop the communication skills necessary for the other subsets of the set of real numbers.

Major Ideas or Content Themes

Numeration and notation comprises a unified and related set of ideas. The content area of numeration and notation is defined by the statements of content themes, which should be the major ideas or concepts about number and the naming or describing of number ideas. The extent to which these themes are recognized and emphasized in program presentation will determine the extent to which numeration and notation can be seen as one content area across the subsets of the set of real numbers and the extent to which common instructional strategies can be utilized throughout the program.

The content themes or major ideas of numeration and notation should not be learned as verbal definitions or as vocabulary exercises. Children will come in contact with the concepts or themes through using the ideas in active laboratory learning experiences. The concepts will be introduced early in the child's study of number and developed in a spiral manner. Each major idea will gain familiarity and strength as it is interwoven with the other contributing strands that go into making up the big idea. The contributing strands may be performance-skill activities that are directed toward and related to the further development of the content theme. As each contributing strand, each sequential application of the idea, is being introduced and developed, the learner should develop those skills that will enable him or her to better communicate the idea and apply it. In this manner children can develop their own structures of meaningful mathematical ideas and useful skills.

The content themes of numeration and notation apply to the set of real numbers and its subsets, regardless of how the subsets are named. For the intents and purposes of the mathematics program of the elementary school, the pertinent subsets might be called whole numbers, common fractions, decimal fractions, and negative numbers rather than the more precise mathematical terms of positive and negative integers and rational numbers. At the elementary level, little can be done to develop meaningfully the concepts of irrational numbers, a subset of the set of real numbers. Meaningful development of those concepts requires a complete understanding of integers and rational numbers: whole numbers and common and decimal fractions. The nature, existence, and treatment of irrational numbers may be introduced to talented children in the upper elementary levels, but this topic may better be left to later study. The study of negative numbers also requires previous knowledge and understanding of other number concepts, depending on the complexity of the negative numbers to be studied. However, some concepts and skills pertaining to naming, comparing, and combining quantities or numbers less than zero or less than some other referent amount (x, N, and the like) can be meaningfully presented in laboratory learning activities *after* concepts and skills with nonnegative numbers have been acquired. Concepts of and skills with nonnegative whole numbers and common and decimal fractions should be *well established* before children encounter either negative numbers or irrational numbers. When or whether concepts and skills involving negative numbers should be introduced and developed in the elementary school is a philosophical value judgment, and as such it should be decided on the bases of its appropriateness and its contribution to the growth and development of individual children.

The following major ideas of numeration and notation involve naming or describing numbers or quantities under various situations.

The rearrangement or change of configuration of a quantity of objects does not alter or change its numerousness.

This idea is one aspect of the concept called *conservation.* Conservation may also pertain to single objects, amounts, or quantities that may be altered in appearance and referred to in terms of length, mass, volume, or weight, but the major idea as it pertains to numeration and notation primarily relates to quantities of single objects, the same kinds of objects that might be moved and counted by a person with that skill in counting. The basic idea of conservation does not involve the use of number names; some mathematics educators believe conservation of number to be a true prerequisite to introducing the first number names to children. After all, the number name for

```
* * *  or  *   *  or  *
           *         *
                     *
```

or any other configuration or arrangement for that many stars must always be communicable and consistent. There is some controversy as to whether the extent of children's understanding of this concept can be accurately measured or ascertained and as to whether the concept can be directly taught. Readers may wish to examine the opinions and research findings that have been published in this regard. Those opinions and findings do not alter the importance of this concept as a persistent theme in the area of numeration and notation. Conventionally, the concept of conservation has received a great deal of attention when the first number names are introduced to children, but the theme persists through all of the learning activities that involve the naming and renaming of number. Because the rearrangement or change of configuration of a fixed quantity does not alter the numerousness of the quantity, we can name the quantity in one of several correct ways by separating, combining, collecting, and regrouping, and we can always return to the original arrangement, configuration, and number name.

The amount of numerousness (number) can be described with quantitative names.

The first task in describing an amount or quantity is to establish the referent unit. What is the object or single unit of quantity? When the single unit, or referent, has been established, number names can be used to describe the amount. The number names are used in the manner of adjectives to describe how many unit objects. When the first whole-number names are introduced to children in the early school years, the idea of using a unit of reference is so obvious that it is almost ignored. The early units of reference are single common objects that can be seen, handled, and understood, and the idea of "oneness" seems to be well accepted and understood by children. Yet, in later learning expectations, programs may be deficient in establishing collections of 10, 100, 1000, and so forth, as referent units when working with greater whole numbers; in establishing or referring to the unit of 1 referent when working with common and decimal fractions; or in establishing the unit of reference in measurement or comparison problems. The idea of conservation of number and the idea that number or quantity can be named or described are basic foundations of the content area of numeration and notation.

There are many names for the same number. There are many ways, both oral and written, of describing the same quantity.

Some mathematics educators have expressed the opinion that the field of arithmetic is merely the study of ways of renaming number through the application of computational operations. Exercises, examples, and problems merely require the renaming of a number that has already been described. While this notion is basically true in that the results of computational operations do rename the quantitative expressions that appear in exercises or that are derived from stated problems, the totality of the idea does not specify the renaming of numbers as conventions or skills that are necessary in the performances of the operations or in simpler arithmetical tasks. In relation to this major idea, there are performance-skill objectives associated with both whole numbers (nonnegative integers) and rational numbers. In naming and renaming nonnegative integers, both combining and separating conventions are used. The first combining convention is apparent when the first number names are developed by utilizing an "and one more" approach. The same approach is used in developing the idea of rational counting.

∗	"One star"	
∗ ∗ —∗∗	"One star and one more—two stars"	
∗∗ ∗ —∗∗∗	"Two stars and one more—three stars"	
∗∗∗ ∗ —∗∗∗∗	"Three stars and one more—four stars"	

This process is continued until a collection of ten is made. From that point, base ten is emphasized and the naming would involve "ten and one more, ten and two more, ten and three more," and so on, until there are two collections of ten. The same combining convention and the "and ＿＿ more" approach applies to combining collections of two (counting by twos), of five (counting by fives), or collections of ten (counting by tens). The use of base ten in our system of naming number is a combining convention. The operations of addition and multiplication call for the combining conventions of renaming number.

The separating convention for renaming whole numbers may be used early to introduce the idea of "and one less" or "what number name comes before ＿＿ ?" and basic ideas of both addition and subtraction. The idea of "and one less" can be developed by beginning with a known number or quantity of objects and removing one object at a time, each time naming the remaining number. It is in this manner that the meaning of the name "zero" can be established for the absence of quantity or the number name for the empty set: "One and one less . . . zero." Other aspects of the combining and separating conventions are described in later paragraphs that deal with other major ideas or content themes.

Regrouping to larger units of numeration is used to name results of the operations of addition and multiplication. The inverse of that regrouping operation is necessary to rename numbers or to think about whole numbers involved in the computational operations of subtraction and division. In order to perform the operation of subtraction as it is applied in an example such as $43 - 16 = \square$, the 4 tens and 3 ones of 43 must be renamed or thought of as 3 tens and 13 ones or units. In order to perform the operation of dividing 27 into 3 equal groups, $3\overline{)27}$, the 2 tens and 7 ones of 27 must be renamed or thought of as 27 ones or single units.

Renaming integers, as *rational numbers* (numbers that can be expressed in the form a/b, where a and b are both integers with the condition that b cannot be zero) is a prerequisite to performing computational operations with common fractions. Of course, the first integer to be renamed as a rational number is 1, and children should be guided through laboratory learning experiences to see and know that there are many names for 1, including

$$\frac{2}{2} \quad \frac{3}{3} \quad \frac{4}{4} \quad \frac{a}{a} \quad \frac{\frac{1}{4}}{\frac{1}{4}} \quad \frac{a+b}{a+b}$$

The skills of renaming 1 as a rational number will be extended to renaming other integers as rational numbers and to renaming those rational numbers, a/b, where a is equal to or greater than b to integers and mixed numerals.

The ability to rename rational numbers with other names for rational numbers is another achievement expectation of the elementary mathematics program. The ideas of equivalent common fractions and of renaming common fractions to names for equivalent fractions are related to the identity element of multiplication—a major idea from the content area of operations on numbers using numerals. The number 1 is the identity element of multiplication, and the major idea is that any number multiplied by 1 results in a product equal to the original number, $1 \times N = N$ and $N \times 1 = N$. The number N may be an integer or a rational number, and since there are many names for the number 1, the multiplier may be any of those names. The resulting product will be another name for the original number. This procedure and the application of the idea is further discussed in the appropriate section of Chapter 9. Other achievement expectations or performance skills to be acquired in regard to renaming rational numbers include renaming rational numbers in the form of common fractions to rational numbers in the form of decimal fractions and vice versa; renaming decimal fractions to percentages and vice versa; renaming ratios to other ratios; and renaming ratios to percentages. The numerals 3/4, 75/100, 0.75, and 75% may all be used to describe the same quantity or number. One of the important ideas of this content theme is that the number names or notation that is used to describe a quantity or number varies with the purpose, situation, and application—what is to be done with the numeral and what is to be communicated.

The idea that there are many names for the same number is perhaps the major content theme of numeration and notation. A great deal of time and effort with appropriate learning opportunities and experiences should be devoted to developing this theme and its associated performance skills spirally throughout the program. In the earliest learning experiences, children will use the simple conventions of combining and separating to find that there are several names for the same number. In later experiences, they should learn to apply specific ideas and skills until they can understand that there are an infinite number of names for any number. The capabilities of naming and renaming number are prerequisites for performing the computational operations that are required to solve problems.

The concept of base ten is the foundation for naming or describing quantities or number in the decimal positional system of numeration that is used throughout the world.

Base *ten* is a particular application of the concept of base as it applies to numeration and notation and pertains specifically to collecting ten smaller units in the system to exchange for the next larger unit. The collecting in tens is consistent from each smaller unit to the next larger unit. Conversely, one larger unit can be exchanged for ten of the next smaller units. This content theme is the basic concept underlying naming and renaming whole numbers and decimal fractions. The idea can be introduced early with quantities between 9 and 99 and meaningfully developed through larger numbers and decimal fractions with the use of appropriate physical object models and pictorial manipulative materials. The concept and performance skills of communication with both oral and written number names are prerequisites for understanding the computational operations. Without understanding of the concept of base ten and its application in our positional system of numeration, it is virtually impossible for children to appreciate the magnitude of quantities or numbers named, or to approximate or estimate reasonable responses to problem situations.

In addition to the use of the concept of base ten in naming and renaming whole numbers and decimal fractions, the concept of base is also applied when working with or studying common fractions and measurement. In working with common fractions, one unit is the referent. The denominators of the common fractions indicate the bases or number of smaller units that must be collected to be exchanged for the unit of one and vice versa. In working with common English standard units of measurement, the use of the concept of base to exchange units of measurement may appear to be even more complex because there is no consistency in the bases of the measurement units. The same problem does not exist in metric measurement. Units of metric measurement were developed with base ten, and work or study activities with the metric system can and should be deliberately related to work and study with the base-ten system of numeration.

In the intermediate or upper levels of the elementary school, some mathematics programs may incorporate the study of positional systems of numeration with bases other than ten. The value of such work may be questioned by some mathematics educators, but such study can be successful in achieving specific goals for children if (1) the real concept of base is emphasized and used; (2) an appropriate model for number is used (see Figure 7.2 in

Figure 7.2

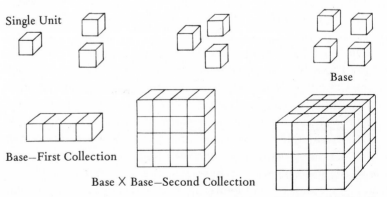

Single Unit

Base

Base—First Collection

Base X Base—Second Collection

Base X Base X Base—Third Collection

which a small cube is used as the model of a single unit); and
(3) care is taken to avoid confusing the names used in our base-
ten system with the names used in the systems being developed
(perhaps completely different names should be used).

Understanding the concept of base, and the application of base
ten in particular, is basic and prerequisite to the total understanding of place or positional value as it is used in reading and writing
numerals. The concept and its application can be introduced
early and should be emphasized spirally as a content theme
throughout the elementary mathematics program.

**Two or more quantities or numbers can be combined, and the
resulting total quantity or number can be named or described.**

This idea or theme does not pertain to the computational operations of addition or multiplication, which are performed on
numerals utilizing established facts and rules of regrouping. It
does, however, refer to the physical operations of combining
quantities, which are the foundations for understanding the uses
of those operations. Initially, the concept is introduced with
the "and one more" idea with single objects. This idea is used
to introduce new number names and leads to rational counting.
The idea and related activities can extend to processes of combining small groups of objects and finding the name of the new
group. The number names for the groups of objects to be
combined may or may not be established. The tasks are to make
the combining effort and to do whatever is necessary to describe
the numerousness of the combination. In many instances, this
will require children to utilize the concept of base ten and the
act of grouping or collecting the objects into tens. When a base-
ten block model for whole numbers is used, the process may
also involve collecting the model pieces that represent ten and
the model pieces that represent one hundred into groups of ten
and exchanging the collections for the proper larger unit piece
of the model. The quantities or numbers to be combined may
be of unequal or equal size. When the original quantities are
small in number and are equal in size, ideas of counting by
multiples can be developed. Same-size quantities to be combined
will also be used to introduce and develop the meaning and
processes of multiplication.

The quantities or numbers to be combined may be less than
one unit, therefore, describable by written rational numbers

in common-fraction or decimal-fraction form. Of course, the oral terms used to describe rational numbers are not distinguishable as either common fractions or decimal fractions. The total of the combination, when two or more quantities that are each less than one unit are combined, may be either less than one unit or greater than one unit.

The oral conversation accompanying these activities would be similar to the following statements:

"Another name for nine and one more is ten."

"Another name for four and two more is six."

"The name for this many is five tens and six."

"Another name for twenty and ten more is thirty."

"The name for this many is three hundreds, seven tens, and five."

"When eight hundreds, four tens, and six is combined with three hundreds, seven tens, and nine, the total number is one thousand, two hundreds, two tens, and five."

"This much is three-fourths of one."

"When one-third and one-sixth are combined, the total is one-half or three-sixths."

"Another name for three-sixths is one-half."

"Three groups of four in each group are ten and two."

In these kinds of activities, the communication is basically oral. If a record is to be kept, that record should not include the use of the operational symbols. Those symbols will be introduced and utilized when the operations on number using numerals are studied formally. The record of the combining may be kept by listing only the total of the combination or the information pertaining to the groups to be combined and the total amount of the combination.

Utilizing this idea as a content theme may not appear to be of major importance to the planners, directors, and presenters of learning experiences for children in elementary mathematics programs. However, if the idea is spirally developed and reemphasized as new types of numerals are being introduced, as the types of numerals being studied become more complex, as problem-solving situations involving those numerals appear, and as the computational operations necessary to solve problems are introduced and developed, understanding of the situations and of the numerals used to describe those situations is more likely to occur. The ideas will be introduced at a simple, premathematical level and a greater potential will exist for children to acquire an intuitive feel for the concepts and the necessary number-naming skills.

A quantity or number can be separated, and the resulting separated quantities or numbers can be described.

This idea or content theme is the inverse of the concept pertaining to combining, which was just described. It does not refer to the computational operations of subtraction or division, which may be applied to specific problem situations involving the separation of one quantity or number into two or more smaller quantities. The idea refers to the physical manipulations of separating a quantity or number into two or more smaller quantities and of separating a quantity or number of objects into groups of unequal or equal sizes. Initially, the idea would be introduced with a small quantity of objects for which the number name is known or can be established; the physical manipulation would involve removing one object, applying the idea of "and one less," and naming the remaining quantity. That kind of activity can be extended to applying the ideas of "and two less," "and five less," "and ten less," or any other small amount if the original quantity of objects is first grouped or collected into the size groups that are to be removed. In those instances where the original quantity is greater than ten, the number should be represented by a model, bundled ice cream sticks or base-ten blocks, which would require ungrouping or exchanging a ten unit, a one-hundred unit, or a one-thousand unit for ten smaller units.

In another early application of the separation of a quantity or number, the description of that separation, and the naming of the original quantity in several ways, children can begin with a small quantity of objects and separate that number of objects into two or more smaller groups.

Five   *****

Four and One   **** *   or   * ****

Three and Two   *** **   or   ** ***

Three and One and One   *** * *   or   * *** *
or   * * ***

Two and Two and One   ** ** *   or   ** * **
or   * ** **

Two and One and One and One   ** * * *   or   *
** * *   or   * * ** *   or   * * * **

One and One and One and One and One   * * * * *

At first it may be desirable to make only two groups, but children
can quickly attempt to make all of the possible small-group combinations to name the original quantity in as many ways as possible.
(One of the projects that may be associated with this activity is to
have children make a number poster "All About Five.") When the
original amount involves greater quantities or numbers of objects,
the children can be directed to make subgroups of either equal or
unequal size. When the original quantity is to be separated into two
groups of equal or unequal size, the situation will be similar to problems that might be solved by the computational operation of subtraction. When the original quantity is to be separated into two or
more groups of equal size, the situation will be similar to problems
that might be solved by the computational operation of division.

The inverse nature of the operations of separating and combining can be introduced and developed by combining the separated
subgroups after the separation has been described and the numbers
in the subgroups have been named. This action will also reinforce
the concept of conservation of number and lay the foundations
for developing addition and subtraction and multiplication and
division as inverse computational operations.

By using physical object models for rational numbers—common
fractions and decimal fractions—the basic concept of equal parts,
which is used in naming quantities less than one unit, can be
established. If solid model pieces are used in this activity, the
original piece (or pieces) cannot be separated, but other model
pieces can be laid on top of or beside the original piece. However,
if paper or cardboard is used to represent the original quantity
or number, the model piece may be folded or cut into equal-size
pieces. Developing the concept of separating one unit or a fractional quantity into equal-size parts is a prerequisite for separating

into unequal size parts. The sizes of the parts must be describable or namable.

The communication accompanying these separation activities is similar to that employed with the activities of combining. The descriptions of the separation and the naming of the subgroups in regard to quantity or size is primarily oral. If written records are to be kept, the records should not involve the use of operational symbols.

Two quantities or numbers can be compared, and that comparison can be described.

When children are first asked to make comparisons, the two quantities or amounts involved should be so different in size that the comparisons can be made visually. Children should be able simply to see that there is a difference in the quantities or amounts. Descriptions of the comparisons employ such terms as *larger, bigger, longer, greater, more, smaller, shorter,* and *less.* "This group (or piece) is _____ than that group (or piece)." General comparative terms will suffice for these initial activities, and the quantities or amounts may be single pieces or groups of similar objects. It is not necessary nor is it recommended that children count or measure objects at this level.

In later comparison activities, the two quantities or amounts of single objects should be so nearly equal in number that a technique or performance skill is required to find out if there is a difference. That technique or performance skill involves matching the objects in the two groups in one-to-one correspondence. Activities that require one-to-one matching of the objects in the two groups lay the foundations for comparison problems that can be solved by the computational operation of subtraction. Those types of problems require one to ascertain the amount of difference between two quantities or amounts and are discussed further in later chapters. However, the concept of comparison in numeration and notation only requires making and describing the comparison of two quantities, numbers, or amounts.

Utilizing physical object models for number also allows a meaningful development of the ideas of comparing two quantities that are each less than one unit. Each of the two fractional quantities can be shown and named, and the comparison can be made. In this manner, children can see that one-eighth of a one unit is definitely smaller than one-half of the same unit. They are, therefore, less likely to be confused when they are asked, "Which is greater, 1/8 or 1/2?" Because quantities or numbers can be compared and that comparison can be described, *the numerals that describe or name quantities can also be compared and that comparison can be described.* Having children record comparisons between quantities or numbers by utilizing the numerals that describe those amounts provides an opportune time to introduce the comparative symbols =, ≠, >, and < so that they are meaningful to children.

Because two quantities or numbers can be compared, a series of comparisons of amounts can result in more than two quantities or numbers being ordered in size.

Ordering quantities or amounts requires that the numbers involved be compared to each other so that they can be arranged in a serial order. The ability to compare two quantities and describe that comparison is a prerequisite for ordering more than two numbers. The initial ordering of amounts or quantities may not require the use of number names. The quantities can be arranged from smallest to largest or vice versa without actually naming the amounts, particularly if the quantities are visually different in sizes. If the quantities are nearly the same size, the comparison skill of matching must be applied. The oral communication skills and vocabulary terms employed in these kinds of ordering activities will be similar to those used in comparison activities.

Because numbers or quantities can be ordered, *the numerals that name or describe numbers can also be ordered.* The first numerals to be ordered will be the single-digit numbers (0, 1, 2, 3, 4, 5, 6, 7, 8, 9), which are introduced with the "and one more" idea. Each of these numerals describes a small group of single objects. After the concept of ten as a collection or unit in our system of numeration is introduced, children can order numerals that are greater than ten by using the idea of comparing the number of ten units. When the numbers of ten units are equivalent, the numbers of single units can be compared to determine which numeral is larger or smaller. The same idea can be applied to comparing and ordering larger whole numbers by first comparing the numbers of largest-sized units (hundred, thousand, ten-thousand units, for example) and then comparing the numbers of the smaller units in turn. An identical procedure can be employed to compare rational numbers written as decimal-fraction numerals. The larger units of the numerals will be compared before the smaller units in the positional-value notations. Ordering rational numbers written as common fractions depends on understanding one unit as the reference, the concept of equal parts, and the concept of how common-fraction numerals are written. This understanding can only be developed through continued reference to and utilization of physical object models for common fractions.

These major ideas or themes can serve as the strands of consistency in the content area of numeration and notation throughout the elementary mathematics program. Concepts and performance skills of communicating about number can be related to these ideas and themes in such a manner that children can develop a consistent structure of mathematical ideas.

Performance Skills

The performance skills that children are expected to acquire in regard to numeration and notation may be categorized as either *prenumeration* or *numeration* skills. The term *performance* implies that the learner is to apply skills to complete defined or designated tasks in a satisfactory manner. The ability to perform on specified tasks is the true test of understanding and knowing. Unless a skill can be applied correctly to a problem situation, it is virtually useless. For example, imagine a child who can recite a series of number names in order, but who cannot correctly associate those names with quantities of objects in a "How many?" problem situation requiring the "and one more" approach to counting. That child possesses a useless skill sometimes called rote counting. The child is not counting and cannot count objects; in other words, he or she cannot apply the skill. The child can only repeat a sequence of number names in a meaningless or useless manner.

Prenumeration Skills

Prenumeration skills involve the student's ability to deal with quantitative situations or problems without using number names or numerals: to apply concepts and skills related to the ideas of conservation of number, to compare two quantities, to match the objects in two groups in one-to-one correspondence, to make two collections of objects equal in number, to collect or group objects into a specified or shown quantity or amount, and to order more than two amounts or quantities in reference to size. It is a fallacy to associate these ideas and skills only with the early years in the elementary mathematics program. These concepts and skills extend beyond the early introduction of whole numbers. They pertain to the other subsets of the set of real numbers and should be a part of the introduction and development of the numeration skills associated with those subsets.

Conservation

To develop and reinforce the concept of *conservation*, children need active laboratory-type learning experiences in which a defined, specific quantity or number is arranged, rearranged into different configurations, and returned to the original arrangement. These kinds of learning opportunities can be initiated and conducted with physical object models for whole numbers, common fractions, decimal fractions, and even negative numbers. Several specific examples may be cited. Young children can be given a specific amount of poker chips. The illustrations in Figure 7.3 show some of the arrangements or configurations they might make by grouping, arranging, or stacking the chips. After each new arrangement, the chips should be returned to the original arrangement. The idea to be developed is that the number of chips does not change. Children might also be given a box filled with small cubes. The filled box indicates that there is a definite number of cubes. The cubes can be removed from the box and arranged into many different configurations. Structures can be built, subgroups can be made, the cubes can be arranged into rows, and so on. Each time the cubes are returned to fill the box, it can be determined that the number of cubes did not change. Similar activities can be conducted with larger quantities or pieces from the base-ten block model. A quantity can be designated, that quantity can be separated into equal or unequal groups, and the subgroups can be combined back into the original amount. Extending the idea of conservation to models representing common and decimal fractions also requires the uses of physical object representations. Consider the illustration in

Figure 7.3

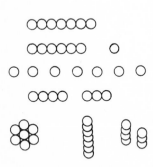

Figure 7.4 of a simple model for common fractions. The pieces of the model can be arranged in units of one as shown in the drawing. The pieces can then be arranged in many different ways: either as units of one or as unequal or equal separated subgroups. Each time, the pieces can be moved back to the original configuration. At much later levels, a quantity representing a missing amount, a negative number, can be treated in much the same manner.

Figure 7.4

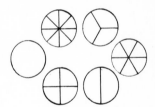

Comparison

Developing the skills of *comparison*, determining which quantity is greater or which quantity is less, has already been briefly described. The activities involve the presentation of two quantities with identical referent units and ascertaining a crude comparison of difference in the more comparative terms of *the same number as, more than,* and *less than* or synonyms for those terms. Initially, the differences are so great that the comparisons can be made visually. Later, the skills of *one-to-one matching* are needed to determine whether or not a difference exists and, if it does, the general nature of that difference. The amount of the difference is not named. These types of learning activities can be conducted with physical object models for whole numbers, common fractions, decimal fractions, things to be measured, and negative amounts.

Equivalence

The skills developed from activities that involve comparing two quantities or numbers are prerequisite to acquiring the skills of *making two amounts or collections equal in number*. One-to-one matching of the elements in the two quantities is first conducted to find out the general nature of the difference in number or amount between the two groups or amounts. Children will have three options in making the two groups equal in number: increasing the size of one of the amounts, decreasing the size of the other amount, or doing both at the same time. Initially, that option may be left to the decision of the children involved. However, to prevent the continued application of only one of the options or to make certain that both of the first two options are employed, specific directions may be given: "Make the number of red chips equal to the number of white chips"; or, "Make Group A the same amount as Group B." The number name of the amount that is "added to" or "removed from" an amount need not be required. Activities in which children make two amounts or collections equal in number may be conducted with physical object representations of whole numbers, common fractions, decimal fractions, things to be measured, or negative amounts.

Grouping

Introducing and developing the concept of base, and in particular base ten, in a meaningful fashion depends on helping children develop and acquire the skills of *collecting or grouping* single objects into a specified quantity or amount. Initially, children are given an unspecified number of single objects, such as chips, counters, sticks, or small cubes, and asked to make as many groups of a specific amount as they can from the number of objects they were given. That specified amount can be shown by a number of fingers, a stack of chips, a pile of sticks, or a row of cubes. Later, emphasis should be placed on collecting in groups of ten—ten is the specified number of objects shown. This idea can be extended to making one large collection from the same number of small groups as there are single objects in each small group, as shown in Figure 7.5.

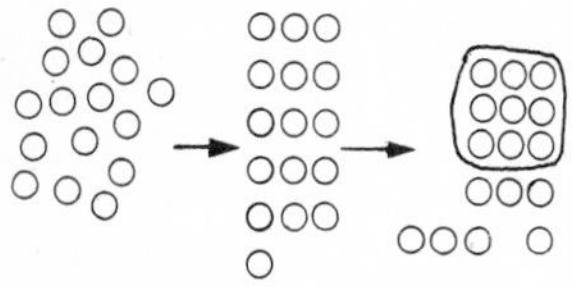

When this idea is consistently applied to specified collections of ten objects, the foundations are laid for understanding the oral and written communication employed in the decimal system of numeration with whole numbers and decimal fractions. However, developing these skills with decimal fractions is facilitated by using some form of the base-ten block model and exchanging ten of the smaller model pieces for one of the next larger pieces of the model and vice versa. Collecting or grouping objects into a specified amount or quantity with common fractions calls for showing or naming a specified unit of one. First activities should require that equal-sized pieces be used in the collections. Later, the specified amount can be less than one unit (for example, the one-half piece or the one-third piece of the model) and much later, the pieces to be combined or collected need not be the same size.

Figure 7.5

Ordering

The concepts and skills of comparing quantities or amounts are also prerequisites to introducing and developing the skills of *ordering more than two amounts or quantities in reference to size*. The skills of ordering physical amounts are prerequisite to the skills of ordering numerals, which describe numbers or amounts. General procedures for introducing and developing those skills in a meaningful manner have been described in previous sections.

Numeration Skills

Numeration performance skills pertain to those capabilities of ascertaining the number names needed to describe a quantity or amount and of communicating about those numbers or quantities: counting, group recognition, and collecting and exchanging units of the decimal system of numeration (using physical object models or pictorial representations). These capabilities require the use of oral number names, the skills of listening and speaking.

Counting

Counting is a procedure, operation, or skill employed to find the answer to the question "How many?" The introduction to rational counting utilizes single objects and an "and one more" approach in much the same manner as the first number names are introduced. In reality, children need only learn to count up to ten objects. After that, counting objects merely requires counting up to ten objects as often as necessary and utilizing the major idea that there are many names for the same number—"ten and two are twelve, three tens and four are thirty-four," and so on. Counting by units of one can be extended to counting by groups or multiples—by groups of two, three, or five, and, most certainly, by groups of ten. Counting units of equal size that are less than one (halves, thirds, tenths, and so on) is an application of the same procedure as counting chips, sticks, or units of ten, one hundred, or one thousand.

Group Recognition

Group recognition is a skill of identifying or recognizing the number of objects in a collection without counting. It also refers to recognizing that two amounts or quantities are equal in size and understanding that the same number name can be employed to describe each group or number. Children's abilities to recognize and name number amounts depends on their perceptions, the size of the number, the pattern in which the quantity is arranged, and their previous experiences with those quantities in laboratory-type activities with physical object models for number. Attempts to develop skills of group recognition are directed toward a de-emphasis of dependence on counting skills by children when those skills are least appropriate: when they are asked to ascertain the number of objects in a recognizable group and when the skill to be employed is a computational operation. It is not unreasonable to expect young children to recognize and name the number, without counting, in the small groups shown in Figure 7.6, especially when the patterns are so easily discernible.

Figure 7.6

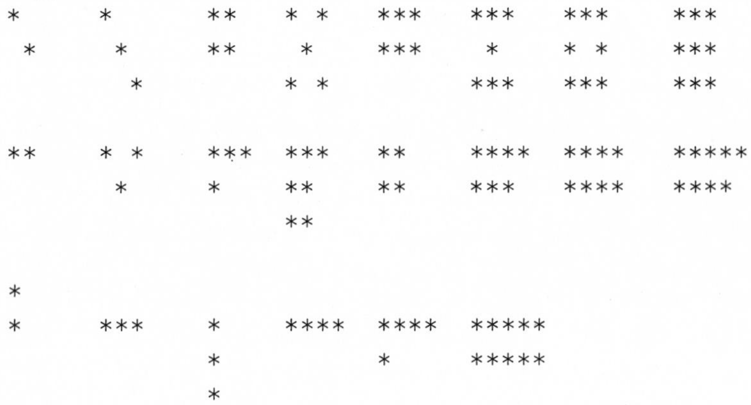

```
*        *        **     *  *    ***     ***     ***     ***
  *        *        **     *      ***      *      *  *    ***
           *                 *  *            ***     ***     ***


**       *  *     ***    ***     **      ****    ****    *****
  *        *        **     **      ***     ****    ****
                   **


*
*        ***      *      ****    ****    *****
                   *              *       *****
                   *
```

After a base-ten model has become familiar to children through its employment in numeration and notation learning experiences, it would be reasonable to expect children to recognize the unit pieces and to identify and name the numbers represented by small amounts of any of the model pieces. The same expectations may be held for children who have had appropriate introductory and developmental learning opportunities with the models for common fractions and decimal fractions. Skills of approximation and estimation depend on a person's ability to visualize the quantities involved. The skills of visualizing quantities are more likely to be attained if the learner has had sufficient experiences with models for number and group-recognition activities.

Collecting and Exchanging Units
General procedures for introducing and developing the capabilities of collecting and exchanging units of the decimal system of

numeration using physical object models for number require consistent emphasis on the concept of ten and the content theme of base ten. These general procedures should have a consistent procedural rule that when a number is to be named, single objects must be collected in groups of ten and groups of ten must be collected into a larger collection of the ten smaller groups. This general procedure also implies a sequence in the use of physical object models. First, the models that have only one units (chips, counters, cubes), which can be collected into rows or stacks of ten, will be used in the learning experiences. The groups of ten consist of single pieces and are not really a unit of ten. Then using ice cream sticks or soda straws, which can not only be collected into groups of ten, but which also can be temporarily bundled into a unit of ten with a rubber band, will help children see that *ten is a unit* in the decimal number system. The grouping and ungrouping of bundles of ice cream sticks will help children rename number and will provide foundations for the operations of addition and subtraction. Finally, the exchangeability of the pieces of the base-ten block model for whole numbers can be utilized.

Communication Skills

Whole Numbers

The ability to communicate about numbers or quantities depends on the development and utilization of listening, speaking, reading, and writing skills. The oral communication skills are introduced first and developed in relation to the learning experiences involving appropriate models for number. For whole numbers, those skills involve ascertaining and using the names for quantities up to and including ten objects (including zero as the name for the absence of quantity), using those names to describe numbers greater than ten and less than ten groups of ten (one hundred) as " ____ tens and ____ ," learning the other names (eleven, twelve, thirteen, . . .) for the numbers greater than ten and less than 2 tens, and learning and using the decade names for 2 tens, 3 tens, 4 tens, and so on. When the learning experiences arrive at the new collection of ten groups of ten objects, the name for that collection (one hundred) is introduced. The new names for units of ten hundred, ten-hundred thousand, and ten-hundred million are introduced when situations, either real or written, involving those quantities are encountered. The structure of the decimal system of numeration is such that a pattern exists in the positional-value system. That pattern might best be described in reference to a base-ten block model for number in which a small *cube* represents the one unit, a *long rod* that is ten times as long as the one cube represents the ten unit, and a *flat* piece that is as large as ten rods placed side by side represents the one-hundred unit. (See Figure 7.7.) The pattern is repeated with the thousand unit, which is represented by a larger cube which is ten of the one units long, ten of the one units wide, and ten of the one units high. Collecting ten of the thousand units makes a long rod to represent the unit of ten thousand, and collecting ten of the ten thousand units to make a flat piece representing the one-hundred-thousand unit. The pattern is repeated with each of the new cube unit representations: one million, one billion, one trillion, and so on. (See Figure 7.8.) In positional value, the pattern appears as hundreds, tens, and ones in each set of units begun with a cube model—one, thousand, million, billion, and so on. (See Figure 7.9.) Being familiar with and understanding this pattern in naming whole numbers and being familiar with the magnitude of the units that are named are necessary prerequisites for meaningful oral communication and for developing the skills of reading and writing whole numbers.

Decimal Fractions

Decimal fractions extend this pattern to units smaller than one, except that the one unit is used as the referent and commas are

Figure 7.7

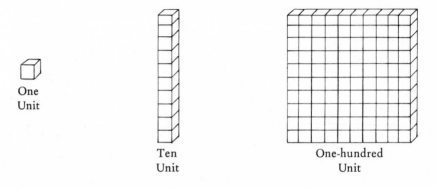

One
Unit

Ten
Unit

One-hundred
Unit

Figure 7.8

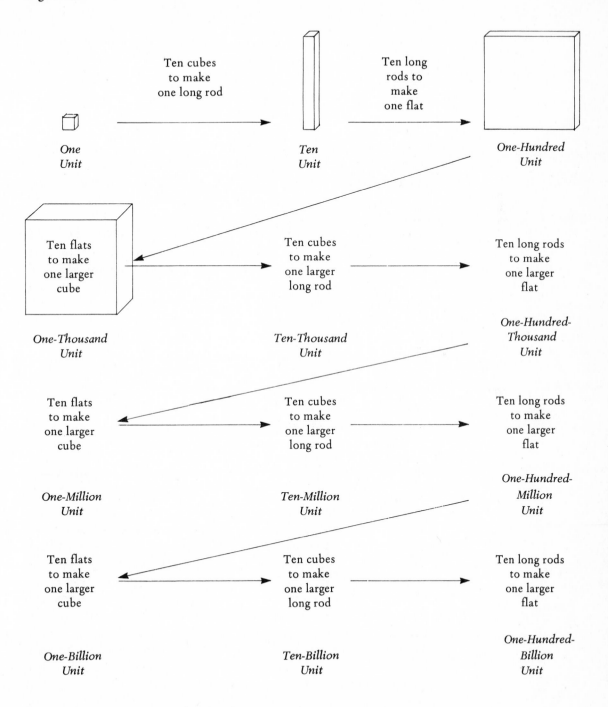

Figure 7.9

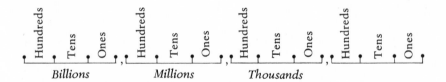

not generally used. The capabilities of reading and comprehending whole numbers and decimal fractions are developed from experiences with the physical object models and recording the numbers of the different-size units in the pieces of the models being displayed. The first numeral-reading activities involve children seeing the one-digit numerals (0, 1, 2, 3, 4, 5, 6, 7, 8, 9) printed on numeral cubes and numeral cards and associating those signs with numbers of objects. When learning activities include numbers greater than ten, collections of ten objects are made and the same digits are used to describe the number of collections of ten objects. Numeral cubes, numeral cards, and place-value charts should be used to help children associate two-digit and three-digit numerals as well as numerals describing even greater numbers, with quantities represented by the models for number.

Reading and Writing Numerals
When the one-digit numerals are being studied, children should be helped to identify and recognize those numerals in their proper form before they are expected to write or draw the numerals. The reversals made by many young children who are attempting to write numerals may be caused by unnecessary haste or early emphasis on writing compounded by the possibility that they are not yet positive about the proper form of the numerals and the possibility that they have not yet acquired the necessary psychomotor coordination. After all, these same children have been urged to learn manuscript writing, and the hand movements that are required to write the first numerals are exactly opposite those used in manuscript writing. (See Figure 7.10.) The argument that reversals are caused by perceptual problems is not logical. That simple argument states that when children look at a numeral such as 2 , they see ƨ , therefore, they write ƨ . The response to that argument is that if certain children see ƨ when they look at 2 , they must write 2 in order to see ƨ .

Figure 7.10

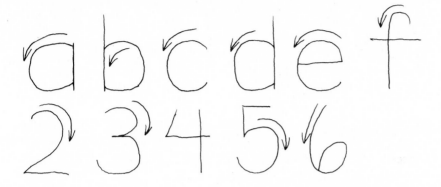

Reversals are very rarely caused by perceptual problems. The cause is much more likely to be that the proper form of the numeral is not firmly fixed in the child's mind, therefore, the reversal is not recognized as incorrect. The child has not learned to read the numeral.

When children have acquired the skills of reading numerals, the skills of writing those numerals will follow quickly. The principal notion is that developing children's abilities to read and to write numerals describing whole numbers and decimal fractions should be based on understanding of the concept of base ten as it is represented by a good physical object model for number and not merely built on or related to the characteristics of place value and the positional value of digits.

Common Fractions
The skills of reading and writing common fractions are introduced and developed in much the same manner. A physical object model, preferably fraction disks or pies, is laid out by the children, who are told to "make pies using equal or same-size pieces in each pie." The pies or units of one are thoroughly discussed using the language and terms that the children have acquired while working with whole numbers. Attention is given to the number of pies being used and to the fact that all of the pies are the same size, each pie is one pie or one unit, before any reference is made to the number of equal pieces in each pie. Then, while pointing to each pie or unit of one, the question "How many pieces in this pie?" can be repeatedly asked. The prerequisite skill needed

for this introduction and development is merely the ability to count the number of pies and the number of pieces in each pie. Depending on the model used, children will not have to count beyond 12 or 16. The basic concepts and skills required to understand and communicate about common fractions can be introduced and developed with a model that includes the one unit, and other units composed of halves, thirds, fourths, fifths, sixths, eighths, tenths, and twelfths.

Discussion with a small group of children about the number of pies and the number of equal-size pieces in each pie will probably not require more than three or four minutes. In the same introductory session, attention can be given to naming the equal-size parts in each pie. The first names given to each of these parts can be vocabulary terms that the children already understand, the number names they used while working with whole numbers. While referring to the pies in a random order, the questioning may proceed in the following manner:

Placing a hand on one pie	"How many pieces in this pie?"	Oral number name is given by a child
Pick up or turn over one piece of the pie	"How many pieces did I pick up (turn over)?"	"One"
Keep a hand or finger on the one piece	"What part of the pie did I pick up (turn over)?"	"One out of ___" (The teacher may have to and probably should utter this phrase.)

This activity continues until all of the children in the small group are consistently responding correctly. Notice that the teacher introduces the phrase "one out of _____." This phrase is used deliberately to avoid the misconceptions that children may have and the misuses they may make about such terms as *half, third,* and *fourth.* Many children use the term *half* incorrectly ("He got the biggest half.") because they have acquired the misconception that half refers to one of two pieces rather than one of two *equal* pieces of a unit or object. They have also heard the terms *third* and *fourth* used to refer to the position of an object in a series of objects. The phrase "one out of _____" is a proper use of a rational number name and it will help children quickly learn to read and to write common-fraction numerals with meaning and understanding.

When children are responding correctly to the questions of the preceding activity, they are ready to begin introductory and developmental activities directed toward reading common-fraction numerals. These same activities should reinforce their use of oral communications and can be extended to practice in writing common-fraction numerals. At some time in the preceding activity, after a child has correctly responded, "One out of ____ ," the child can be handed a unit-fraction numeral cube (a cube with the unit fractions 1/2, 1/3, 1/4, 1/5, 1/8, and 1/10 on the six faces of the cube) and asked, "Where on this cube does it say one out of ____ ?" If the child can read whole numbers, he or she will be able to show the correct numeral on the cube to the other children in the group. The numeral should be read orally as "one out of ____ ." Other children can then be asked to respond to the same questioning about other pies. When children can identify the proper numeral and give the correct oral name, they are ready to proceed to learning experiences directed toward associating the unit-fraction numerals on the cube with pieces in the model. Some additional learning acquisitions can be expected from the activities that have been described. In the processes of the activities, the teacher will find from questioning that the children can identify and show multiparts of one unit (two out of three, three out of four, five out of five or one pie, and so forth), that the children can identify and name the pieces of the model that are not named on the unit-fraction numeral cube, and that many of them will be able to write the common-fraction numerals to describe the pieces in the model (1/3, 1/6, 2/4, 4/5, and so on).

After successful experiences with these learning opportunities, children can be directed toward learning experiences in which they are asked to associate both oral and printed common-fraction names with number or quantity, to combine both equal and unequal fractional parts, to compare two fractional parts of one pie, to develop many names for the same number (many names for 1 and equivalent fractions), and to order fractional amounts. The developmental procedure is from meaningful oral communication to reading to writing common-fraction numerals through learning activities directed toward the concept of equal parts, identification, association of numeral to quantity, naming and renaming, combining, comparing, and ordering.

General Goals

The general goals of the content area of numeration and notation can be stated simply in reference to the oral and written vocabularies that are to be introduced and developed. The goals pertain to the understanding and use of symbols in communication. Stated in general terms, the goals are not specific in reference to types of numerals, complexity of numerals, or the age or grade levels at which specific performance skills are to be emphasized. The goals should apply to whatever type or complexity of numerals are being studied at a particular time and to all levels of instruction. The following four general goals refer to the vocabularies that are to be acquired and the performance skills that will demonstrate proficiency:

Listening: When a child hears an oral number name, that child will show that quantity with a model for number with which he or she is familiar.

Speaking: When a child is shown a quantity represented by a model with which he or she is familiar, that child will orally state one or more of the commonly accepted names for that number.

Reading: When a child is shown a printed numeral (not in written words), he or she will show that quantity with a model for number with which he or she is familiar.

Writing: When a child is shown a quantity represented by a model with which he or she is familiar, that child will write (not in words) the commonly accepted, most precise, printed numeral that names or describes that number or amount.

When a child can demonstrate these proficiencies with a specific type of number and the associated numerals at a defined level of complexity, that child will have acquired the basic competencies for that segment of this content area. The learning opportunities and experiences of the content area should be directed primarily toward acquisition of these competencies. At the same time, the learning activities can be directed toward or related to the major ideas or content themes of the content area.

The general goals can be used for evaluation. Observation and questioning by the teacher during the process of the children's participation in the learning activities will reveal the extent to which children have acquired proficiency at the level at which they are working. The performance competencies stated in the general goals are prerequisites to the computational operations on number using numerals. Unless children understand the numerals with which they are to work, it is almost futile to expect them to understand the computational operations—from the establishment of facts to the application of rules and procedures and the uses of those operations to solve problems. Therefore, it seems reasonable to make certain that children have acquired the proficiencies stated with the types of numerals to be involved in the operations. For example, before children begin the formal work of establishing addition facts, they should be able to demonstrate these performance skills with whole numbers up to 20; before children begin the formal work of establishing the "harder" multiplication facts, they should be able to demonstrate these proficiencies with whole numbers to 100; and before children are asked to perform any computational operations with common fractions, numeration and notation skills with common fractions should be evident.

Materials for Instruction

In addition to conventional printed textual materials, an active laboratory-type approach to instruction in elementary mathematics utilizes a wide variety of devices, which are intended to make possible (1) an earlier introduction of major ideas or concepts; (2) a more meaningful and understandable development of concepts and skills; (3) practice opportunities that are more interesting and motivating to children; (4) learning experiences (introductory, developmental, and practice) that allow applications of ideas and skills at the personal, developmental level of children; and, perhaps more important, (5) greater attainment of basic ideas and skills on the part of individual children.

In an active laboratory-type elementary mathematics program, printed textual materials are utilized in manners quite different from conventional textbook-oriented programs. Teachers and large groups of children in their classrooms will not use the same segments of the textual materials at the same time, for the same purposes, or in the same manners. Teachers may use the textual materials as guidebooks to determine the general content ascribed to the age or grade level being taught, as resource materials that suggest instructional approaches, and as a source of evaluative-practice exercises for children. After being introduced to and developing ideas and skills through laboratory activities, children might be directed to printed textual materials as references or for reinforcement reading, to satisfy their curiosity about their own abilities, or for evaluative-practice exercises. The exercises or examples in printed textual materials are very similar to those on standardized tests or other commonly used evaluative instruments, and the textual exercises can be used to develop familiarity with those types of items.

Types of Materials

Devices and materials necessary to introduce, develop, and practice the ideas and skills of numeration and notation in an active laboratory approach may be classified as physical object models, pictorial manipulatives, and recording materials. Physical object models for number are the basic materials for laboratory learning experiences involving numeration and notation. Pictorial manipulative materials are necessary to generate numerals to be used with the models, to practice reading numerals, and to practice the applications of concepts and skills. The recording-keeping devices are needed to practice writing skills as well as for evaluative purposes.

It may not be possible or necessary to obtain all of the materials listed in the following charts before initiating an active learning approach to the concepts and skills of numeration and notation. However, a greater variety of models and pictorial materials will make possible a greater variety of learning opportunities and activities. Some of the items will already be available in the school's learning center or classrooms, other items need to be purchased, some substitute items may be easily obtained, and teachers and children in the classroom might construct other necessities. Some teachers may find additional devices and materials that could be useful. The items on the following lists were selected because of their multiple uses, not only in the content area of numeration and notation but also for introducing, developing, and practicing other concepts and skills related to children's acquisition of familiarity with the main ideas of the real number system.

Whole Numbers

Physical Object Models
"Stackables"—poker chips, counters, small cubes

"Bundleables"—ice cream sticks, tongue depressors, soda straws

"Exchangeables"—base-ten blocks

Other—graduated centimeter rods

Pictorial Manipulatives
Picture number cards

Numeral cubes—(0, 1, 2, 3, 4, 5) and (0, 6, 7, 8, 9, 10)

Numeral cards—(0, 1, 2, . . ., 15), (numerals greater than 20, less than 100), (numerals greater than 100)

Abacus

Place-value chart
Odometer

Number line

Hundred board or chart with numeral tags 0 to 100

Dominoes

Common Fractions

Physical Object Models
Part of a unit—fraction disks or pies, fraction squares, plastic squares (two colors), sheets of paper, squared paper

Part of a group—poker chips, small cubes

Pictorial Manipulatives
Fraction picture cards

Fraction numeral cards

Fraction numeral cubes—(unit fractions: 1/2, 1/3, 1/4, 1/5, 1/8, 1/10), (multipart fractions), (combinations of unit

Other—graduated centimeter rods

Fraction dominoes

Fraction number lines

Decimal Fractions

Physical Object Models
Base-ten block model (the cube representing 1000 in use for whole numbers is used as model for 1 with decimal fractions)

Squared paper (to construct model)

Pictorial Manipulatives
Decimal picture cards

Decimal numeral cards

Place-value chart

Decimal numeral cubes—(0.1, 0.2, 0.3, etc.), (0.01, 0.02, 0.03, etc.), (0.001, 0.002 etc.)

Decimal number line

Integers (±)

Physical Object Models
Pan balance, small cloth or paper bags, small objects with equal weight

Pictorial Manipulatives
Number line—
$$\cdots \quad -3 \; -2 \; -1 \; 0 \; +2 \; +2 \; +3 \quad \cdots$$
Numeral cube—(0, 1, 2, . . ., 5)

Sign cube—(+ and −)

Recording Devices
Recording devices are not cited specifically for each of the types of numerals because those paper-and-pencil devices are basically the same for practicing the writing of various numerals and recording numbers that occur in different learning activities. The two- and three-column recording sheets that have been shown in preceding chapters can be used to describe and record units of different sizes and to record comparisons between numbers. Specially designed sheets or blank sheets of paper can be used for other recording necessities.

Positive and Negative Integers
Readers are probably familiar with or can anticipate the nature of most of the materials listed for whole numbers, common fractions, and decimal fractions. Many of those materials have

3. Matching activities
   a. Number to number or quantity to quantity
   b. Oral name to number and number to oral name
   c. Oral name to printed symbol to number and number to printed symbol to oral name
   d. Writing printed symbols for number
4. Comparing two quantities or numbers
   a. Visual comparisons
   b. Comparison by one-to-one matching
   c. Using comparative symbols to describe comparisons
5. Ordering
   a. Ordering quantities or numbers
   b. Ordering numerals
6. Grouping and regrouping to rename quantities or numbers
   a. Combining smaller units to make the next larger unit
   b. Combining two or more quantities or numbers and naming the total
   c. Regrouping a larger unit into smaller units
   d. Separating a quantity into two unequal-size parts
   e. Separating a quantity into two or more equal-size parts
   f. Writing numerals to describe all of the above

Similarities in Activities

Activities and games directed toward the further development of concepts and the practice of performance skills can also be consistent in type throughout the study of the various subsets of numbers. Concepts and performance skills can be reinforced and practiced through activities and games that involve the following:

1. Showing the number when the name for that number is given orally or when the printed numeral is shown with some pictorial manipulative device.
2. Obtaining quantities and grouping ("What you show is what you get") when numerals are generated in a random manner with numeral cubes, numeral cards, or spinners and the quantities to be obtained are pieces of a physical object model. Procedural rules can require grouping to facilitate naming the total amount that has been obtained. Records can be kept.
3. Matching number picture cards to number picture cards. Matching number picture cards to numeral cards. Matching

numeral cards to numeral cards (can be different numerals for the same number).

4. Giving away and regrouping ("What you show is what you give away") when the object is to start with a quantity or number represented by a physical object model and give amounts of it back to a "bank" until the quantity is diminished to zero. Amount to be given away is shown by a numeral generated in a random manner by numeral cubes, numeral cards, or spinners. Records of amounts started with, amounts given away, and amounts remaining may be kept.

5. Comparing number picture cards to number picture cards. Comparing number of total spots on dominoes. Comparing numeral cards to numeral cards. Comparing numerals generated in a random manner with other numerals generated in a random manner. Physical object models can be used to verify the comparisons. Records may be kept of the comparisons.

6. Ordering number picture cards. Ordering dominoes by total number of spots on the dominoes. Ordering numeral cards.

In such developmental activities and games, children can apply ideas and skills in manners that are appropriate to their ages and grade levels. The activities and games are intended to be interesting and motivating and should precede the practice-evaluative exercises and examples appearing in textbooks and workbooks or on worksheets and dittoed pages.

The nature of pupil-made projects, in which children apply ideas and skills, can also be consistent throughout the various periods or units of study in the content area of numeration and notation. Those projects may include constructing pictorial manipulative materials to be used in the instructional program, making number and numeration games, making number posters to show different names for the same number, constructing models for number, and making simple graphs to show comparisons of number.

Examples of Learning Experiences

The following activities and games are suggested as useful types of learning experiences. Each example involves one type of numeral or number, and readers are encouraged to extend the examples to the other subsets of numbers.

Show the Number Two to four children. Numeral cards with numerals greater than 100 and less than 1000 and a base-ten block model for number. Numeral cards are placed face down on the table. Each child takes a numeral card and shows the number, using pieces from the model. Each child checks every other child for correctness. Children who are correct keep their numeral card. Children who are incorrect return their numeral card to the pile. All pieces from the model are also returned to the pile, and the procedure is repeated.

Matching Two to four children. Set of fraction dominoes. Dominoes are placed face down on the table and mixed. Each child draws five to seven dominoes. One domino is taken from the pile and placed face up. Each child in turn tries to play one of his or her dominoes by matching one end of a domino to one end of the domino train on the table. Only the ends of the domino train may be played on. Equivalents are allowed in the matching, and the child must describe the match. A physical object model may be kept nearby to verify challenged matches. When a child cannot play, he or she must draw one domino from the remaining pile. If possible, that domino is played in that turn. First child to play all of his or her dominoes wins the game.

Comparing (Greatest Decimal Fraction) Two to four children. A deck of numeral cards containing four cards each of 0, 1, 2, 3, 4, 5, 6, 7, 8, and 9. Each child has a sheet of paper marked off with four places and a decimal point, as shown in Figure 7.12. The deck of cards is mixed and placed face down in the middle of the table. Each child, in turn, draws one card and places it in one of the places on the piece of paper. Once placed, the cards cannot be moved. After each child has drawn and placed four cards, the numerals are compared to determine which describes the greatest number. A base-ten block model can be used to verify comparisons. A scoring procedure acceptable to the children may be used. After each round of play, the used cards are placed in a separate pile, and the procedure is repeated.

Figure 7.12

Combining (Two Common Fractions) Two children. Two fraction numeral cubes with 1/2, 1/4, 3/4, 1/8, 3/8, and 5/8 on the six faces and a physical object model for common fractions that includes appropriate pieces. Each child rolls one of the cubes and takes the amount described on the numeral cube from the model. Children then combine the amounts they have taken and describe the total. After each turn, pieces of the model are returned to their proper places on the table and the procedure is repeated. Records of amounts taken and totals may be kept.

Figure 7.13

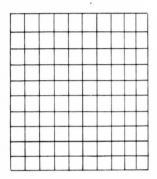

Separating (Cut away 100) Two to four children. Each child has a pair of scissors, a piece of squared paper (see Figure 7.13) that has 10 small squares in a row and 10 rows (100 small squares), and two numeral cubes with the numerals 0, 1, 2, 3, 4, and 5 on the six faces. Each child rolls the two numeral cubes in turn and makes the smaller two-digit numeral possible. (For example, if a 2 and a 3 are rolled, the numeral made is 23; if a 0 and a 5 are rolled, the numeral made is 05 or 5.) The child then cuts that amount from his or her paper and writes the numeral describing the amount on the cut off piece. The first child to cut away the entire piece may be declared the winner. The last numeral rolled need not be the exact amount left, it need only be greater. That last quantity is given its proper name. As an activity of further interest, the pieces that are cut by each child can be used as a puzzle to make a 100 square. A record can be kept of the amounts that are left after each turn and the amounts that are cut away (the record may look like a series of subtraction examples).

Ordering Two to four children. One set of regular dominoes. Dominoes are placed face down on the table and mixed. One domino is taken and placed face up on the table. First child to "play" is told to take a domino and place it on either side of the first domino, or if it has the same total number of spots to place it on top of that domino. Attention can be given to which domino has more spots and which domino has less spots, thus establishing an order. Each child is to draw a domino in turn and place it where it belongs in the order (Figure 7.14). When all of the dominoes have been placed, each stack can be examined to determine if all of the dominoes in that stack have the same total number of spots. Attention might also be called to the nature of the distribution.

Figure 7.14

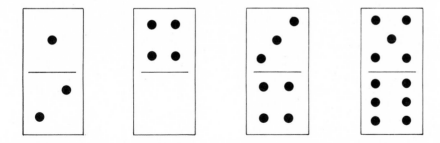

Suggested Activities

1. Examine a textbook or a teacher's manual from a commercially produced textbook series to ascertain the topics, bits of content, exercises, and expectations that apply to the content area of numeration and notation.
2. Ascertain the types of instructional materials, physical object models, and pictorial manipulatives that are suggested for use.
3. Construct one or more pictorial manipulative materials that would help children develop some concept or acquire some skill of numeration.
4. Teach one of the games or activities involving numeration and notation from this chapter or from preceding chapters to one or more children.
5. Select one major idea or content theme from the content area of numeration and notation and list the performance skills that are associated with that theme throughout the elementary mathematics program.
6. Select a general age or instructional level for children and begin a collection of appropriate activities, games, and projects pertaining to the development of communication concepts and skills for the area of numeration and notation.
7. Refer to the section "Examples of Learning Experiences" in this chapter. For each example, devise a similar activity or game that deals with a different subset of numbers.

Chapter 8

Operations on Collections of Objects

The content area operations on collections of objects deals with the possibilities that exist in the majority of quantitative problem-solving situations that children are likely to confront in their study of elementary mathematics. The learning experiences and activities included in this content area involve the actual manipulation of objects by children in order to solve problems or to rename numbers. The objects to be manipulated are the pieces of physical object models for number. The nature of the model to be used depends on the nature of the numbers and numerals in the problems. In the learning experiences and activities of the content area, children will perform physical operations, manipulations, with the pieces of physical object models for number for the specific purpose of ascertaining responses to questions about problems that are structured with those concrete materials.

The purposes and procedures of this content area should not be misconstrued as being synonymous with the topic "operations on sets," which may or may not be dealt with in contemporary commercially produced textual materials used in many elementary mathematics programs. The nature of the content in the topic "operations on sets" is generally descriptive, illustrative, and definitive in regard to defining, naming, and showing the elements that belong to sets, disjoint sets, subsets of a set, the union of two or more sets, and the intersections of two or more sets. Quite often the topic only deals with describing situations, and little is done to apply the ideas to quantitative problem situations that require solutions. Operations on sets and operations on collections of objects are related in purposes and procedures only if the elements of the sets are pieces from a physical object model and are used to illustrate a quantitative problem.

Unfortunately, performing operations on collections of objects, models for number, is rarely dealt with as a specific topic or area of study in the elementary mathematics program. For one reason or another, mathematics educators and classroom teachers seem averse to using concrete physical materials in elementary mathematics programs beyond the early primary level. Some feel that the use of such materials is a sign of weakness or lack of intellectual development on the parts of children; others feel that understanding should have been acquired earlier and that the time and effort needed to develop understanding of basic ideas and skills with concrete materials at the current level might better be spent on introducing and developing other ideas and skills or on practicing facts, rules, and operations in more abstract manners. Others believe that such activities are not necessary for children to attain the achievement expectations of the program. Yet one need not look far to find a significant number of children at the intermediate and upper grade levels who seem able to perform computational operations with numerals and find answers to exercises or examples, but who cannot determine when those operations could or should be used to find solutions to quantitative problems or who cannot explain or demonstrate understanding of how or why the operation works. Children who can cite facts and who can perform computational operations with different types of numerals but do not know when those facts and operations can and should be applied in attempts to solve problems have acquired semiuseless skills. They can, of course, apply those superficial skills to common achievement-testing situations, thus giving a false indication of their prowess with these basic skills. Children who can cite facts and perform operations but who cannot demonstrate how those facts were derived or established and how and why the operation is performed have not acquired basic foundational concepts and skills.

When learning experiences and activities that deal with performing operations on collections of objects are not omitted entirely from school or classroom programs, they often are sporadic and used to (1) briefly introduce the technical skills of the computational operations, (2) quickly demonstrate or illustrate quantitative problem situations, or (3) assist or attempt to assist slow learners or children who are having difficulty to acquire at least some of the performance expectations. In many instances children who have the capacities to memorize facts and operational rules are not given opportunities to see and understand those facts and rules illustrated by models for number. When concrete objects are used as exploratory materials or for demonstration or illustration, the objects utilized often are not consistently good physical object models for the numbers involved. The objects themselves may be distracting to the learning situation, or the ideas to be emphasized cannot be displayed well with those materials. Treating operations on collections of objects as a pertinent content area is an attempt to spirally develop major ideas or concepts in a consistent manner throughout the elementary mathematics program.

Importance of the Area

The importance of and purposes for considering operations on collections of objects as a major area in the elementary mathematics program lie in (1) further developing or reinforcing the concepts, ideas, and performance skills of numeration and notation; (2) developing foundations for understanding and the technical skills of the fundamental computational operations of addition, subtraction, multiplication, and division—operations on number using numerals; and (3) modifying and improving the approach to helping children develop problem-solving abilities.

Concern for Structure

A concern for an emphasis on structure is quite common in the professional literature dealing with elementary mathematics programs. In regard to elementary mathematics programs, *structure* may be described as the patterns and relationships that exist within and between identified concepts, ideas, and performance skills. A consistent recurrence of a phenomenon is a *pattern*. *Relationships* exist when the same idea, fact, generalization, or procedure applies to different concepts, situations, or performance skills. The learning opportunities of children in an active laboratory-type elementary mathematics program should include the search for important patterns and relationships, distinct and direct references to those patterns and relationships as they recur in a spirally planned program, and application of those patterns and relationships in new situations. Patterns of importance in elementary mathematics programs might be classified in the following ways:

1. *Patterns that appear in arrangements or configurations of numerical symbols.* These patterns are evident in the ordering of number names, the application of the base-ten concepts, and the positional-value notations of the decimal system of numeration. They can be seen in the sequences of numerals as they appear in various charts. Some of these patterns and relationships are reinforced or further developed while performing and recording the results of operations on collections of objects. Patterns also can be seen in listing certain kinds of numbers, such as even and odd numbers, multiples of numbers, triangular numbers, square numbers, and so forth.

2. *Patterns that appear in organized collected data.* Through scrutinizing or studying data that have been collected from a particular laboratory-type activity and organized in charts or otherwise, patterns might be discerned that lead to the formulation of generalizations, facts, or rules pertaining to the activity. Activities of this type might be directed toward establishing an order for numbers or numerals, establishing arithmetical facts, introducing and developing computational operations, developing formulas through problems involving measurements, and ascertaining functions in which one variable x has a direct and constant relationship to another variable y. Foundations for ascertaining the patterns and relationships that apply to establishing arithmetical facts and the computational operations performed with numerals are introduced in the operations to be performed on physical objects.

3. *Patterns that appear in quantitative problem situations.* One of the major purposes of emphasizing operations on collections of objects as a content area to be spirally developed throughout the elementary mathematics program is to help children recognize generally analogous quantitative problems. Analogous quantitative problems are similar in structure or in the nature of the problem situation. When children are capable of analyzing problem situa-

tions and of recognizing or identifying quantitative problems as similar to other problems, their potential for solving problems will be increased. Generally, the analogies are to be made from a confrontation with a more complex problem, in terms of the numbers involved, to a simpler problem with familiar numbers.

Concern for an emphasis on structure in elementary mathematics programs has two aspects. First, there is a desire to help children develop their own correct and consistent structure of mathematical ideas, structure that should be as complete as possible. Second, if children are to develop correct and consistent structures of mathematical ideas, there must be a consistency of structure in the instructional program. That consistency not only emphasizes a search for patterns and relationships, but also should attempt (1) a material coherence with retention of form, continued use of well-selected physical object models; (2) a solidity or firmness of continued emphasis on major concepts, ideas, or content themes; (3) density of and intensity on the ideas and performance skills that are related to content themes; (4) constant adherence to identified philosophical and instructional principles; (5) harmony or compatibility between the content and the instructional endeavors of the major areas or topics to be studied in the program; and (6) harmony or compatibility between the concepts, ideas, and skills to be introduced and developed within each of the major content areas.

Concepts and Skills

The learning experiences and activities of performing operations on collections of objects, by the inherent nature of utilizing physical object models for number and communicating about the operations and their results, will reinforce and further develop children's concepts and skills in the area of numeration and notation. Those same learning experiences and activities will build the foundations for developing children's understanding of the fundamental operations of addition, subtraction, multiplication, and division. Children's understanding of the arithmetical facts and rules that are utilized in performing the fundamental operations depends on their knowledge of the characteristics of the decimal system of numeration as exemplified in physical object models for number. Furthermore, as they perform operations using pieces of those models (collections of objects) in order to solve structured problems, they will be able to see facts, rules, and generalizations pertaining to the operations in a real sense. The grouping, regrouping, and exchanging of numerical units will be real and will be performed in a physical manner before the abstract manipulation of numerical symbols in computational operations is expected.

Problem Solving

Helping children to develop problem-solving abilities continues to be a major goal of elementary mathematics programs. In an active laboratory-type elementary mathematics program it is the primary goal inherent in the general objectives of developing familiarity with the main ideas of the real number system, geometry, and algebraic foundations. It is the goal of applying concepts and skills to real situations. Although problem solving is an integral part of the other major content areas, the content area of operations on collections of objects is directed distinctly toward modifying and improving instructional procedures and approaches intended to help children acquire skills in problem solving. Modification implies changing from established procedures to some other approach. Improvement implies increasing children's abilities to solve quantitative problems. Although children's attitudes toward problems and the tasks of solving problems may be related to their solution skills, performance is the basic criterion measure. Before examining a suggested alternative, consider the traditional and conventional text approaches to problem solving in elementary mathematics programs.

Traditional Approach

For many years a traditional approach to helping children learn to solve problems followed a sequence of first expecting children to master one of the computational operations at some difficulty level and then expecting them to apply that computational skill to oral or printed problems. Children were introduced to one difficulty level of a computational operation and were expected to learn the facts and rules for performing that computation by working a sufficient number of exercises and examples. After spending some period of time and effort on the computational exercises, they were given or assigned "word" problems, which could be solved with the same computational operation that had been studied most recently. In some instances, the computational operations needed to solve the problems were at approximately the same level of difficulty. In other instances, the sequence of word problems increased in difficulty in regard to the size or type (0 in a numeral, multipart fractions, mixed numbers, and so forth) of numbers that were involved. In any case, children were expected to apply the computational skills they had just learned. Thus, traditionally, word problems were classified as addition, subtraction, multiplication, or division problems, according to the computational operation that a proficient adult would utilize to arrive at a solution, and children did not encounter certain types of problems until they had been introduced to the operation that a proficient adult would use to solve them. Children did not encounter "multiplication" problems, problems that involved combining several numbers of equal size, until they had studied the multiplication operation, nor did they encounter "division" problems, problems that involved separating one amount into equal-size parts, until they had studied the division operation. At later levels, when problems became more complex, the problems were further classified as one-step, two-step, ... n step problems according to the number of separate operations to be performed in order to arrive at the correct solution.

The fallacies of classifying problems according to adult-level computational solutions and of delaying children's introductions to various kinds of problems may be illustrated by citing one problem and considering how children of different age or grade levels might solve it. The problem would be considered a "division" problem by traditionalists, yet children can solve it by using other operations they have learned. The problem could be stated in several ways, but it entails giving a group of 4 children a bag of candy with the number of pieces of candy (24) marked on the side and asking how many pieces of candy each child will get if they share the candy equally. Each group of 4 children except the youngest group is told that they cannot open the bag until they know how many pieces of candy each child should receive. The youngest group of children, perhaps five years old, will simply open the bag without paying attention to the numeral on the bag and distribute the pieces of candy one at a time to each child. Another group of children, perhaps a year older, would look at the numeral 24 on the bag and might use one of several procedures. They might substitute 24 other items for the 24 pieces of candy and then use the same one-to-one matching approach that the youngest children used. Or, they might use a procedure in which they counted in turn ("one, two, three, . . ., twenty-four"), either while distributing the substitute items or while they each raised an additional finger in turn. Each of the following solution procedures might be used by successively older children who have become familiar with the uses of other operations. One group might determine that it would take 4 pieces of candy to go around the group once, and, therefore, might count by multiples of 4 until they reached 24 ("four, eight, twelve, . . ., twenty-four") and notice how many number names they said or how many times they went around. Using the same idea of 4 pieces of candy to go around once, they might add $(0 + 4 = 4, 4 + 4 = 8, 8 + 4 = 12, . . .)$ and count the number of times they added 4. Another group, noting the numeral 24 on the bag and using the idea that it would take 4 pieces of candy to go around the group once, might subtract $(24 - 4 = 20, 20 - 4 = 16, . . .)$ and count the number of times they subtracted 4. An older group might use the multiplication idea that 4 groups of some number equals 24 $(4 \times \underline{} = 24)$; and finally, some older group might simply say, "24 divided by 4 is 6." Children of different age groups solved the problem by matching, counting, adding, subtracting, multiplying, and dividing. How can the problem be classified as a "division" problem, and why should problems of this nature be deferred until children have formally studied the operation of division?

In this traditional approach to problem solving, children's difficulties did not become apparent until they were assigned problems requiring different computational operations or solutions in "mixed practice problems." These problems required children to decide what operations had to be performed to arrive at a solution, and a significant number of children, for one reason or another, could not make the correct decision and, thus, could not solve the problems. More capable children were able to recall and associate the mixed problems with previous similar problems or could pick out key words in the problems that were associated with operations to be performed. Those children could make proper decisions about methods for solution. Other children devised their own rules for deciding which operation to use. Some relied completely on finding key words such as *altogether, difference, each, total*, and the like. Some based their decision on the numbers in the problem: if there were more than two numbers, add; if there were two numbers about the same size, subtract; and if there were two numbers, one large and one small, flip a coin and either multiply or divide. These decision procedures primarily applied to problems with whole numbers. Sometimes they led to a correct solution procedure, and sometimes they did not. The ability to decide on an appropriate procedure or operation for solving a problem is the first necessity in problem solving. Obviously, the selected operations must be performed correctly, but that is the second step in solving problems.

The procedure traditionally used to help children learn to solve problems, either before they encountered word problems or after difficulties became apparent, might be called an analytical approach. Children were asked to analyze the problem by answering questions similar to the following, either to themselves or to the teacher: "What is given?" "What is asked?" "What operation are you supposed to use?" On written word problems, children could be helped to respond correctly to the first two questions. They could simply read or have read to them those appropriate parts of the stated problem. However, the third question was often met with silence. If the child who was having difficulty knew the answer to that question, that child would have attempted the operation. Met with silence to that question, the teacher might further explain or reread the problem to no avail, and was often left with only that one encompassing direction to give the child, "Think!" The traditional analytical approach was stymied at this point because the children were not prepared to think about analogous problems in a real or visual sense or about alternative procedures for possible solutions.

Conventional Text Approaches

Contemporary printed textual materials often use a conventional approach in which topics dealing with the development of an operation are introduced with a problem situation. Introducing topics with problem situations is an attempt to make the study more real and interesting and to relate computational operations to problem situations. The problem situations in the materials are enhanced with pictures and illustrative problems referring to what authors believe are common experiences of the children— going to stores, having a paper route, eating out, and traveling. Problems deal with setting or situation. Unfortunately, in most instances practically all of the problems or questions involve the same operation (the operation of the content topic) for solution.

Some emphasis is given to writing and using number sentences, and the suggestion is often given to write a number sentence about the problem before attempting solution procedures. In order to write those number sentences, children must be able to answer the last question of the analytical approach, "What operation is to be used?" The procedure for helping children learn to solve problems continues to be analytical, and the problem-solving capabilities of children do not appear to be enhanced.

Suggestions from Literature

Reports of research studies and opinions that appear in the professional literature directed toward elementary mathematics educators suggest several general ideas or specific techniques that might be utilized to increase children's abilities to solve quantitative problems. Some of these techniques are used currently by concerned teachers. The reported ideas and techniques suggest that classroom teachers of elementary mathematics do the following:

1. Teach children to read the language of mathematics in problems. Correlational studies show that reading ability is related to the ability to solve written word problems, and why not? Children cannot solve a written problem if they cannot read it.
2. Arrange the language of problems so that the order in which numerical data are presented enhances a child's ability to solve the problem. Present the data in the same order that they will be written in the computational operation that is used to solve the problem.
3. Work on increasing children's abilities to compute. Children cannot arrive at correct solutions to problems unless they can perform the computational operations correctly.
4. Use a systematic approach in which problems are discussed and diagrammed and responses are estimated before computation is performed.
5. Develop children's abilities to generalize the meaning of an operation on number and to formulate original statements to express these generalizations.
6. Allow children to write and solve their own problems.
7. Allow children to formulate their own solution procedures and to discuss those procedures with other children.
8. Help children to use an equation approach in which they write number sentences to describe the problem.

9. Present problems orally. This procedure is not only more lifelike, it will be especially helpful to children with reading disabilities.
10. Emphasize quantitative vocabulary study so that children are better able to communicate about problem situations.
11. Use manipulative objects to demonstrate and illustrate problems.
12. Use drawings to illustrate problem situations. The drawings might be of objects, or they might be diagrams of sets.

Although these suggested ideas and general procedures may be helpful, they appear to supplement an analytical approach—to help children analyze the problem in order to decide which operation to perform. The suggestions do not imply a change or modification in the general approach. Several of the most helpful suggestions are integral aspects of the suggested approach to developing children's problem-solving abilities that follows.

A Suggested Approach

The suggested modification involves a "total picture" or nature-of-the-problem approach rather than a fragmented one. The numerical data in the problem are not of immediate importance. Neither are key or clue words related to computational operations. Problems are not classified as addition, subtraction, multiplication, or division problems; the computational operations are regarded as technical skills for possible application in solution attempts. The implications are that several different operations might be used to solve the same problem and that all problems can be solved by an operation as simple as counting. All types of quantitative problems are introduced early in the elementary mathematics programs. The quantitative problems are modeled or structured with pieces of good physical object models for number, and emphasis is placed on developing the relationships between the operations that are performed on the pieces of the physical object models (operations on collections of objects) and operations on number using numerals (the computational operations). The operations that can be performed on collections of objects in quantitative problem situations are limited to combining, separating, and comparing.

Modeling Problems   When children are first confronted with a quantitative problem that has been modeled or structured with pieces of a physical object model for number, they can see the original quantities that are involved in the problem and can better understand the nature of the question. When children comprehend the problem situation, they can apply the performance skills they have acquired to the solution of the problem. Structured or modeled problems can be solved first by moving or manipulating the model pieces in accordance with the nature of the problem—combining, separating, or comparing—and describing the nature of the result. Children can use the performance skills that they have acquired. It is the role and responsibility of the teacher to introduce children to more efficient and effective technical skills. The introduction and development of more efficient and effective technical skills in regard to time, effort, and accuracy are related to and associated with the operations that are performed on the physical object pieces in the modeled problems.

Charting the Approach The chart in Figure 8.1 attempts to diagram the changes in emphasis of this approach to helping children increase their problem-solving abilities. It should be apparent that the major emphasis is on ascertaining the nature of the problem so that it may be related to analogous problems regardless of the nature of the numerical data in the problem. When children are confronted with a problem situation, their major task is to ascertain or recognize the "total picture." Confrontation implies that the children accept the problem as one they would like to solve. It is meaningful and real to them. Recognition of the total situation requires a determination of the nature of the starting point of the problem. Does the problem start with one group or collection (number), or does it start with two or more groups or collections (numbers)? If a problem begins with only one group or collection, that number can only be separated; therefore, the problem is a *separation* problem. If a problem begins with two or more groups or collections, those numbers can be either combined or compared, and the problem is either a *combination* problem or a *comparison* problem. Thus, the three major types of problems are *combining, comparing,* and *separating.* Children should learn to classify problems in that manner rather than as addition, subtraction, multiplication, or division problems.

When the problem has been identified as belonging to a major type, children can look at it in more detail. If the problem is a

Figure 8.1

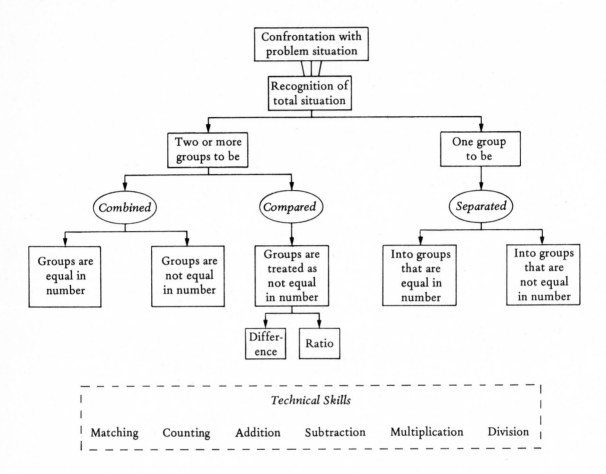

combining problem, does it deal with equal-size groups or does it deal with unequal-size groups? In either case, the task is to find the total of the combined amount. If the problem is a separating problem, does it deal with unequal-size groups and ask, "How much is left?" in a take-away situation, or does it deal with equal-size groups and ask either, "How large is each group?" or, "How many equal-size groups?" If the problem is a comparison problem, does it deal with finding the difference between two numbers or with finding the ratio between two numbers? Once these kinds of questions have been answered, available technical skills can be applied. For each of the two subcategories in each of the major types of problems, there are several technical or performance skills that can be employed to arrive at correct responses.

Type of Problem	*Performance Skills*
Combining groups that are equal in number	Combining objects and counting
	Collecting, grouping, and naming
	Adding
	Multiplying
Combining groups that are unequal in number	Combining objects and counting
	Collecting, grouping, and naming
	Adding
Comparing two unequal groups to determine the difference	Matching one-to-one and counting
	Subtracting
Comparing two unequal groups to determine a ratio	Matching N-to-N and counting
	Subtracting
	Dividing
Separating one group into two unequal groups to find a remainder	Separating objects and counting
	Regrouping, separating, and naming
	Subtracting
Separating one group into two or more equal-size groups	Separating by counting N objects into each group and counting the groups
	Separating by making N equal groups and counting the number of objects in each group
	Subtracting
	Dividing

Major Ideas or Content Themes

The major ideas or content themes of numeration and notation that involve communicating about nonnegative integers, common fractions, and decimal fractions are further developed and reinforced in the learning experiences and activities directed toward performing operations on collections of objects. The operations that are performed with pieces of physical object models for number provide continuous opportunities for children to communicate both orally and in written form about the numbers that the models exemplify. The concepts of base ten and positional value and the performance skills associated with those concepts will be required in describing the numbers involved in the operations and the results of the operations that are performed with the models for whole numbers and decimal fractions. The concepts of equal parts and different names for the same number and the performance skills associated with the development of those concepts will be applied to the operations that are performed on the pieces of models for common fractions. Observation of a classroom engaged in an ideal active laboratory-type elementary mathematics program might fail to detect distinct differences between the learning experiences and activities directed toward the goals of numeration and notation and those directed toward the goals of operations on collections of objects. Instructional materials, especially the models for number, are similar; the learning experiences and activities of the two content areas are integrated; and, the content themes and performance skills of the two areas are related. As indicated in Chapter 9, the same statements might be made about the content areas of operations on collections of objects and operations on numbers using numerals.

Operations on collections of objects is suggested as a major content area because of the importance of developing children's problem-solving abilities in as complete a manner as possible. The major ideas or themes of the content area pertain to different types of quantitative problem situations. Each of these types of problems can be introduced early in the program, and the concepts and skills associated with understanding and solving that type of problem with different types of numerical data can be spirally developed throughout the program. The types of problems will remain constant throughout the program, but complexity will increase in regard to the numerals in the problems, the inclusion of both relevant and irrelevant data, the need to rename the quantities involved numerically, and the complication of needing two or more operations to solve one problem. The six types of problems, two subcategories from each of three major types, can be stated as content themes or major ideas.

Two or more unequal-size quantities (numbers) can be combined, and the total of that combination can be named.

As with the other content themes, this major idea is to be spirally developed throughout the program with analogous problems. The problems are to be structured or modeled with those physical object models that are most characteristic of the numbers and numerals that children have been or are studying. Within each of the subsets of the set of real numbers (whole numbers, common fractions, and decimal fractions) studied in this content area, there is a logical sequence in the complexity of numbers and numerals to be introduced and developed. Therefore, there is a logical sequence in the nature of the physical models or in the pieces of one physical object model to be used in modeling or structuring problems. That sequence depends on the nature of the numbers to be represented, the nature of the regrouping that will be necessary in the combining process, the nature of exchanging of smaller unit pieces of the model for larger units after the combining has taken place, and, in regard to common fractions, the extent of exchanging of units (renaming) that must be done before the combining takes place.

For whole numbers, the first combining experiences should involve counters, poker chips, small cubes, or single sticks or straws. Combinations that result in quantities or numbers greater than ten could then be represented by collecting objects into stacks, rows, or piles of ten objects and single objects in order to name the combinations properly. As the whole numbers to be combined become greater, models consisting of bundles of ten sticks and single sticks or the base-ten blocks would be used.

For all of the problems dealing with common fractions, a complete fraction-pie model can be used. The sequence of problems would be similar to combining same-size unit fractions; to combining unit fractions and multipart fractions having the same size fractional unit, extending the combinations to one unit or a complete pie; to combining two or more multipart fractions having fractional units of the same size, extending the combinations to amounts greater than one unit; to combining two or more fractional amounts with fractional units of different sizes; to combining mixed numbers. After some experiences with providing these activities, teachers may find that many children have the numeration and notation skills to deal with mixed problems and it will not be necessary to provide distinct and separate activities for each type of problem.

The model to be used for all structured or modeled problems involving decimal fractions is a base-ten block of some type. The sequence of problems depends on the amount of exchanging of ten smaller units for the next larger unit that is required after the combining takes place.

Two or more equal-size quantities (numbers) can be combined, and the total of that combination can be named.

The only real difference between this major idea and the last is that the problems to be structured and spirally developed throughout the elementary mathematics program involve groups of quantities of the same size. For whole numbers, the sequence of structured problems to be encountered by children ranges from combining quantities or numbers that can be described by one-digit numerals, to combining numbers described by two-digit numerals, to combining numbers that are described by three-digit numerals, and so on. For problems involving common fractions, the sequence of structured problems begins with combining N groups of a quantity described by a unit fraction, to combining N groups of a quantity represented by a multipart fraction, to combining N groups of a quantity described by a mixed number, to combining N and a fractional amount of any of the above quantities. Problems pertaining to combining a number of same-size quantities described by a decimal fraction are sequenced according to the amount of exchanging of units that is required after the combining takes place in order to most effectively name the total of the combination.

One quantity (number) can be separated into two unequal parts, and the result of that separation can be described.

The structured problems pertaining to this content theme employ the idea of "taking away," in which the problem starts with a specified quantity or amount, a specified amount or quantity is to be removed or taken away, and the question to be answered is "How much is left?" For structured problems involving whole numbers, the sequence for spiral development is related to the nature and extent of regrouping or exchanging of a larger numerical unit for ten of the next smaller numerical units that must take place before the separation can be done. Naturally, the sequence also proceeds from smaller numbers to greater numbers. Modeled problems that start with smaller quantities or numbers will precede problems that start with greater numbers. Regardless of the size of the beginning number, problems that require no exchanging of units and problems that require only one exchange will precede problems that require several exchanges. If children are familiar with the physical object models used to structure the problems and are proficient with the performance skills of numeration and notation, extensive sequencing of the structured problems to be undertaken need not be delineated specifically into the types of regrouping a ten unit to ones, regrouping a one-hundred unit to tens, and so on. Also, if that familiarity is present, the nonexistence of a numerical unit of a particular size in the starting quantity ("Start with 2 hundreds and 3 ones, take away 6 tens and 5 ones") should not cause great difficulty. For problems involving common fractions that are structured with a fraction-pie model, the sequencing will be related to the nature of the exchanging of model pieces that must take place before the separation can be accomplished. Initial problems will require no exchanging for an equivalent amount. A second type of problem will require exchanging the starting amount for an equivalent amount of the fraction unit named in the amount to be removed. A third type of problem will require renaming the amount to be removed in terms of the fractional unit used in the starting amount. And, a fourth type of problem will require renaming both of the amounts cited in the problem. It should be noted that children will be able to arrive at solutions to the structured problems without actually renaming amounts or without actually performing all of the intended exchanges. For problems that require separating a quantity or number named by a decimal fraction, the sequence of modeled problems is very similar to the sequence of problems dealing with whole numbers. The introduction and development is related to the extent and nature of the exchanging of a larger numerical unit for ten of the next smaller numerical units.

One quantity (number) can be separated into two or more equal parts, and the result of that separation can be described.

Structured problems pertaining to this major idea or theme are of two types. In one type, the size of each of the separated groups is known and the task is to find out how many of those size groups can be made from the original group. In the other type, the number of groups to be made is known and the task is to find how many or how much will be in each group. As in the preceding major idea, the sequence of spiral development of problems involving whole numbers depends on the nature and extent of the regrouping or exchanging of larger units to smaller units that must occur before the separations can take place. Through observation, the teacher may find that one type of problem is no more difficult for children than the other. Children may appear to be equally adept at answering "How many groups?" and "How many in each group?" with structured problems. When data from the problems are recorded in an organized manner, it might be pointed out that the records of the two types of problems have the same information and appearance. This observation or generalization will be particularly helpful when the formal operation of division is introduced and developed as a technical procedure for arriving at solutions to these problems.

Three major types of problems within this major idea or theme involve common fractions. One type, perhaps the first to be introduced, begins with a whole number quantity, represented by one unit of the fraction-pie model, that is to be separated into equal-size fractional parts. (At a later level, the initial quantity may be a mixed number.) Initial problems of this type would require finding how many pieces of a particular size unit fraction can be separated from a small whole number: "How many pieces of this size can be made from N pies?" Problems would then increase in complexity or difficulty by changing the sizes of the equal subparts to multipart fractions. A second type of problem begins with a fractional quantity that is to be separated into N equal parts. Problems of this type are initiated best with a unit-fraction piece of the model that is to be separated into a specified number of equal parts: "Start with ½. Make 4 equal parts. How big is each part?" Structured problems can then be extended to starting with a quantity illustrated by multiparts of the same size, which can be described by a multipart fraction, and separating that quantity into N equal parts. Even more complexity is added when the original quantity is to be separated into N and a fraction of N (3½) equal parts. Problems of this type may also include separating a small whole number, represented by fraction pies, into N equal parts: "Start with 3 pies. Make 4 equal parts. How big is each part?'' The third type of problem within this major idea involves finding a part of a part—a fractional part of a fractional quantity: "Start with 'three-fourths'. Separate it into 3 equal parts. How much is two-thirds of three-fourths?" Problems of this type can also be extended to mixed numbers. Structured problems in which decimal fractions are used to name the numbers involved are related to both the concepts and skills that are involved in problems with whole numbers and in problems with common fractions. The types of problems are similar to those described for common fractions: partitioning a whole number into fractional parts; separating a fractional part into N equal parts; and finding a fractional part of a fractional part. Each type of problem is extended to include mixed numbers. The model used and the nature of the exchanging of the pieces of that model are similar to the activities with structured problems pertinent to whole numbers.

Two numbers (quantities) can be compared in regard to size, and the result of that comparison can be described.

Some of the first quantitative experiences that young children have in elementary mathematics programs involve comparing two quantities. In the earliest of those activities, children may simply compare two quantities in regard to a characteristic, such as size, amount, length, capacity, or weight, without reference to specific number names. Those activities are directed toward developing general ideas or procedures of comparing and using comparative terms, such as *bigger, smaller, more than, less than, longer, shorter, taller, heavier,* and *lighter.* In very early activities, children begin using one-to-one matching of the elements or objects in two different groups. Unfortunately, the activities of matching in one-to-one correspondence often are not carried on after children learn the first number names and the operation of counting. One-to-one matching of the elements in two collections of objects representing numbers is the basic physical operation used in comparisons to find differences. The structured problems directed toward this major idea or theme are deliberately modeled so that there are differences in quantity or number between the two groups involved. The task in each problem is to find the amount of the difference. There are two sequential physical manipulations involved in arriving at the solution naming the amount of difference. The first of these operations entails matching the elements or objects that represent the two quantities in one-to-one correspondence. Matching the pieces of the models representing the two quantities, insofar as possible, will reveal that a difference exists. The second operation is directed at finding the amount of the difference and can be conducted in one of two ways. In the first, pieces of the larger quantity that have not been matched with pieces of the smaller quantity can be moved aside, and the number name for that amount can be determined. This procedure is similar to the "take away" idea of separating one group into two unequal groups, and the formal record will have the same appearance. For example, "Which group is larger?

A: ✳✳✳✳✳✳✳
B: ✳✳✳✳

A: ✳✳✳✳✳✳✳ or B: ✳✳✳✳ How much larger?" The written record of the problem which is shown in the margin, may have the same appearance as a "take away" problem, $7 - 4 = 3$. Thus, it can be generalized that the operation of subtraction can be utilized as a technique for solving. In the second method, pieces of the model can be "added" to the smaller amount until it is equivalent to the larger amount. The formal record for the problem may be written as $4 + \square = 7$. Thus, the so-called missing-addend problems and exercises, which apparently cause children some difficulty, can and probably should be approached as comparison problems. After the record has been written in the formal manner ($4 + \underline{\quad} = 7$), children must be helped to develop procedures for finding the unknown quantity. Initially, with simpler problems, counting skills or application of the addition facts will suffice. Later however, children should be encouraged to apply ideas from algebraic foundations to arrive at solutions. These ideas include the nature of equality and equivalence and procedures for maintaining equality or equivalence in quantitative statements (number sentences or equations). In this case, the same number can be added to or subtracted from both sides of the statement of equivalence, both quantitative amounts or number names, without destroying the statement of equivalence: $4 + \square - 4 = 7 - 4$ or $4 + \square + (-4) = 7 + (-4)$ leading to $\square = 3$. The directions to "subtract" or to "transpose" are not sufficient to develop meaning and understanding. Spiral development of this major idea or theme throughout the elementary mathematics program and through the subsets of whole numbers, common fractions, and decimal fractions only entails increasing the size and complexity of the numbers involved.

Two numbers (quantities) can be compared in terms of a relationship of ratio between the two amounts, and that comparison can be described.

A rational number describes the relationship between two numbers or quantities that can be counted, integers, in the form a/b where a and b are integers with b not equal to 0. In this content theme, the idea of matching the elements, objects, or pieces of a model for number in one-to-one correspondence is extended to developing correspondences or ratios of two-to-one, three-to-one, three-to-two, and so on; and, if the referent quantity is reversed, correspondences or ratios of one-to-two, one-to-three, two-to-three, and so on. When comparing the relationship of ratio between two amounts or quantities, one of the quantities serves as the referent number. That referent amount is extended from a single object (1) to a group or collection of objects, which is treated as one quantity. The intent is to arrive at a statement of ratio that is easily understood or communicated. The original relationship or comparison is observed, the referent unit is established, comparisons are made with the physical objects using the referent amount, and the relationship of ratio is stated. In regard to whole numbers, the units used are units of the decimal system of numeration and the referent amount may be any whole-number amount. The referent amount may be one of the quantities (numbers) to be compared, or it may be a common factor of the two numbers or quantities. For example:

"What is the ratio relationship of group S to group T?"

S	T		
*******	**	→	$\dfrac{8}{2}$
** **	**		
** **		→	$\dfrac{4}{1}$

"What is the ratio relationship of group C to group F?"

C	F		
********	******	→	$\dfrac{9}{6}$
***	***		
***	***		
***		→	$\dfrac{3}{2}$

Activities directed toward ascertaining ratio relationships between quantities or numbers that can be described with decimal fractions are quite similar to those involving whole numbers. The only difference is that the ratio comparisons are made between fractional amounts. However, as with the larger quantities or amounts, which can be described with whole numbers and which are to be compared to ascertain a ratio relationship, the problems involving decimal fractions are to be structured with pieces of a base-ten block model for number. The referent amount can be one of the original quantities, or it may be a common factor of both of the numbers. Ratio comparisons involving common fractions also utilize fractional quantities as the referent units, either unit-fraction pieces or multipart fractions. By using an appropriate referent amount, the original statements of comparisons involving two common fractions can be evolved to a simpler ratio statement. For example:

"What is the ratio relationship of A to B?"

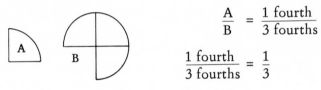

$$\frac{A}{B} = \frac{1 \text{ fourth}}{3 \text{ fourths}}$$

$$\frac{1 \text{ fourth}}{3 \text{ fourths}} = \frac{1}{3}$$

"What is the ratio relationship of A to B?"

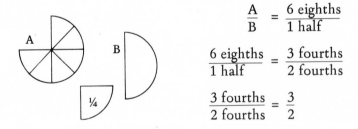

$$\frac{A}{B} = \frac{6 \text{ eighths}}{1 \text{ half}}$$

$$\frac{6 \text{ eighths}}{1 \text{ half}} = \frac{3 \text{ fourths}}{2 \text{ fourths}}$$

$$\frac{3 \text{ fourths}}{2 \text{ fourths}} = \frac{3}{2}$$

Performance Skills

Recognizing Problems

The major performance skills in this content area pertain to recognizing analogous problems regardless of the types of numerals involved in the quantitative situations. Children are expected to recognize and differentiate between problems that involve combining, separating, or comparing. They also are expected to be able to ascertain whether (1) combination problems deal with combining unequal-size groups or with combining equal-size groups, (2) separation problems deal with separating one quantity into two unequal amounts in take-away situations or with separating one quantity into equal-size parts (in the latter case, they should also be able to tell whether the task is to ascertain the number of groups or the size of each group), or (3) comparison problems deal with finding the difference in size between two quantities or with finding the ratio relationship between two numbers. Developing these performance skills helps children improve their problem-solving abilities by acquiring skills that help them *program*—or determine the nature of—problems, and, thus, become more proficient at deciding which technical skills may be applied toward solutions. The attainment of these skills is best accomplished by children through an early introduction to the various types of problem situations and the spiral development of analogous problems throughout the program.

Dealing with Number

Other performance skills inherent in this content area are the skills of numeration and notation that were described in Chapter 7. In the processes of performing operations on collections of objects that are models for number in order to solve modeled or structured problems, children will be given opportunities to name numbers orally by naming or describing the original quantities of the problems, renaming the original quantities when necessary, and naming the numbers or relationships derived as solutions to the problem. In recording procedures, they will be given opportunities to write the various numerals. Learning experiences directed toward solving structured or modeled problems by performing operations on pieces of models for number provide opportunities for children to utilize the concept of base in the collection or exchange of model pieces. Problem-solving tasks will require exchanging smaller units for a larger unit and exchanging a larger unit for smaller units. All of these experiences and activities may be regarded as opportunities for children to develop and reinforce the performance skills of numeration and notation.

Materials for Instruction

The materials for instruction that can be used most effectively by children to acquire the concepts, ideas, and skills of solving structured problems by performing operations on objects include many materials suggested for use in the area of numeration and notation as well as activity or pictured-problem cards. Problems are to be structured with pieces of the physical object models for number that best illustrate or demonstrate the nature of the numbers involved and that permit the performance of the operations in an effective, understandable manner. Children must be able to see the general ideas of the operations.

Physical Object Models

Suggested physical object models for quantities that can be named or described by whole numbers are limited to chips, bundles of ten sticks and single sticks, and base-ten blocks. All of the combining, separating, and comparing problems dealing only with whole numbers can be structured with those models. Familiarity with those models will enable children to perform the operations successfully. For similar reasons, the fraction-pie model is sufficient for structuring problems involving common-fraction numerals. The general ideas of combining, separating, and comparing problems can be introduced and developed with this model. A model of fraction squares could be used, but children appear to have more difficulty in recognizing both the unit-fraction parts and the one unit. The best available model for decimal fractions is a set of base-ten blocks in which the largest piece (preferably a large cube) is used as the model for one. When using this model for problems involving decimal fractions, extreme care must be taken to help children identify and constantly refer to the model piece representing one in order to name and use the other pieces.

Pictorial Manipulatives

If the procedure selected to introduce problems is first to generate numerals and then to model the problems in reference to those numerals, pictorial manipulative materials may be used to generate the numerals in a random manner. Materials used to generate numerals randomly may include numeral cubes, numeral cards, or some other device such as a spinner. The teacher may control the complexity of the problems by controlling the numerals on the cubes, cards, or other devices.

Recording Results

Recording devices will not be used in the first problem-solving activities for any type of problem or at any new level of complexity. In initial activities, emphasis is placed on observing correct and proper operational procedures and communicating the description of the result orally. After children have demonstrated that they understand the nature of the operations and can communicate orally, they may be asked to record their observations and findings in writing. The recording devices look like the record-keeping sheets used in the learning experiences of numeration and notation, as can be seen in Figure 8.2.

Activity Cards

Activity or pictured-problem cards can be prepared by the teacher or by children and can be used repeatedly by individual children or small groups of children. Each card contains a picture of a problem and as few words as possible. Those few words give simple directions and ask appropriate questions. Pictures on the cards show the models that are to be used in the problems and illustrate the pieces of the models that are to be used. General procedures for making and using these cards and illustrations appear in later sections of this chapter. The advantages in using activity cards to picture or structure problems lie in (1) the careful planning that can go into preparation of the cards, (2) the fact that the pictured problems make it unnecessary to generate numerals to be used in the structured problems, a procedure that may cause difficulty for some children, and (3) the possibilities of using the cards over and over during the same school year and in following school years. Sets of activity cards of pictured or structured problems can be planned and prepared to

Figure 8.2

Combine

	COMBINE		
1.	6		
2.	10		
3.	13		
4.	26		

Name _____

COMBINE I		
A	B	Total
4	2	6
3	7	10

Name _____

COMBINE II		
N groups	Size groups	Total
2	6	12
3	8	24

Name _____

Separate

	SEPARATE
1.	3
2.	0
3.	9

Name _____

SEPARATE I		
Start with	Take away	Left
3/4	1/4	2/4
5/8	1/2	1/8

Name _____

SEPARATE II		
Start with	N groups	Each group
12	3	4
24	6	4

Name _____

Compare

	COMPARE
1.	1/3
2.	3/8
3.	3/4
4.	1/6

Name _____

COMPARE I		
L	S	Dif.
5	3	2
12	7	5
23	16	7

Name _____

COMPARE II		
A	B	Ratio
8	2	4/1
1/2	3/4	2/3
.6	.8	3/4

Name _____

cover a wide range of complexities with one type of problem (for example, combining equal groups) with one subset of numbers (for example, whole numbers), or they can be planned and prepared to deal with one general level of difficulty with one subset of numbers (for example, combining less than ten equal groups, each group larger than 10 but less than 100).

Common Strategies or General Procedures

The basic instructional strategy of this content area is to confront children with modeled problems or problems that can be structured with pieces of physical object models for numbers and require them to solve the problems through manipulation of the model pieces. The strategy involves introducing the different types of problems early in the program and spirally developing each type of problem through different levels of complexity throughout the program. Emphasis should be placed on helping children recognize analogous problems regardless of the numerical data or complexity of numbers that appear in the problems.

Oral Problems

Several general procedures might be utilized, including oral or verbal problems that are to be structured and solved, problems that are to be structured from numerals generated with pictorial manipulative devices, and problems that are pictured on activity cards. The use of oral problems is generally built around one specific level of difficulty with one subset of numbers. A group of children is given a physical model for that subset of numbers and presented with an orally stated problem. The children are expected to use the model to structure and solve the problem without using a computational operation. The problem may be stated by the teacher or by one of the children. When the operation with the objects has been performed correctly, the problem has been solved and perhaps some discussion of the problem has occurred. At this point another problem is stated. For those schools or classrooms with the necessary equipment, sets of problems may be tape-recorded for use by small groups of children. Some teachers may want to use printed or written word problems in this manner. Oral or written problems that do not contain specific numerical data can be used to give children practice in determining the general nature or types of problems (combine, separate, compare). These problems can also be used as developmental activities.

Pictorial Manipulatives

Problems structured from numerals that are generated with pictorial manipulative devices generally deal with one subset of numbers. Children are given the pictorial manipulative devices (numeral cubes, numeral cards, or spinner, for example) with which to generate numerals, the appropriate model for number, and directions for the procedures to be followed. The complexity of the problem is controlled by the numerals that can be generated. After the necessary numeral(s) is/are generated, children structure or model the problem with the appropriate pieces of the model and solve the problem without using a computational operation. After children complete one problem and agree on the operations and the solution, they may generate another problem. For example, four children are given a base-ten block model for number and three numeral cubes, each with the numerals 0, 1, 2, 3, 4, and 5 on the six faces. They are to roll the three cubes, make a three-digit numeral, and show the number named by that numeral with pieces from the base-ten block model. Then, they are to share equally the amount that they have shown. If the numeral they make is 352, they must exchange pieces of the model in order to distribute the amount into 4 equal groups. Each child in the group must be satisfied or assured that he or she has received the same amount as the others before another numeral is generated and the procedure repeated.

Pictured Problems

Some pictured problems on activity cards are illustrated in the following section. Each illustration is intended to be an example of one pictured problem from one of the two subcategories of the three major types of problems, and each illustration pertains to one subset of numbers: whole numbers (WN), common fractions (CF), or decimal fractions (DF). As stated previously, one set of activity cards can be prepared to cover the range of complexities in one type of problem with one type of numbers or numerals. Sets of activity cards may also be prepared to deal with one level of complexity with one type of number or numeral. To use the activity cards, children are given the appropriate model(s) for number (those needed or pictured on the cards), a set of activity cards, and a record-keeping sheet if a record is to be kept. The children are to lay out the pieces of the model as they are pictured on the card and to solve the problem by following the directions or answering the questions on the card without performing a computational operation. In order to solve the problem, children may need to collect or exchange pieces of the model, so a complete model must be available. A classroom teacher using different sets of activity cards dealing with all of the different subcategories of problems (comparing, separating, and combining) and with one subset of numbers, particularly whole numbers, may find that children are equally proficient with the different types of problems.

Whether one general procedure is used primarily or whether some combination of the procedures is utilized, emphasis should be placed on the similarity of problems within and between the different subsets of numbers. Attention given to analogous problems is a major factor in helping children acquire and develop skills in problem solving.

Examples of Learning Experiences

Several examples of learning experiences or activities directed toward having children perform operations on collections of objects that are pieces of physical object models for number have been discussed in the preceding sections of this chapter. The examples in this section are similar in approach, are in accord with the common strategies or procedures that have been cited, and are of two types—problems that are to be structured from numerals that are generated with pictorial manipulative devices and problems pictured on activity cards. When considering the following pictured-problem activity cards, keep in mind that children are to solve each problem by first laying out the model pieces as they are pictured on the card and then performing operations with or on the pieces according to the directions given or questions asked.

Activity Cards

Combining Unequal Groups

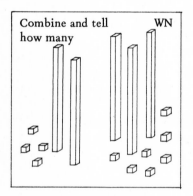

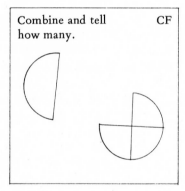

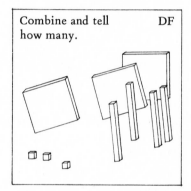

Combining Equal Groups

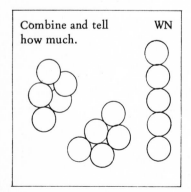

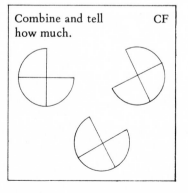

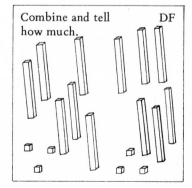

Separating into Two Unequal Groups

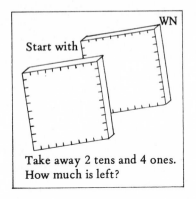

WN

Start with

Take away 2 tens and 4 ones.
How much is left?

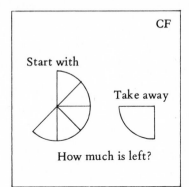

CF

Start with

Take away

How much is left?

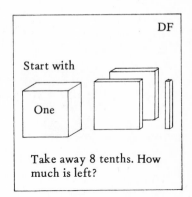

DF

Start with

One

Take away 8 tenths. How
much is left?

Separating into Equal Groups

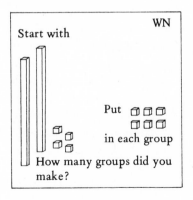

WN

Start with

Put

in each group

How many groups did you
make?

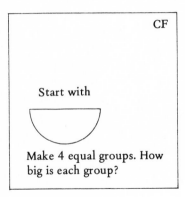

CF

Start with

Make 4 equal groups. How
big is each group?

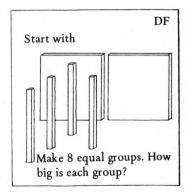

DF

Start with

Make 8 equal groups. How
big is each group?

Comparing Two Groups—Find the Difference

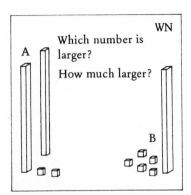

WN

A

Which number is
larger?

How much larger?

B

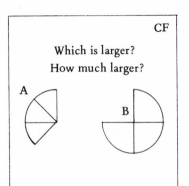

CF

Which is larger?
How much larger?

A

B

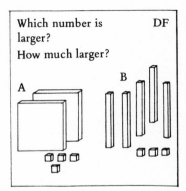

DF

Which number is
larger?

How much larger?

A

B

Comparing Two Groups—Find the Ratio

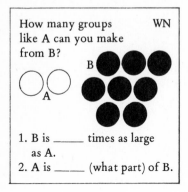

How many groups like A can you make from B?   WN

B
A

1. B is _____ times as large as A.
2. A is _____ (what part) of B.

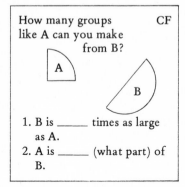

How many groups like A can you make from B?   CF

A

B

1. B is _____ times as large as A.
2. A is _____ (what part) of B.

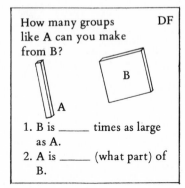

How many groups like A can you make from B?   DF

A

B

1. B is _____ times as large as A.
2. A is _____ (what part) of B.

Generating Numerals

As with the pictured-problem activity cards, each of the following examples is intended to illustrate the kinds of learning experiences that can be provided in regard to the different types of problems. In these activities, however, problems are to be structured with pieces of models for number after numerals have been generated with pictorial manipulative materials. Directions for each of the learning activities are given orally in a simple, understandable manner either by the teacher or by some child who is familiar with that particular type of problem and activity. After the numerals generated with pictorial manipulative devices have been used to structure a problem with pieces of the model for number, the solution or result of the problem is obtained through manipulation of the model pieces. In the initial activities of each type, questions may be asked to guide or direct the problem-solving processes of performing operations on the collections of objects. Later, teacher observations of the children's procedures and questions may focus on making certain that children understand the procedures and can demonstrate them.

Each of the learning experiences or activities is planned and presented in a manner that provides opportunities for children to continue the activity after each problem is modeled and solved. Each child engaged in a particular activity is encouraged to check or observe the operations performed and results obtained by other participating children and to question or challenge the operation and result when doubtful. It should not be necessary for the teacher to be constantly present at the scene of the activity to check or assure correctness. A good learning experience or activity flows with the interest, initiative, and participation of the children involved.

Combining Unequal Groups (Common Fractions)   One child or a small group of children. A fraction pie or disk model, a record-keeping sheet (as shown in Figure 8.3), and two pairs of fraction numeral cubes. One pair of the cubes has the numerals 1/3, 2/3, 1/6, 5/6, 1/12, and 5/12 on the six faces of each cube. The other pair of numeral cubes has 1/2, 1/4, 3/4, 1/8, 3/8, and 5/8 on the six faces of each cube. (To distinguish between the two pairs of cubes, the numerals on one pair can be written in a different color from those on the other pair.) The fraction pie model is laid out on the table. One child selects a pair of the numeral cubes and rolls them. The model pieces described by the numerals are taken from the model by the child and placed together. Then the child must determine a correct name for the total amount. Preferably, that name should be in terms of the smallest units combined. After the name or numeral describing the total amount has been given correctly, the combination can be illustrated on the record-keeping sheet. If more than one child is participating in the activity, they will take turns. At a later stage, a record-keeping sheet requiring numerals may be used.

Figure 8.3

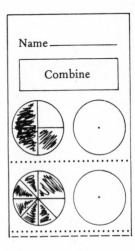

Combining Equal Quantities (Decimal Fractions) One child or a small group of children. A base-ten block model for decimal fractions, a numeral cube with the numerals 0, 1, 2, 3, 4, and 5 on the six faces, and a set of decimal-fraction numeral cards (complexity to be determined by the teacher) including such cards as $\boxed{0.43}$ and $\boxed{0.09}$. A record-keeping sheet requiring data collection in terms of numerals may also be used. The model is made available and the numeral cards are mixed and placed face down on the table. The child draws a numeral card and shows the numbers named or described with pieces of the model. This establishes the size of groups. Then the child rolls the numeral cube. The numeral shown on the cube is the number of groups of the established size that must be modeled. The combining of groups is then performed by the child with the rule that all possible exchanges of ten smaller units for the next larger unit must be made. After the combining and exchanging has been completed, the child is to name the amount. If more than one child is participating in the activity, they can take turns or each child can work independently but side by side with others.

Separating One Group into Two Unequal Groups (Whole Numbers—"Give away") Two to four children. A model for number consisting of bundles of ten sticks and single sticks and a numeral cube with the numerals 0, 6, 7, 8, 9, and 10 on the six faces. Record-keeping sheets requiring the use of numerals may also be used. Each child is given the same amount (number) of the model, perhaps seven bundles of ten sticks. The object of the game is to find which child will give away all of his or her sticks first. Each child plays in turn, rolling the numeral cube, and giving away the number of sticks named by the numeral rolled by taking that number of sticks from his or her group and putting them in a central repository. The rule is that a bundle of ten sticks must be ungrouped when necessary. At the end of each turn, each child must name the number he or she has left. If record-keeping sheets are used, the data should include "Start with, Give away, and Number left" for each playing turn. To win the game, a child does not have to roll the numeral describing the exact number of sticks left, only a numeral describing a number equal to or greater than that amount.

Separating One Group into Equal Groups (Whole Numbers) One child or a small group of children. Chips or counters that can be stacked into groups and a numeral cube with the numerals 0, 1, 2, 3, 4, and 5 on the six faces. Record-keeping sheets requiring the use of numerals may also be used. Each child takes 24 chips, which must be shown as two stacks of 10 chips and 4 single chips. One child rolls the numeral cube (turns can be taken). Each child (all participants) must then regroup his or her chips by putting the number of chips described by the numeral on the rolled cube in each small group, preferably laid out in rows. Participating children are to observe the results of others and to agree on the correct number of groups that were made. Placing 5 chips in a group and determining the number of groups will introduce the idea of a remainder in such situations. After each separation, the chips should be returned to two stacks of 10 and 4 singles. If record-keeping sheets are used, the data should include "Start with, Size of each group, and Number of groups" for each regrouping. A modification of the activity involves using the numeral rolled to define the number of equal-size groups to be made. In that case the number of chips in each equal group is to be determined.

Comparing Two Groups to Find the Differences (Decimal Fractions) Two to four children. A base-ten block model for number is made available and decimal fraction numeral cards are mixed and placed face down on the table. Each child draws a numeral card and shows the number described by the numeral on the card with pieces of the model. Comparisons are then made between the modeled numbers. After the comparison(s), the model pieces are returned to their original place. Several variations in procedures may accompany or follow the comparison(s). In a gamelike manner, the child who shows the greater number may be allowed to "keep" the numeral cards. At the end of the game, the child with the most cards wins the game. If two children are participating, they may keep a record of the comparisons using numerals and comparative symbols. If more than two children are participating, the winner (or loser) of the comparisons may be allowed to order the numeral cards and perhaps record the order of the numerals.

Comparing Two Quantities to Find the Ratio (Common Fractions) Two children. A fraction pie or disk model and two pairs of fraction numeral cubes. One pair of the cubes has the numerals 1/3, 2/3, 1/6, 5/6, 1/12, and 5/12 on the six faces of each cube. The other pair of numeral cubes has 1/2, 1/4, 3/4, 1/8, 3/8, and 5/8 on the six faces of each cube. Record-keeping sheets requiring the use of numerals may also be used. The fraction pie model is laid out on the desk or table and each child takes one of the cubes from the same pair. (After each comparison, pieces from the model will be returned to their original place and children can, if they wish, use the other pair of cubes.) Each child rolls the numeral cube he or she has taken and shows the number named on the cube with pieces from the model. Together, the children determine the ratios of the larger amount to the smaller amount and of the smaller amount to the larger amount (or they can ascertain one or the other of the ratios). They might vary the activity by always determining the ratio of the amount shown by one particular child to the amount shown by the other child. If a record-keeping sheet is used in this variation, the data should include "The amount shown by (A)," "The amount shown by (B)," and "The ratio of A to B (A/B)" for each comparison.

Suggested Activities

1. Review the textual materials for one age or grade level in the elementary mathematics program to see what types of word problems are presented. Classify those problems according to the categories described in this chapter.
2. In regard to activity 1, pay attention to the types of numerals (subsets of numbers) that are involved in the problems. Select one or more of the types of word problems and devise one or more ways of introducing that type of problem with structured or modeled quantitative situations.
3. For one of the subsets of numbers—whole numbers, common fractions, or decimal fractions—make a set of pictured-problem activity cards that covers the range of complexity involved in one or more of the following:
   a. Combining unequal-size quantities
   b. Combining two or more equal-size quantities
   c. Separating one quantity into two unequal quantities
   d. Separating one quantity into two or more equal-size quantities
   e. Comparing two quantities to find the difference in size
   f. Comparing two quantities to find the ratio in size
4. For one of the subsets of numbers—whole numbers, common fractions, or decimal fractions—devise several learning experiences directed toward structuring or modeling problems with numerals that are generated with pictorial manipulative devices for one level of complexity in regard to one or more of the following:
   a. Combining unequal-size quantities
   b. Combining two or more equal-size quantities
   c. Separating one quantity into two unequal quantities
   d. Separating one quantity into two or more equal quantities
   e. Comparing two quantities to find the difference in size
   f. Comparing two quantities to find the ratio in size

5. Select one general level of difficulty in regard to whole numbers—problems involving numerical data given as one-digit numerals, two-digit numerals, three-digit numerals, and so on. Then select one problem category and devise a set of pictured-problem activity cards that deals specifically and rather completely with that subset of whole numbers and that single problem category.

6. Refer to the section "Examples of Learning Experiences" in this chapter and, in particular, to those examples utilizing pictorial manipulative devices to generate numerals for problems. Each example involves one type of numeral—whole numbers, common fractions, or decimal fractions. Devise learning experiences of the same type for the other two types of numerals.

Chapter 9

Operations on Numbers Using Numerals

The operations to be performed on numbers by using numerals that name or describe those numbers are the fundamental computational operations of addition, subtraction, multiplication, and division. Before completing the elementary mathematics program, children are expected to perform those computational operations with whole numbers, common fractions, decimal fractions, and mixed numerals (numerals with a whole-number part and a fraction part). Some more-talented children or children in a more comprehensive program, such as an active laboratory-type program is intended to be, might also be expected to achieve the rudimentary skills of these operations with positive and negative rational numbers. Children who are even more talented might be introduced to the ideas of rounding irrational numbers appearing in decimal-fraction form to a nearest specified numerical unit and treating those rounded numerals in computational operations just as they would treat decimal-fraction numerals and mixed decimal-fraction numerals. The goal of helping children develop and acquire skills in the computational operations is an integral part of the more general goal of helping children develop familiarity with the main ideas of the real number system.

Performing a computational operation involves the mental recall of facts, concepts, rules, and generalizations and their application in a specific procedure or algorithm. The basic facts established for the nonnegative integers (whole numbers) are also utilized in performing the computational operations with the other subsets of numbers or numerals in the set of real numbers. No new basic facts are necessary to perform the computational operations of addition, subtraction, multiplication, or division with common-fraction numerals, decimal-fraction numerals, or mixed numerals. Similarly, the concepts and related skills of naming numbers, renaming numbers, base ten and positional value and the rules and generalizations that pertain to the regrouping of numerical units in computational operations with whole numbers also apply to the computational operations to be performed on decimal-fraction numerals. Therefore, demonstrated proficiencies on the part of children with the concepts and related skills of numeration and notation are prerequisites for the introduction and development of the computational operations.

Traditionally, a major portion of the elementary mathematics program has been devoted to children's study and practice of the computational operations with whole numbers, common fractions, and decimal fractions. In some instances, the entire program has been dominated by the computational operations—beginning with the memorization of facts and extending through difficulty levels based on steps involving the nature and size of numbers, regrouping ("carrying" and "borrowing"), the necessity of renaming numbers, and the complexity of rules to be applied. Children proceeded through the operations of addition, subtraction, multiplication, and division with whole numbers, common fractions, and, finally, with decimal fractions. Quite often the isolated facts and rules of the operations were rotely memorized and practiced on abstract printed exercises or examples. The apparent goals were to prepare children to respond correctly to the abstract stimuli of printed computational exercises and examples and, if possible, to apply the computational operations they learned to printed word problems.

Importance of the Area

Children's study of the basic arithmetical facts and the fundamental computational operations with whole numbers, common fractions, and decimal fractions continues to be a major content consideration of modern elementary mathematics programs. The ability to perform the computational operations is part of the basic skills to be acquired in the elementary school program. However, those skills go beyond merely finding correct answers to printed computational exercises or examples. When quantitative problems are to be solved, performing a computational operation is the second step, the necessary step to arrive at a solution to the problem. After *programming*, arriving at a decision about the nature of the problem and deciding on an appropriate solution procedure, the numerical data in the problem must be *processed* with one or more computational operations. The primary skill that children should be helped to acquire in regard to computational operations is the capability to determine when each computational operation may be appropriately used as a solution procedure for problem situations.

In addition to the basic skills of being able to ascertain when computational operations are to be used and being able to perform the algorithms of the operations to arrive at correct results, children in an active laboratory-type elementary mathematics program are expected to understand the algorithms of the operations. Rules for procedures in the operations are not only to be followed, they also are to be understood in terms of how and why the rules "work." Thus, the natural sequence of development is from the concepts and related skills of numeration and notation to the concepts and related skills of operations on collections of objects to the concepts and related skills of operations on numbers using numerals.

Prerequisite Skills

The emphases, time, and efforts, given to each of the fundamental operations of addition, subtraction, multiplication, and division with each of the subsets of numbers or numerals (whole numbers, common fractions, and decimal fractions) will vary with the individual capabilities of children and their mastery of the prerequisites for introduction and development of particular operations with particular subsets of numerals. If the major concepts and related performance skills of numeration and notation are mastered to the point where performance skills can be demonstrated, children will have much less difficulty with the facts and algorithms of the operations. Since the basic facts of addition, subtraction, and multiplication with whole numbers are the basic facts used in division of whole numbers and in the four fundamental operations with common fractions and decimal fractions, those facts must be mastered before the operations with greater whole numbers (two- and three-digit numerals) and the operations with common and decimal fractions are introduced. Mastery of the facts by children implies more than being able to find the answers to fact stimuli (given addends, factors, and so forth) by counting or by referring to a table and more than being able to immediately recall correct responses to the stimuli. Complete mastery means that children understand the facts *and* can demonstrate, reestablish, and verify them with appropriate physical object models for number.

The Facts

The process of recalling a correct response to a basic arithmetical fact stimulus is not an act of performing the computational operation to which that fact pertains. The process of recalling an arithmetical fact is similar to the act of recalling any other fact, whether that fact has been established by observation of a physical phenomenon or whether that fact simply has been verbally communicated. The arithmetical addition facts comprise all of the possible combinations of two addends from the numerals 0, 1, 2, 3, 4, 5, 6, 7, 8, and 9 and the total or sum associated with each combination. The arithmetical subtraction facts are the inverses of the addition fact statements in the following manner: sum − addend = missing addend. The arithmetical multiplication facts comprise all of the possible combinations of two factors from the numerals 0, 1, 2, 3, 4, 5, 6, 7, 8, and 9 and the total amount or product associated with each combination. Only after children have mastered the basic arithmetical facts should they be expected to apply those facts in performing operations on numbers using numerals. Unfortunately, it is not difficult to find children in elementary classrooms who are attempting to perform computational operations with larger whole numbers or even with common or decimal fractions and who are counting on their fingers or elsewhere or referring to fact tables to find the facts that are needed in the operations.

Concerns About Common Fractions

Currently, many mathematics educators are concerned about how much emphasis should be placed on computational operations with common fractions in elementary mathematics programs. Their concerns are related to programmatic, arithmetical, utility, and societal factors or considerations. Programmatically, the topics of naming rational numbers and performing computational operations with rational numbers, particularly common fractions, have been described as the most poorly taught topics in the elementary mathematics program. This accusation is based on the less than acceptable performances of children and young adults on various levels of standardized-testing instruments. The incompetencies of children and young adults and the criticism of "poor teaching" are related and are probably due to improper programmatic or instructional procedures. In many instances, the topics of naming quantities with common fractions and of performing computational operations with common fractions are treated as if they were unrelated to other mathematical ideas. Deficient programs fail to utilize

1. children's previously acquired concepts, vocabulary, and communication skills and computational skills with whole numbers to introduce and develop meaning for and understanding of common-fraction numerals and operations with those numerals
2. physical object models to represent or illustrate either the fractional quantities to be named or the quantitative problems to which the computational operations with common fractions can be applied as solution procedures (for example, observations of children's records for structured problem activities like those in "Operations on Collections of Objects" in which a fractional part of a fractional part is to be found—1/2 of 3/4, 3/4 of 2/3, and so forth—should reveal the generalization that the operation of multiplication can be used to solve these separation problems)
3. analogous problems (combine, separate, or compare) involving whole numbers to introduce problems involving common-fraction numerals
4. the properties of number in operations and other major ideas to develop understanding of and proficiency in the procedures of the operations.

Instead, instructional reliance often is placed on demonstrations with pictures and "special" rules to be rotely applied in the different computational operations with common fractions. Consider the following examples of special operational rules that can be memorized and applied without understanding to arrive at correct responses to computational exercises involving common fractions:

To add or subtract common fractions, change the fractions to equivalent fractions with a common denominator, add or subtract the numerators, and keep the common denominator.

To multiply common fractions, multiply the numerators and multiply the denominators. If one of the numbers to be multiplied is a whole number, give it a denominator of 1.

Mixed numbers must be changed to improper fractions before they are multiplied.

The word *of* in exercises with common fractions means "times" or "multiply."

To divide with common fractions, invert the divisor and multiply. If one of the numbers is a whole number, give it a denominator of 1 first.

Unfortunately, rules that have no meaning are often forgotten or misapplied by children.

The argument may be presented that, based on the criteria of achievement and utility, the time and effort spent by teachers and children on introducing, developing, and practicing computational operations with common fractions might be better spent elsewhere. If the primary goal is to help children learn to apply computational operations to quantitative problems as solution procedures, perhaps we should help children learn to rename common fractions as decimal-fraction equivalents and help them to learn to add, subtract, multiply, and divide with decimal-fraction numerals. This argument has strong support in several current trends and events. The availability of hand-held calculators makes converting common fractions to equivalent decimal fractions and calculations with decimal fractions easier, faster, and more efficient than performing computations with common fractions using paper and pencil. This is especially true when complex or unrealistic common fractions, such as 3/7, 8/11, or

5/13, are involved. One of the more frequent uses of common fractions in this country has been in relation to measures and measurement situations. The inevitable move to adopt the metric system of measurement, which utilizes base-ten and decimal-fraction notation, not only implies different learning experiences and activities for children in the content area of measurement, but also an earlier introduction of decimal-fraction notation and quantitative problems involving decimal fractions. Arithmetic as a branch of mathematics deals with computation using numerals. Arithmetical computations with decimal-fraction numerals involve the same numerical concepts and skills and the same operational rules, generalizations, and procedures as computations with whole numbers; arithmetical computations with common fractions, on the other hand, involve additional concepts, rules, and procedures.

The preceding arguments may also be regarded in a societal sense. There are few opportunities for adults in our society to apply computational operations with common fractions to real problems, and as the metric system of measurement becomes more popular, there will be even fewer opportunities. When common fractions appear in complex problem situations, adults often convert those common fractions to equivalent decimal fractions before performing the applicable computational operations. In their efforts to make computational operations with common fractions meaningful and to relate them to problem situations, some classroom teachers have employed primarily measurement situations and problems of construction and cooking. These procedures may seem appropriate because it undoubtedly will be some time before the metric system of measurement is universally accepted.

It is not suggested here that computational operations with common fractions should be deleted from elementary mathematics programs, but rather that a great deal of thought and planning should be directed toward the emphases, time, and efforts that are given to introducing, developing, and practicing these technical skills in relation to quantitative problem situations. If and when the metric system of measurement is nationally adopted, the people of this country, like the people in other countries that use the metric system, will continue to use simple common-fraction names to describe fractional parts and will continue to encounter quantitative problem situations that involve simpler common fractions. The concepts and performance skills pertaining to performing the computational operations of addition, subtraction, multiplication, and division can be introduced, developed, and established with unit and multipart common fractions having denominators of 2, 3, 4, 5, 6, 8, 9, 10, and 12. The applications of properties of number in operations, which are cited later as major ideas or content themes for this content area, can also be further developed in a spiral plan with fractions having those denominators. In addition, study of unit fractions and multipart fractions with those denominators will allow further development of algebraic foundations as they relate to writing quantitative statements—number sentences or equations—and to procedures for solving incomplete or open quantitative statements involving fractions or unperformed divisions written as fractions for unknowns. Perhaps the weakest reason for retaining computational operations with common fractions in the elementary mathematics program is that such exercises and examples continue to be presented on standardized-testing instruments. More substantial and realistic reasons for retaining computational operations with common fractions as topics for study in the elementary mathematics program include the further development of children's problem-solving abilities and the extension of major mathematical ideas.

Concerns About Calculators

The accessibility of hand-held calculators poses other concerns and considerations in regard to goals or objectives, content, and instructional procedures pertaining to performing operations on number using numerals. Should the hand-held calculator be used in the elementary mathematics classroom, and, if so, how should it be used? Is it necessary for children to learn and memorize the basic arithmetical facts so that they can be immediately recalled? And, is it necessary for children to learn to perform the computational operations with whole numbers and decimal fractions quickly and accurately? What content topics or procedures, if any, should be dropped from or deemphasized in the elementary mathematics program? What content topics or procedures, if any, should be added to, emphasized more, or extended in the program?

There is no substantial reason that can be realistically supported for banning the hand-held calculator from the learning activities of the elementary mathematics classroom. However, if calculators are available to some children, efforts should be made to make them accessible to all. The uses made of hand-held calculators (and other hardware) should contribute to the totality and efficiency of the program as it helps children develop and acquire a unified and related structure of mathematical ideas and performance skills. Children should continue to learn the basic arithmetical facts and to commit those facts to memory so they can be immediately recalled when needed. Knowledge of those facts will be useful and necessary in simple day-to-day quantitative problem situations, in performing computational operations when a calculator is not available, in estimation situations, and in ascertaining whether a result is reasonable when a calculator has been used to perform an operation. As implied in the preceding sentence, children should also continue to learn the "when, why, and how" of performing the computational operations with whole numbers, simple common fractions, and decimal fractions. It is unreasonable to assume that a culture will evolve in which all people will constantly have at their disposal a hand-held calculator with which to solve their quantitative problems, or a culture in which people will accept the calculations of machines without question.

Initially, in primary or early intermediate level mathematics classrooms, children might use hand-held calculators to practice facts or to verify the results of their computational efforts. Later, when children have demonstrated their proficiencies in programming and processing solutions to quantitative problems, when they have shown that they can perform the computational operations by applying facts, rules, and operational procedures in a paper-and-pencil approach, they might use hand-held calculators to expedite or speed up the processes of solving problems. The calculator then serves as a tool.

Estimation

Developing children's abilities to estimate solutions for quantitative problems and results or answers for computational exercises has been a goal of the elementary mathematics programs for some time. In some problem situations, a reasonable estimation of the result may be all that is required. In other instances, an estimated answer may be used to determine the reasonableness of the computed or calculated results. Estimation serves as a crude form of verification. Since the uses of calculators and computers are subject to human input errors, it seems reasonable to suggest that processes and procedures of estimating reasonable results for computational exercises and quantitative problems should be more heavily emphasized in the content and instructional procedures of elementary mathematics programs. Learning experiences and activities directed toward improving children's abilities to estimate may pertain to problems or examples involving whole numbers, common fractions, or decimal fractions and should initially involve physical object models for number. The early use of physical object models in activities or experiences requiring estimation may help children acquire the ability to visualize problem situations without models.

The following discussion involves estimating reasonable answers to multiplication examples containing numerals describing whole numbers and mixed decimal-fraction numerals. In the initial activities, physical object models for number are used to develop meaning and understanding of the operation of multiplication with whole numbers. As they record the results of operations on collections of objects in which equal-size groups (whole numbers) are combined, teachers and children might observe and generalize the following ideas in regard to factors and products:

Factors Are (Smallest to Largest):		*Product Is:*
1-digit numerals	$\begin{cases} 0 \times 0 = 0 \\ \quad \text{to} \\ 9 \times 9 = 81 \end{cases}$	1-digit or 2-digit numeral
2-digit numerals	$\begin{cases} 10 \times 10 = 100 \\ \quad \text{to} \\ 99 \times 99 = 9801 \end{cases}$	3-digit or 4-digit numeral
3-digit numerals	$\begin{cases} 100 \times 100 = 10{,}000 \\ \quad \text{to} \\ 999 \times 999 = 998{,}001 \end{cases}$	5-digit or 6-digit numeral
4-digit numerals	$\begin{cases} 1000 \times 1000 = 1{,}000{,}000 \\ \quad \text{to} \\ 9999 \times 9999 = 99{,}980{,}001 \end{cases}$	7-digit or 8-digit numeral

And the pattern continues.

The generalization can be made that the same facts that are used in multiplying ones (one-digit numerals) are used in multiplying tens, hundreds, thousands, and millions. From the activities utilizing physical object models to represent the equal-size groups or numbers, teachers and children might also generalize that (1) groups of single objects multiplied by a one-digit numeral may require grouping the objects into collections of ten objects; (2) groups of objects including units of ten that are multiplied by a one-digit numeral may require one or more exchanges of 10 ten units for 1 one-hundred unit; and (3) a similar pattern continues in multiplying larger numerals. Ideas about the nature of factors and the resulting products can be related to the base and positional-value concepts of the decimal system of numeration. By using these ideas and generalizations, children can better estimate products in multiplication of whole numbers. The generalizations also apply to multiplying mixed decimal-fraction numerals. In those applications, only the whole-number values in the mixed numerals are to be considered, and the estimation is similar to estimating products for whole numbers. Consider the example of $8 \times 27.4 = \square$. Since 27 is nearest in tens to 30, the whole number part of the mixed-decimal numeral product will be close to 240 (8×30).

Solving Problems

Although the learning experiences and activities of this content area appear to be directed toward helping children acquire and apply basic arithmetical facts as well as procedural rules in computational algorithms, the major purpose of the content area is to help children learn to use or apply the facts and computational operations in quantitative problem situations. In an active laboratory-type elementary mathematics program, the facts and most of the computational operations should be introduced and developed through the use of structured problem situations. As the problem is solved by manipulating the objects, a record is kept of each of the moves—grouping, regrouping, exchanging, and so forth. As recording procedures are organized and shortened, an algorithm or computational operation evolves.

Algorithms from Data

In some instances, a completed record of one type of activity will reveal a pattern in the organized data, which will indicate a method or procedure of solution. Figure 9.1 shows a record-keeping sheet for an activity involving common fractions. The fraction-pie model was laid out on the table and a small group of children was given a unit-fraction numeral cube (1/2, 1/3, 1/4, 1/5, 1/8, and 1/10 on the six faces) and a numeral cube with 0, 1, 2, 3, 4, and 5 on the six faces. The procedure was to first roll the unit-fraction numeral cube to describe the size of pieces that were to be taken. By studying the data on the record sheet, an operational procedure or algorithm for solving that type of problem could be discovered. (At a later time, the fraction numeral cube used could contain multipart fractions.)

Algorithms Using Major Ideas

In other instances, an algorithm may be developed by referring to and using major mathematical ideas. Consider a laboratory-type activity in which children have been separating a whole number quantity into equal-size fractional parts in order to answer the question "How many groups?" By using and manipulating a fraction-pie model for common fractions, the children are able to arrive at the correct number of groups for each situation. (A numeral cube with the digits 0, 1, 2, 3, 4, and 5 was rolled to describe the number of pies to start with, and a unit-fraction numeral cube was rolled to describe the size of the parts—groups—to be made.) Yet, the procedure for the operation of division with common fractions, particularly with a common-fraction divisor, that can be used to find the number of groups was not completely evident in the record that was kept. At that point, the teacher might suggest that they find or develop a way to determine the number of groups without using the physical object model and that, in fact, the model limits the activity to certain fractions. The idea is to use the mathematics that the children know to find an arithmetical way to do the division. A good first step might be to write several of the problems that the children have solved as division statements: $3 \div 1/2 = 6$; $4 \div 1/3 = 12$; $2 \div 1/5 = 10$; and so on. Then an incomplete example to be solved without the model can be written—for example, $7 \div 1/4 = \square$. The question is "How many pieces the size of 1/4 can be made from

Figure 9.1

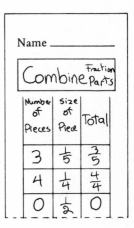

$1/4\overline{)7}$ $\dfrac{7}{1/4}$

7 pies?" and the task is to perform the division. It should be pointed out that $7 \div 1/4$ describes a quantity or names a number and that the quantity or number could be described in two other ways, as shown in the margin. Children who have been working on the activity probably will be able to answer the question. "There are 28 pieces the size of 1/4 in 7 pies." However, the remaining task is to arrive at a method of arithmetical operation that will serve as a procedure for all problems of this type. (Later the same operational procedure can be extended to applications involving division of a fraction by a whole number and division of a fraction by a fraction.) Noting that they do not know how to divide by a fraction, the teacher may suggest that perhaps the quantity could be renamed in such a way that the division could be performed. "What is the easiest number to divide by?" "1." "Then why not try to rename the quantity so that the divisor is 1?" At this point, the major mathematical ideas (content themes) to be employed should be reviewed with the children. The major ideas are:

1. There are many names for the same number.

   a. $\dfrac{7}{1/4}$ names a quantity or number, and it is to be renamed.

   b. There are many names for 1.

$$2/2, 3/3, \ldots, N/N, \frac{1/2}{1/2}, \frac{2/3}{2/3}, \ldots, \frac{a/b}{a/b}$$

2. The identity element of the multiplication operation is 1. Any number multiplied by 1 has a product equal to the same number.

$$1 \times 3 = 3 \quad 27 \times 1 = 27 \quad N \times 1 = N \quad 2/2 \times N = N$$

$$9 \times N/N = 9 \quad a/b \times 1 = a/b \quad \frac{a}{b} \times \frac{c}{c} = \frac{ac}{bc} \quad \text{or} \quad \frac{a}{b}$$

$$\frac{c/d}{s/t} \times \frac{a/b}{a/b} = \text{another name for the quantity or number } \frac{c/d}{s/t}$$

3. Any number divided by 1 is that same number.

$$N \div 1 = N \quad 1\overline{)N} \quad N/1 = N \quad \frac{a+b}{1} = a + b \quad \frac{a \times b}{1} = a \times b$$

$$\frac{a/b \times c/d}{1} = a/b \times c/d$$

4. For every number other than 0, there is another number such that when the two numbers are multiplied, the product is 1.

$$\square \times 1/3 = 1 \quad 1/5 \times \square = 1 \quad 4 \times \square = 1 \quad 3/8 \times \square = 1$$

$$a/b \times \square = 1$$

This idea is called the *multiplicative inverse*, and the number selected as the factor is called the *reciprocal* of the known factor. These terms may have been introduced earlier when children were working with multiplication of common fractions, but they are not necessary to develop the idea. Use of such terms only provides for quicker and more specific communication after children understand the idea.

The tasks are now to apply these major ideas to the situation of $\dfrac{7}{1/4}$ in a sequential manner:

Situation	*Idea*
$\dfrac{7}{1/4} \times 1 = \dfrac{7}{1/4}$	$N \times 1 = N$
$\dfrac{7}{1/4} \times \dfrac{4}{4} = \square$	Selecting another name for 1 so that after the multiplication is performed,
$\dfrac{7}{1/4} \times \dfrac{4}{4} = \dfrac{7 \times 4}{1}$	the divisor will be 1. There are many names for 1. For every number, there is another number such that when the two numbers are multiplied, the product is 1.

$$\frac{7}{1/4} \times \frac{4}{4} = \frac{7 \times 4}{1} = 7 \times 4 \qquad N \div 1 = N$$

The major ideas and procedures utilized with this type of problem or example can then be extended to use with other types of problems and examples involving division with common fractions:

$$2/3 \div 4 = \square \qquad\qquad 3/4 \div 2/3 = \square$$

$$\frac{2/3}{4} \times \frac{1/4}{1/4} = \frac{2/3 \times 1/4}{1} \qquad \frac{3/4}{2/3} \times \frac{3/2}{3/2} = \frac{3/4 \times 3/2}{1}$$

$$\frac{2/3 \times 1/4}{1} = 2/3 \times 1/4 \qquad \frac{3/4 \times 3/2}{1} = 3/4 \times 3/2$$

The operation of multiplication with common fractions, which was introduced and developed earlier, can then be performed. Notice that there are no abstract or meaningless rules such as "To divide with common fractions, invert the divisor and multiply" or "To divide with common fractions, multiply by the reciprocal of the divisor," only the application of major mathematical ideas. With other computational operations and/or with other types of numerals, different major mathematical ideas are the foundations for developing algorithms. For example, the major ideas of base ten and positional value are the vital, basic ideas for developing the procedures for all of the computational operations with whole numbers.

Learning Experiences

In an active laboratory-type elementary mathematics program, children's learning experiences directed toward practice with the computational operations, particularly with the facts of addition, subtraction, and multiplication, are childlike or game-like activities. (The "basic facts" of division are not developed or emphasized *per se*. The operation of division is approached through its relationship to multiplication: separating one quantity into equal-size groups is the inverse or opposite of combining equal-size groups or numbers into one quantity, and the division operation is the inverse of multiplication. The facts and procedures of multiplication and subtraction are employed in the technical operation of division.) The childlike or gamelike practice activities primarily utilize pictorial manipulative materials and, in some instances, recording or score-keeping devices. Appropriate physical object models for numbers should be available for children to find answers to their own questions, to settle their disputes or challenges, and for purposes of verification. Although some practice activities might employ abstract printed materials, such as pages of exercises or examples in textbooks, in workbooks, or on dittoed sheets, those types of materials are best used as evaluative or testing devices. Before beginning a unit of study, teachers might use such materials to assess individual children's competence or areas of difficulty. Appropriate learning experiences and activities could then be selected for children of varying capabilities. Each child's performance on such evaluative devices can be analyzed to determine a current level of competence. Practice activities for each child should start at or below that demonstrated achievement level and proceed to tasks of greater complexity. It is reasonable to expect each child to acquire the skills of performing the computational operations with whole numbers, common fractions, decimal fractions, and mixed numerals only if attention is given to a sequential development of skills with each child.

Major Ideas or Content Themes

The major ideas or content themes of operations on number using numerals are neither the basic arithmetical facts associated with the computational operations nor the procedures or algorithms of the operations. Knowledge of the basic facts and performance of the algorithms are technical skills for children to acquire. The major ideas of this content area are consistent mathematical themes to be spirally developed throughout those aspects of the program that deal with the computational operations. With few exceptions, those major ideas or themes pertain to the properties of number in operations and the relationships between operations, particularly the inverse operations. The major ideas or content themes are to be used in ways that help children establish and master the facts, understand the procedures or algorithms of the operations, learn to perform the operations accurately, and employ the operations in appropriate situations. Each of the ideas or content themes can and should be dealt with as the complexity of the operation(s) to which it pertains increases in terms of the numerals involved. When a major idea or theme is being used with more complex numerals, review of and reference to the use of that idea with simpler numerals is an appropriate instructional procedure. In some elementary mathematics programs, these major ideas are used sporadically or studied as vocabulary exercises emphasizing names, definitions, and examples. The meaningful development and utilization of these major ideas is of greater importance in an active laboratory approach to learning mathematics than in a formal language approach in which names and definitions for the ideas are stressed. The following discussion of content themes or major ideas uses technical terms, but classroom efforts are directed at meaningful communication and uses of the ideas.

Only like numerical units can be added or subtracted.

As with the other content themes described in this section, this major idea pertains to the number names or printed numerals that appear in computational exercises or examples. The idea should be introduced at an early level when children are working with addition and subtraction of whole numbers—ones are added to ones, tens are added to tens, hundreds are added to hundreds, and so on—and when the procedures of the two operations are being illustrated or represented by physical object models for whole numbers. Note that the idea applies only to like numerical units and not to like objects. However, when good physical object models for number are used, the objects to be combined are alike. In problem situations, children may be asked to add or subtract numerals describing quantities of unlike objects. It is possible to add 16 apples to 13 oranges to find the total number of pieces of fruit, but the operation of addition is performed on numerals and only like numerical units can be added. When children encounter problems or exercises involving addition or subtraction of common fractions, the idea is again emphasized; the solution procedure may first require renaming the quantities or numbers to like numerical units. In order to add (or subtract) 1/2 and 1/3, the numbers must be renamed to like numerical units. The idea is also extended to adding and subtracting decimal-fraction numerals. The old rule of "keep the decimal points in a straight line or under each other" merely established an efficient procedure for adding or subtracting like numerical units. Algebraic expressions or equations involve variables named by letters (a, b, c, . . ., x, y, z) or other symbols. Those letters or symbols describe quantities and are to be considered numerical units. The quantities named by a and b are obviously to be considered different quantities and, therefore, different numerical units, which cannot be actually added or subtracted as long as they are named in that manner. Similarly, the variables x and x^2 describe different quantities and are not like numerical units.

The identity element of addition is 0.

When 0 as one addend is added to another addend, the sum is identical to the other addend. When children are establishing the addition facts, this idea may be one of the first generalizations that they observe, and they should be helped to recognize this idea or generalization as *one* fact. The idea must be extended to zeros as they appear in whole numbers greater than 9 that are to be added (10, 20, 30, . . .; 100, 200, . . .; 203, 580, 1000, 2034, 2304, 2340; and so forth). If the idea is well developed with whole numbers, children will have little difficulty applying it to addition with common fractions or decimal fractions.

The order in which two addends appear or the order in which they are considered does not affect the associated sum.

This is the commutative property of addition, $a + b = c$ and $b + a = c$. The ordering of two addends does not become evident or apparent until the addition operation is indicated either in a number sentence ($2 + 3 = \square$ or $3 + 2 = \square$) or in computational form, as shown in the margin. If children are introduced to addition facts with incomplete number sentences or with fact stimuli in computational form, this idea may be difficult for them to comprehend because in printed form there is an obvious order to the addends. They may see the following computations as more than one addition fact.

$$\begin{array}{ll} 23 & 15 \\ +15 & +23 \\ \end{array}$$

$$4 + 3 = 7 \quad 3 + 4 = 7 \quad \begin{array}{cc} 4 & 3 \\ +3 & +4 \\ \hline 7 & 7 \end{array}$$

Similarly, if children are presented with fact tables arranged according to a single addend (the addition fact tables of 0, 1, 2,

3, . . . , 9), this major idea is not being introduced when it ought to be, nor is it being used early as it ought to be. In an active laboratory-type program, the addition facts are introduced with a procedure in which the order of the addends is of no consequence or is not evident. Consider an activity in which children are to "show the facts," which is directed toward helping them to establish (discover) the facts for themselves. Initially, children need not record the facts they observe. One child or a small group of children is given an amount of poker chips of at least two different colors and two numeral cubes, each with the digits 0, 1, 2, 3, 4, and 5 on the six faces of the cube. The child is to roll the two numeral cubes at the same time. The numeral on one of the cubes tells how many chips of one color to take and the numeral on the other cube tells how many chips to take of another color. The object is to determine the total number of chips taken. (If two children are participating, one child may roll one of the numeral cubes while the other child rolls the other cube, and each child can take or show chips of different colors.) An addition fact is shown for each pair of addends that is rolled. There is no order in the addends that are shown on the numeral cubes. To make certain that children see the idea, the teacher may point at one shown fact and ask, "Is this 5 and 2, or is it 2 and 5?" The expected response is: "It's both," or, "It doesn't make any difference." The addends 5 and 2 have the same total (sum) as 2 and 5. (This activity also introduces and develops the idea about zero as an addend, previously described in the second statement.) When recording procedures are utilized in the activity, children may write each observed fact in two ways, altering the order of the addends. Seeing and understanding the idea when they are using one-digit numerals as addends will not only reduce the number of facts to be committed to memory by children, it also will allow them to apply the idea to additions of larger whole numbers, common fractions, and decimal fractions.

When more than two numerals are to be added, the numerals can be grouped two at a time in any manner for the additions without affecting the sum.

This is the associative property of addition, $(a + b) + c = d$ or $(a + c) + b = d$ or $(b + c) + a = d$. The idea of the commutative property of addition $(a + b = b + a)$ is an integral part of this idea. This major idea may be introduced early with one-digit addends in an activity similar to that described in the third statement. One way would be to use two numeral cubes with the digits 0, 6, 7, 8, 9, and 10 on the six faces of each cube and add the rule that the total chips must be grouped as a stack of 10 and single chips. When numerals such as 8 and 7 are rolled, the 8 chips of one color are stacked with 2 chips of the other color (or 7 chips of one color are stacked with 3 of the other color) and 5 chips remain as singles. Thus, the original two addends may be seen as three addends. Another way to alter the activity is to use three different numeral cubes as described and chips of three different colors. The three cubes are rolled, three different colors of chips are used to show the three numbers to be added, and any two groups can be combined first. In both variations of the activity, as well as in other activities, attention can and probably should be given to adding or grouping addends with sums of 10. This major idea is used in conjunction with the idea in the first statement to explain how and why the algorithm for addition works for whole numbers greater than 9 and for decimal fractions. Consider the following example, the illustrations of expanded notation, and the manner in which the additions would be done. Each original numeral is actually treated as three addends, each of a different numerical unit.

423	4 hundreds 2 tens 3 ones	400 + 20 + 3
278	2 hundreds 7 tens 8 ones	200 + 70 + 8
+304	+3 hundreds 0 tens 4 ones	+300 + 00 + 4

When the additions are performed, like units are added. Addition of decimal-fraction numerals is performed in the same manner. The concept of grouping addends in order to perform the addition operation more efficiently is often forgotten or ignored when common fractions are to be added. If attention were given to the idea, some children might have less difficulty with pencil-and-paper operations, and others might be able to arrive at correct responses through mental calculations without paper and pencil. Given the example (preferably derived from a problem situation) $3/4 + 1/3 + 1/4 = \square$, some children, because of habit or because they were directed to do so, would rename the three fractions to like units and then perform the additions. Those who understand the major idea involving the grouping of addends simply would add the 3/4 and 1/4 (getting 1) and then add the 1/3. Later in the mathematics program, when children who understand this idea encounter longer algebraic expressions or equations, they will have little or no difficulty in grouping addends of like numerical units for purposes of addition or subtraction.

The identity element of multiplication is 1.

When any factor N is multiplied by a factor of 1, the product is identical to the factor other than 1 ($1 \times N = N$ and $N \times 1 = N$). Children will be quick to see and understand this major idea when they are establishing the multiplication facts in laboratory-type learning experiences. This idea may be one of the first generalizations they observe, and they should be helped to recognize and use the idea as *one* fact. With multiplication involving whole numbers greater than 9, the idea is extended to 1 as it appears in any place or position in a base-ten numeral and to multiplying by 1 ten, 1 hundred, 1 thousand, and so on. One group of any quantity is that quantity; ten groups of any quantity increases that quantity by one power of 10; and so on. The idea and skills are applied in a similar manner in multiplication involving decimal-fraction numerals. Children who understand this idea will have very little difficulty in multiplying a common fraction by 1. However, when renaming common fractions to equivalent fractions and when performing the operation of division with common fractions as described previously, application of the concept that there are many names for 1 must be stressed. A number can be multiplied by any of the names for 1. In the process, that number merely has been renamed.

When one of the factors to be multiplied is 0, the product is 0.

Children who study the multiplication facts in a rote or abstract manner often have difficulty with the "facts" about 0 in multiplication and with multiplying larger whole numbers when 0 appears in one or more places in one or both of the numerals. When children are actively establishing or discovering the multiplication facts in a laboratory approach, this idea (along with the identity element of multiplication) will be one of the first generalizations they observe, and they should be helped to recognize and use the idea as *one* fact. The idea pervades all types of numerals or quantitative symbols that may be involved in an operation of multiplication, and also applies to the use of any of the many names for 0 that might be used as a factor (4 − 4, 0/N, and so on).

The order in which two factors appear or the order in which they are considered does not affect the associated product.

This is the commutative property of multiplication, $a \times b = p$ and $b \times a = p$. As with addends in addition, the ordering of two factors does not become apparent until the example is written either in number sentence form or in computational form. To avoid children's confusion about multiplication-fact statements like $4 \times 8 = \square$ and $8 \times 4 = \square$, to introduce this idea, and to use it to reduce the number of multiplication facts that children must commit to memory, early learning experiences and activities should provide opportunities for children to see and understand it. The activity of "Making Arrays" is an excellent laboratory-type activity for helping children establish or discover the multiplication facts. In it they will be able to see and understand the identity element (1) of multiplication, the use of 0 as a factor, and the commutative property of multiplication ($a \times b = b \times a$). At the first level of this activity, a child or a small group of children is given an amount of chips or small cubes and two numeral cubes with the digits 0, 1, 2, 3, 4, and 5 on the six faces of each cube. The directions are to roll the numeral cubes and make an array of chips. The numeral on one of the rolled cubes tells how many chips or cubes to put in a row, and the numeral on the other cube tells how many rows like that to make. The object is to determine the total number of chips in the array. To determine the total number or product, children should be encouraged to regroup the chips or cubes into rows of ten when possible so that they can see the product as "_____ ten(s) and _____" rather than counting the single chips or adding. In that manner, children are more likely to arrive at correct totals (especially when the numerals 6, 7, 8, 9, and 10 are later used as factors or appear on the numeral cubes to be used), the concept of base ten is reinforced, and regrouping of *ones* to *tens* in multiplication is introduced. For some children, counting and addition may be less precise, and this procedure deemphasizes counting when dealing with the facts. When the two numeral cubes are rolled at the same time, or even when the numerals rolled are alternately used to show the number in each row and the number of rows, there is no order in the factors

Figure 9.2

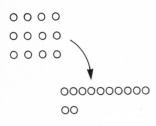

27	3486
X3486	X 27

.59	13.47
X 13.47	X .59

that are shown. To make certain that children see the commutative idea, the teacher may point to an array that has been made, such as that in Figure 9.2, and ask, "Is this 3 rows of 4 chips, or is it 4 rows of 3 chips?" The expected response is: "It's both," or, "It doesn't make any difference." Three rows of four chips and four rows of three chips have the same total. In this same activity, children will quickly see that the total is 0 when either the number of chips in a row is 0 or when the number of rows is 0; and that if one of the factors is 1, either the number of rows or the number of chips in a row, the total or product is the other factor. Later, when children are multiplying whole numbers greater than 10 or decimal-fraction numerals, they will use this idea in arranging the computational forms of the operations so that the computation can be performed in the easiest, shortest, or most efficient way (see margin). In regard to common fractions and quantitative problems involving them, children should utilize this idea to see that they must use similar computational procedures to solve the exercises or examples derived from problems that involve finding (1) the amount when N groups of a fractional amount are to be combined, (2) the size of a quantity when a whole-number amount is to be separated into a fractional amount, and (3) the amount of a fractional part of a fractional quantity (a separation problem). The order of the factors does not affect the product.

	3/5 of 15	2/3 of 3/4
	or	or
5 X 3/8	3/5 X 15	2/3 X 3/4
	or	or
	15 X 3/5	3/4 X 2/3

When more than two numerals (factors) are to be multiplied, the factors and resulting products can be grouped for multiplication two at a time in any manner without affecting the result or product.

This is the associative property of multiplication ($a \times b) \times c = p$ or $(a \times c) \times b = p$ or $(b \times c) \times a = p$. Of course, the idea also applies to situations in which there are more than three factors, and the number of possible groupings for multiplication of factors and resulting products increases. The idea of the commutative property of multiplication ($b \times a = a \times b$) is an integral part of this idea. This idea is sometimes introduced when children are studying the multiplication facts, particularly with the factors 6, 8, or 9. When children encounter those factors in the multiplication facts, they are sometimes encouraged to think of the factor as a product or to rename the factor in terms of another multiplication fact(s). For example, $6 = 2 \times 3$; $8 = 2 \times 4$ or $8 = 2 \times 2 \times 2$; and $9 = 3 \times 3$. Then, when facts involving those factors (6, 8, or 9) are introduced or when the products cannot be recalled, the "thinking" procedures could be similar to the following:

$$6 \times 7 = \square \qquad 6 \times 7 = \square \qquad 9 \times 7 = \square$$
$$(2 \times 3) \times 7 = \square \qquad (2 \times 4) \times 7 = \square \qquad (3 \times 3) \times 7 = \square$$
$$2 \times (3 \times 7) = \square \qquad 2 \times (4 \times 7) = \square \qquad 3 \times (3 \times 7) = \square$$
$$2 \times 21 = \square \qquad 2 \times 28 = \square \qquad 3 \times 21 = \square$$

However, these procedures are likely to detract from the development and acquisition of the facts by children. A more appropriate activity for introducing and developing this idea might actually involve three factors as in the activity "Build Rectangular Solids." Notice that this activity also involves geometric and measurement ideas and skills. One child or a small group of children is given an amount of small cubes of the same size and three numeral cubes with either the digits 0, 1, 2, 3, 4, and 5 or 0, 6, 7, 8, 9, and 10 on the six faces of the cubes. The three numeral cubes are rolled and the numeral on one cube tells how long the rectangular solid is to be, another numeral tells how wide the solid should be, and the third numeral tells how high the solid should be. The rectangular solid should be built in all possible ways and the object is to determine how many small cubes there are in the solid. Figure 9.3 shows three of the possible constructions if the

Figure 9.3

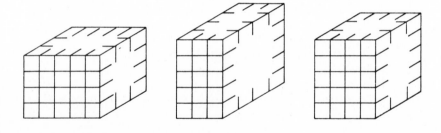

Figure 9.4

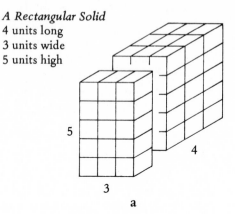

A Rectangular Solid
4 units long
3 units wide
5 units high

Solid separated to
show solution:
$$3 \times 5 = 15$$
$$4 \times 15 = 60$$
$$(3 \times 5) \times 4 = 60$$

a

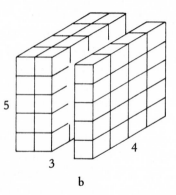

b

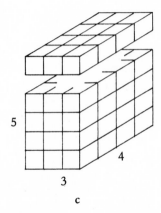

c

Solid separated to show solution:
$$4 \times 5 = 20$$
$$3 \times 20 = 60$$
$$(4 \times 5) \times 3 = 60$$

Solid separated to show solution:
$$3 \times 4 = 12$$
$$5 \times 12 = 60$$
$$(3 \times 4) \times 5 = 60$$

numerals 3, 4, and 5 are shown on the rolled cubes. If more than
one child is participating in the activity, each may construct
the solid in a different way. Initially, the children may determine
the number of small cubes in each construction simply by dis-
mantling the solid and arranging the cubes in rows of ten. Later,
however, children should be helped to use an arithmetical procedure, multiplication, to determine the number of cubes used and
to see that the operation can proceed in several ways with different groupings of the factors as shown in Figure 9.4a, b, c. Notice

that each of the illustrations starts with a rectangular solid that is 4 units long, 3 units wide, and 5 units high. A fourth factor can be involved if several solids of the same size are built and the given task is to find the total number of small cubes in all of the solids. After children see and understand this idea as it is represented with a physical object model and involving smaller whole numbers, they should have little difficulty extending its use to more complex problems, including measurement situations, greater whole numbers, and common-fraction or decimal-fraction numerals.

When the sum of two or more numbers is to be multiplied by a number, the same total will be obtained if the sum of the addends is found first and then the multiplication performed, or if each addend is first multiplied by the number and the sum of those products is then obtained.

This is the distributive property of multiplication over addition, $f(a + b + c) = fa + fb + fc$. Actually, this major idea also applies to numbers or terms that are to be subtracted and multiplied, $f(a - b) = fa - fb$; and to a series of terms that are to be either added or subtracted and multiplied, $f(a - b + c + d - e) = fa + fc + fd - fb - fe$. Simple quantitative problems involving smaller whole numbers might be utilized to introduce this idea. For example, 3 friends are returning the same kind of reusable bottles or containers for the deposit. Each friend has a different number of bottles. How much will they receive in returned deposit money? Traditionally, such problems have been called "two-step" or "three-step" problems depending on the number of separate computational operations necessary in the solution procedures. Many such problems involving either addition or subtraction or both and multiplication can be used soon after children have acquired the necessary arithmetical facts. The idea is most necessary and useful in helping children see and understand how and why the operation of multiplication with larger whole numbers works. Consider the following multiplication exercise in which a three-digit numeral is to be multiplied by a one-digit numeral. The three-digit numeral is thought of as the sum of three different numerical units and illustrated in expanded notation. Each quantity (number) of different numerical units in the three-digit numeral is multiplied independently by the one-digit factor.

$$\begin{array}{r}\boxed{\begin{array}{r}347\\ \times\ 5\end{array}}\end{array}$$

3 hundreds 4 tens 7 ones   or   5(3 hundreds 4 tens 7
$$\underline{\times 5}$$ ones) is 15 hundreds +
15 hundreds 20 tens 35 ones   20 tens + 35 ones

$$\begin{array}{r}300 +\ \ 40 + 7\\ \times\ 5\end{array}$$ or   5(300 + 40 + 7) = 1500 + 200 + 35

$$\overline{1500 +\ \ 200 + 35}$$

     ② ③

$$\begin{array}{r}347\\ \times\ \ \ 5\\ \hline 35 = 5 \times 7\\ 200 = 5 \times 40\\ 1500 = 5 \times 300\\ \hline 1735\end{array}$$

$$\begin{array}{r}3\ \ \ 4\ \ \ 7\\ \times\ \ \ \ \ \ \ 5\\ \hline 1\ \ 7\ \ 3\ \ 5\end{array}$$

The idea is extended and further applied with problems and
computational exercises in which both of the factors are two-
or more-digit numerals. For example, 56 × 34 is treated as
(30 + 4) × (50 + 6) in the following manners:

$$\begin{array}{r}(50 +\ \ 6)\\ \times\ (30 +\ \ 4)\\ \hline 200 +\ \ 24\ = 4(50 + 6)\\ 1500 + 180\ = 30(50 + 6)\\ \hline 1700 + 204\end{array}$$

$$\begin{array}{r}56\\ \times\ \ 34\\ \hline 24 =\ \ 4 \times 6\\ 200 =\ \ 4 \times 50\\ 180 = 30 \times 6\\ 1500 = 30 \times 50\\ \hline 1904\end{array}$$

     or

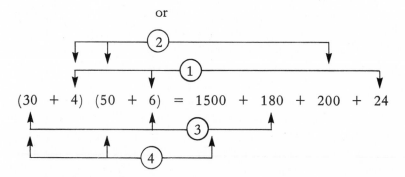

The idea can be pictured (for one-digit or two-digit factors) by
drawing the exercises on squared paper. Figure 9.5 is an illustration of the computation 23 × 35. Making drawings of this kind

for multiplication examples with whole numbers and with decimal-fraction numerals is an appropriate project for children. The only differences in applying this idea to multiplication of decimal

Figure 9.5

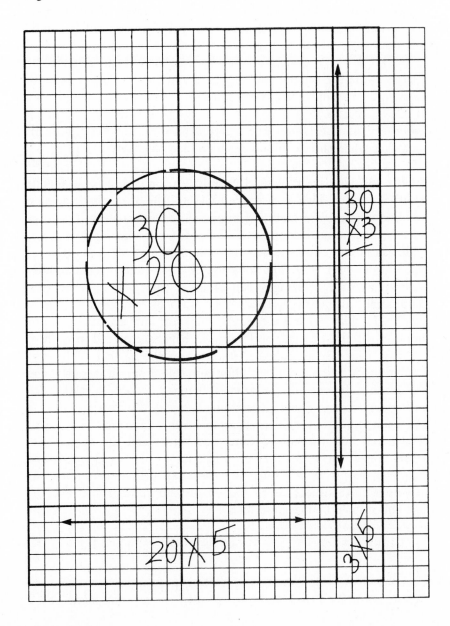

fractions are that the numerical unit sizes are different and that the unit size of 1 must be established, preferably as 10 tenths and 100 hundredths in a ten-by-ten-unit square. Understanding of this idea should be developed thoroughly before children try to apply it to problems or examples involving common fractions, such as $3(1/2 + 3/4)$ or $1/2$ of $(2/3 + 5/6)$. However, those problems can be illustrated with physical object models and drawings. At the later intermediate or upper levels of the elementary mathematics program, children will be required to apply this idea to algebraic expressions and ideas such as $a(b + c)$ and $(a + b)(a + b)$. At that level, the application of the idea should be related to its use with whole numbers and can also be made more meaningful through the use of drawings. (See Figures 9.6 and 9.7.)

Figure 9.6

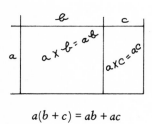

$$a(b + c) = ab + ac$$

Figure 9.7

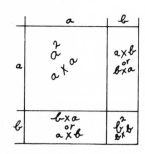

$$(a + b)(a + b)$$
$$= a^2 + 2ab + b^2$$

For every number (numeral), there is another number (numeral) such that when the two numbers are added, the sum is 0.

This is the additive inverse, $4 + (-4) = 0$ or $N + (-N) = 0$. The additive inverse idea is not identical to the idea that addition and subtraction are inverse computational operations. This idea may be introduced soon after the study of negative integers is undertaken and can be extended to applications of $-4 + (+4) = 0$ and $-N + (+N) = 0$. The idea may be introduced meaningfully with an activity utilizing a pan balance, objects of equal weight, a numeral cube with 0, 1, 2, 3, 4, and 5 on the six faces, and a sign cube with + and − (three each) on the six faces. Equal amounts of the objects, preferably in bags, are placed in each of the two pans of the balance, resulting in the balance of $N = N$. The numeral cube and sign cube are rolled simultaneously and the amount in one of the pans is changed according to the sign and the numeral. The sign is to be associated with the numeral, and each move is to be interpreted as an "addition." Thus, successive rolls of +3 and −3 (and vice versa) and the appropriate moves result in a maintained balance, $(+3) + (-3) = 0$ and $(-3) + (+3) = 0$. A similar activity may utilize a number line of integers, an object to be moved on the number line, and the sign and numeral cubes described.

$$\ldots -5 \quad -4 \quad -3 \quad -2 \quad -1 \quad 0 \quad +1 \quad +2 \quad +3 \quad +4 \quad +5 \quad +6 \quad +7 \ldots$$

The object is placed at 0 as a starting point, the two cubes are rolled simultaneously, and the proper moves are made. Each move is considered to be an "addition." Regardless of the point at which an object starts on a particular move, two successive moves involving the same numeral and different signs (positive or negative), will result in the object returning to its starting point, actually an addition of zero with the two moves. Some teachers and mathematics educators may not consider this a major idea to be emphasized in the elementary mathematics program, but the idea can be meaningfully introduced and it can be spirally developed throughout the program with greater whole numbers, common fractions, and decimal-fraction numerals to serve as a foundation for its later use in more complex mathematical endeavors.

For every number (numeral) other than 0, there is another number (numeral) such that when the two numbers are multiplied, the product is 1.

This is the multiplicative inverse, $3 \times 1/3 = 1$; $1/5 \times 5 = 1$; $3/4 \times 4/3 = 1$; $N \times$ the *reciprocal* of $N = 1$. This idea should be observed, generalized, and emphasized when children are studying the processes of multiplication with common fractions. Its use in meaningfully developing the processes of division with common fractions has been described earlier in this chapter. At later levels in the program, children may utilize the idea in solving complex incomplete or open number sentence statements or equations by multiplying the quantitative statements on both sides of the equal sign by the *reciprocal* of one of the quantities to simplify the expression or to solve for a specified unknown.

Subtraction and addition are inverse (opposite) operations ($6 + 5 = 11$ so $11 - 6 = 5$ and $11 - 5 = 6$).

The major use of this idea is probably in abstract adult-level verification procedures for either of the operations. Results of subtraction operations can be verified (or questioned) by addition, and results of an addition operation can be verified (or questioned) by subtraction. (If the second operation does not verify the first, the only implication is that one or both of the operations has been improperly performed.) An earlier use of the idea is to help children learn the addition and subtraction facts. Some children may think of and learn the subtraction facts in an additive manner—"What is the missing addend?" In their earliest activities of performing operations on collections of objects, children should be given opportunities to see and understand that combining and separating are inverse or opposite operations. While emphasizing this idea, children will separate a combined quantity to verify the combination and will combine separated quantities to verify the separation process. When recording techniques are associated with these activities, addition and subtraction will be derived as the operations for dealing with these problems. Similar combining and separating activities with physical object models should be the bases for children establishing, developing, and learning the basic addition and subtraction facts. Fact families $(4 + 5 = 9, 9 - 4 = 5,$ and $9 - 5 = 4)$ and the inverse relationship are developed early through such learning experiences. If both combining and separating collections of objects and addition and subtraction are emphasized as inverse operations early in the program, foundations will be laid for further utilization of the idea with larger whole numbers, common fractions, and decimal-fraction numerals. And, it is not unreasonable to expect children to employ the idea that subtraction and addition are inverse operations to verify solutions to problems or results of computational exercises involving not only whole numbers, but also common fractions and decimal fractions. Requiring verification of solutions is realistic in regard to lifelike situations and provides variation in practice. Children should be held responsible for the correctness and accuracy of their solutions to problems and exercises, and this requires either complete mastery of skills or application of verification procedures instead of dependence on adults (teachers) for checking, correcting, or indicating errors.

Multiplication and division are inverse (opposite) operations $(3 \times 9 = 27$ so $27 \div 3 = 9$ and $27 \div 9 = 3)$.

As with the inverse operations of addition and subtraction, the major use of this idea is in abstract adult-level verification procedures for either of the operations. Multiplication operations can be performed in attempts to verify results of division operations and vice versa. As proficiency with each of the operations increases, proficiency with the verification procedure utilizing the inverse operation will also increase. It is unreasonable to expect a child to check the result of one operation with performance of another operation if that child is not proficient in one or the other.

Like the addition-subtraction inverse idea, this idea can and should be introduced and emphasized early in the mathematics program by two related types of activities. One of those types of activities involves performing operations on collections of objects in which equal-size groups are to be combined and in which one quantity is to be separated into equal-size groups. The acts of combining and separating are inverse physical operations. That idea can be developed and emphasized by activities that require children to separate a combined quantity into groups of the original equal size and to recombine the equal-size groups that were separated. As recording procedures and the algorithms are developed and derived from these activities, the inverse relationship between multiplication and division should be stressed and utilized. In the second type of activity, children combine small equal-size groups (pieces of physical object models) or numbers to establish, develop, and learn the basic multiplication facts. (Refer to "Making Arrays" on p. 245.) After children have demonstrated the ability to make arrays and to find the total number in each array by rearranging the array into collections of ten, they may be asked to separate the new arrangement into groups of the original size and to determine how many groups there are. Although the basic division facts are not emphasized, taught, or utilized in an active laboratory-type elementary mathematics program, fact families can be derived and the relationship between multiplication and division certainly can be introduced, developed, and stressed. Extending the use of this idea to applications in quantitative problem situations, exercises, and examples and to verification procedures with greater whole numbers, common fractions, decimal-fraction, and algebraic expressions requires that a solid foundation be laid early with realistic learning opportunities and experiences.

Several additional mathematical ideas might be mentioned. They have not been ascribed as major ideas or content themes either because they are inherent or obvious in other ideas or in the processes of the program, because they are not subject to spiral development throughout the program, or because they are of minor importance and are handled in other manners. One of those mathematical ideas is *closure* as it pertains to specific computational operations and subsets of the set of real numbers. A set or subset of numbers is *closed* in regard to an operation if, and only if, the result of the operation is always an element of the same set or subset as the set named, described, or illustrated by the possible component elements or numbers involved in the operation. For example, the sum of any two or more nonnegative integers is always a nonnegative integer; therefore, the subset of nonnegative integers is closed in regard to addition. However, the difference between any two nonnegative integers is not always a nonnegative integer ($6 - 9$ = a negative integer); therefore, the set of nonnegative integers is not closed in regard to subtraction. In order to be arithmetically complete, a set of numbers must be closed in regard to the fundamental operations. Perusal of the following chart will indicate why the development of the main ideas of the real number system is a major general objective of the elementary mathematics program.

Subset of Set of Numbers

Operations	Nonnegative Integers	Negative Integers	All Integers	Rational Numbers
Addition	closed	closed	closed	closed
Subtraction	not closed	not closed	closed	closed
Multiplication	closed	not closed	closed	closed
Division	not closed	not closed	not closed	closed

Ideas about the nature of the results of operations performed with various kinds of numbers or numerals should naturally evolve in the process and conduct of learning experiences and activities dealing with the operations. Attention can be called to the nature of those results, but it does not seem necessary or appropriate to introduce the idea of *closure* early in the program nor to develop the idea spirally throughout the elementary mathematics program. The concepts can be dealt with only after children are familiar with the types of numerals that can emerge as results.

Another pair of arithmetical ideas not considered to be content themes apply to the relationship of addition to multiplication and the relationship of subtraction to division. Counting, addition, subtraction, multiplication, and division are all unique operations. The real relationship between multiplication and "repeated" addition is not that multiplication is a short procedure for addition, but that both operations can be used to solve problems that involve combining equal-size numbers. The process of multiplication with whole numbers and decimal fractions does require the addition of partial products, but that is a part of the uniqueness of the multiplication operation. The same general point applies to the relationship between division and subtraction. The operation of subtraction, as well as the operation of multiplication, is required in the process of division with whole numbers and decimal-fraction numerals. The real relationship between division and "repeated" subtraction is that both operations can be used to solve problems in which one quantity or number is to be separated into equal-size groups or in which two numbers or quantities are to be compared to make a ratio statement.

In an active laboratory-type elementary mathematics program, "repeated" addition is neither a prerequisite nor a developmental procedure for introducing and developing the multiplication facts or operation. Those facts, rules, and procedures can be developed meaningfully without giving attention to "repeated" addition (or to counting in multiples). In fact, the procedures of "repeated" addition may be more difficult than multiplication for some children. Similarly, "repeated" subtraction is neither a prerequisite nor a developmental procedure for introducing and developing the operation of division.

Performance Skills

The performance skills that apply to this major content area have been implied or described in preceding chapters or in sections of this chapter. Ideally, on completion of the elementary mathematics program, children would be able to (1) apply all of the computational operations as solution procedures to quantitative problem situations involving whole numbers, common fractions, decimal fractions, and mixed numerals and (2) arrive at correct responses or results to abstract printed examples or exercises requiring addition, subtraction, multiplication, or division with those subsets of numbers. Realistically, because of the differing characteristics of individual children, those objectives cannot be achieved by every child. However, each child, regardless of his or her current age or grade level, should have opportunities to progress toward those objectives in accordance with his or her currently demonstrated performance skills.

Providing for Pupil Abilities

Learning experiences and activities should be directed toward meaningful improvement of the current abilities of every child. Each child should have opportunities and be encouraged to work with problems of all types and with the computational operations needed to solve those problems. Those opportunities need not involve large or complex numbers. One computational operation with one type of number or numeral need not be mastered completely before children are introduced to other operations with the same kind of numerals or to the same computational operation with other kinds of numerals. In every case, actual prerequisites of understanding and performance should be considered.

The Basic Facts

The basic arithmetical facts of addition, subtraction, and multiplication pertaining to whole numbers are prerequisites for the introduction and development of those operations and the operation of division with larger whole numbers and with decimal fractions. The same facts are prerequisites for the operations of addition, subtraction, multiplication, and division with common fractions. The facts should be mastered first, but once a subset of those facts has been learned, additional applications can and should be made. Each child's power with the concepts and facts that he or she has acquired should be increased immediately. It is unreasonable to expect children to apply facts that they do not know to more complex computational operations, whether those operation stimuli are related to quantitative problems or not. It is also unreasonable to expect children to apply the basic facts that they have learned or mastered to new types of problems or to different types of numerals when those "new" ideas appear as concepts or applications completely unrelated to those that have already been introduced and developed.

Making Facts Easier to Learn

Learning experiences, activities, and procedures of an active laboratory-type approach to elementary mathematics are planned, selected, and conducted with the aim of making it easier for all children to master the basic arithmetic facts. Ease in learning the facts is facilitated by

1. meaningfully introducing and developing the facts through representation in problem situations with concrete physical object models
2. utilizing the properties of number in the operations and other major ideas to reduce the number of facts that children must commit to memory
3. approaching (introduction, development, and practice) the facts in subsets that are reasonable learning segments in terms of the numbers or numerals that are involved and the number of facts that are to be attained or mastered in that segment
4. building on and utilizing the concepts and performance skills that children have already acquired
5. practicing the facts in childlike and gamelike ways

The first skill that children should attain in regard to the introduction and development of the computational operations is the ability to demonstrate the basic facts with concrete physical object models for number as in the activities of "Show the Facts" and "Making Arrays" described in the preceding section of this chapter. Those activities help children to establish subsets of the addition and multiplication facts. In those activities and in the recording procedures that accompany them, the subsets of facts are controlled by the numerals on the cubes that are rolled. The facts of each subset should be established and practiced nearly to mastery by children before another subset is undertaken. Consider the chart in Figure 9.8 as it pertains to the subsets of addition facts, the addends involved in each subset of facts, the utilization of the properties of number in the operation (particularly the identity element of addition and the commutative property of addition) and other ideas, the number of facts in each subset, and the total number of facts that children must commit to memory.

Figure 9.8 *The Addition Facts*

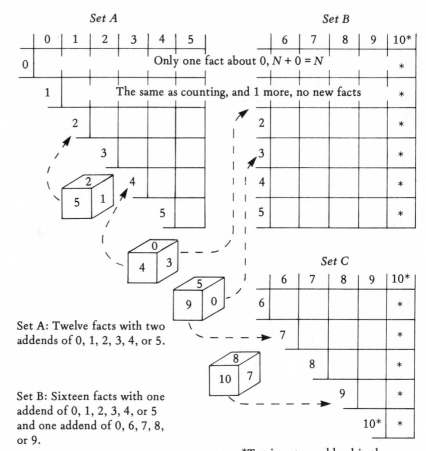

Set A: Twelve facts with two addends of 0, 1, 2, 3, 4, or 5.

Set B: Sixteen facts with one addend of 0, 1, 2, 3, 4, or 5 and one addend of 0, 6, 7, 8, or 9.

Set C: Ten facts with two addends of 6, 7, 8, or 9.

*Ten is not an addend in the basic addition facts. However, using 10 as an addend at this time will allow practice and reinforcement of renaming the numbers 10 through 20.

Mastery of Facts

If the facts are to be mastered to the point that children are to immediately recall the responses to fact stimuli (two addends), they must be practiced in activities and games that demand immediate recall instead of counting. Children should be made aware of this expectation and encouraged, even directed, to commit the facts of each subset to memory. Practice activities and games with each subset of facts can be controlled and directed with selected numeral cubes, numeral cards, dominoes, and other pictorial manipulative materials.

After each subset of addition facts is learned to the point where a child is hesitant or unsure about only one or two responses, the basic facts of subtraction related to that subset of facts can be emphasized. This procedure allows the child to utilize the inverse relationships between combining and separating groups of objects and between the addition facts and subtraction facts. Stressing the relationships between addition and subtraction facts immediately after one subset of addition facts is learned rather than delaying subtraction until all of the addition facts have been dealt with, not only permits an earlier introduction of the operation, but also facilitates pupil mastery of those facts.

In an active laboratory approach, the basic facts of multiplication also are introduced, developed, practiced, and learned in subsets determined by the nature of the factors involved. The chart in Figure 9.9 presents those subsets with the assumptions that ideas about 0 in multiplication, the identity element of multiplication, 2 as a factor (the problem situation, representation with physical objects, and total amount are identical to addition facts in which the two addends are the same), and the commutative property of multiplication are utilized in the learning processes of children.

Division

The basic arithmetical facts of division need not be developed, practiced, or committed to memory by children. Instead, division can be approached as a unique operation by stressing the inverse problem situations of separating one number into equal-size groups and of combining equal-size groups into one quantity and by emphasizing the relationship of the division operation to multiplication. The division operation and symbolism are introduced with those inverses, and division ideas initially can be dealt with after each subset of multiplication facts has been well learned by children. After children can make the necessary arrays and rearrange the objects in the arrays to groups of ten (and single objects), the inverse ideas can be employed by asking children to regroup the newly arranged amount into the original subgroups. Three ways of describing this quantitative situation as an arithmetic expression should be illustrated or demon-

Figure 9.9 *The Multiplication Facts*

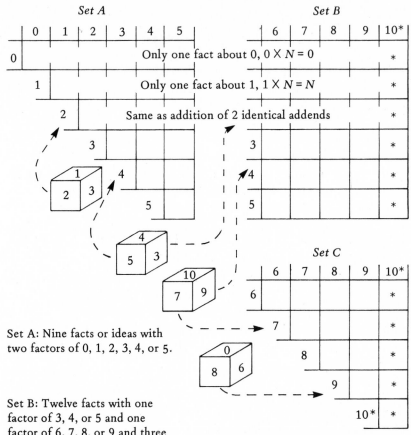

Set A: Nine facts or ideas with two factors of 0, 1, 2, 3, 4, or 5.

Set B: Twelve facts with one factor of 3, 4, or 5 and one factor of 6, 7, 8, or 9 and three continued ideas.

Set C: Ten facts with two factors of 6, 7, 8, or 9.

*10 is not a factor in the basic multiplication facts. However, using 10 as a factor at this time will allow practice and reinforcement with base ten and the decade names twenty, thirty, forty, . . . for 2 tens, 3 tens, . . . and the idea of 100.

strated simultaneously. Each of those expressions seeks the same unknown. Consider the situation in which 8 chips were placed in each row, 3 rows were made, the chips in the array were arranged to 2 rows of 10 chips and 4 single chips, and the direction now requires that the 24 chips be rearranged into 3 equal groups. How many chips will be in each group? The arithmetical expressions are shown in the margin. Appropriate oral communication should accompany each written expression:

$3 \times \square = 24$

$24 \div 3 = \square$

$$3\overline{)24}^{\square}$$

"3 groups of some number is 24."

"3 times some number equals 24."

"24 separated into 3 equal groups puts the same number in each group."

"24 divided by 3 is some number."

The same ideas of utilizing inverse relationships and of writing the three arithmetical expressions should be continued when problems and examples involve greater whole numbers, common fractions, decimal fractions, and mixed numerals. The division operation with whole numbers and decimal-fraction numerals will also require application of the process of subtraction. The need for and use of subtraction in the division operation should be developed and derived from structured problem situations employing physical object models for numbers.

Dealing with remainders in division situations is another skill to be acquired by children. Depending on the problem situation, some remainders are merely "left-overs" as in: "3 children are to share 11 marbles equally. How many marbles will each child get?" Some remainders are used to adjust the response, as in: "12 eggs can be placed in each carton. How many cartons are needed to store 79 eggs?" And, some remainders are converted to fractional amounts of the divisor and actually become a quantitative part of the response as in: "5 candy bars are to be shared equally by 3 children. How much candy will each child receive?" In abstract printed division examples or exercises, children generally proceed from merely citing remainders to converting remainders to fractional quantities to be included in the response or quotient.

The Operations

Extending children's performance skills to capabilities of performing the computational operations with larger whole numbers, common fractions, decimal fractions, and mixed numerals requires application of the basic facts, techniques of renaming numbers, and the rules and procedures for regrouping numerical units in the decimal system of numeration. The major ideas pertaining to renaming numbers and to regrouping numerical units, which are introduced and developed as topics for study in the content areas of numeration and notation and operations on collections of objects, should be spirally developed and utilized throughout the time that attention is given to children's acquisition of the computational operations. Proficiencies with these ideas and skills and with the major ideas and skills of this content area should allow children to perform mental calculations to solve problems that go beyond recall of basic facts.

Verification Procedures

Children participating in an active laboratory-type elementary mathematics program should also be expected to become proficient in a variety of procedures for verifying solutions to problems and responses to computational exercises. Those procedures can and should include verification by (1) demonstration by and manipulation of physical object models for number, (2) application of an easier operation that has been previously mastered, (3) utilization of one or more of the properties of number in the operations, and (4) performance of the inverse computational operations.

Reading and Writing Symbols

In order for children to understand and meaningfully perform operations on number using numerals, they must become familiar with the printed or written symbols. Reading and writing skills must be established, and those skills should be directed toward quantitative expressions including number sentences and equations as well as examples presented in computational form. It is in the content area of operations on numbers using numerals that children will encounter a full array of the quantitative, operational, comparative, and descriptive symbols necessary to develop familiarity with algebraic foundations. Helping children develop and acquire procedures for solving incomplete number sentences and equations should also be a concern for teachers in this content area.

Materials for Instruction

Other than the abstract printed computational examples or exercises and word problems, which might be used for practice purposes and which should be used for evaluative purposes, the instructional materials to be employed in this content area are identical to the materials used to introduce, develop, and practice the ideas and skills of numeration and notation and operations on collections of objects. Appropriate physical object models are used to illustrate structured problems from which the facts and computational procedures are derived. The pictured-problem activity cards described in the preceding chapter may be used for these purposes. Pictorial manipulatives such as numeral cubes, numeral cards, or other devices may be used to generate the numerals to be used in the problems, examples, or exercises. Pictorial manipulative materials, such as number picture cards, numeral cubes, numeral cards, dominoes, and play money, can also be used in activities and games that provide opportunities for children to practice basic ideas, facts, and operations.

Common Strategies or General Procedures

General procedures for introducing, developing, practicing, and evaluating pupil growth or achievement with the basic arithmetical facts and the computational operations on number using numerals have been cited or described in previous paragraphs. With the exception of the division operation, a common instructional strategy involves the introduction and development of the three other computational operations, particularly with nonnegative integers or whole numbers. Development of the fundamental operations with common fractions and mixed numbers with common fractions calls for a different type of physical object model and for different procedures for renaming or regrouping numbers. Yet, the operations with common fractions are derived from the same types of quantitative problem situations, utilize the same basic arithmetical facts, and require application of the same properties of number in operations. Solving problems and performing operations with decimal-fraction numerals and mixed decimal-fraction numerals is very similar to performing the same operations with whole numbers. So similar, in fact, that if children are proficient with the operations on whole numbers, they will be able to perform the operations with decimal fractions and mixed decimal fractions with little difficulty. The only new idea will be in dealing with the sizes of the numerical units, but this can be dealt with effectively through the proper use of models and drawings. The early introduction of problems involving metric measurements and money also will greatly alleviate these difficulties.

The common strategies or general procedures involving the operations of addition, subtraction, and multiplication with whole numbers may be summarized in two component considerations: attention to the basic facts and attention to developing the algorithms of the operations.

Mastery of the Basic Facts

1. Basic facts and their meanings are established by children using chips, counters, small cubes, or other models for number and numeral cubes or cards to generate numerals.
2. Facts are introduced, developed, and practiced in subsets, which depend on the numbers (addends and factors) involved. Regrouping with numerical units of base ten is stressed.
3. Major ideas, properties of number operations, and relationships are utilized to reduce the number of facts that children must commit to memory. When facts are recorded, those ideas are noted.
4. Practice of facts is with childlike activities and games (instead of rote drill) with the goal of immediate recall. Continued counting to find responses is discouraged. Communication in practice activities and games is oral.
5. Practice and evaluation on abstract printed examples occurs only after children have demonstrated proficiency and immediate recall of responses in other practice and evaluative activities and games.

6. Mastery of the basic facts is a prerequisite for performing the operations with larger numbers.

Developing the Algorithms

1. Each of the algorithms is developed in a logical sequence, which depends on the sizes of the numerals and the extent of the regrouping of numerical units that is involved.
2. Meanings and uses of the algorithms or rules and procedures for the computational operations are derived from problems structured with models for whole numbers and the combining and separating movements with the model pieces that are necessary to solve the problems.
3. Keeping records of the movements (combining, separating, and exchanging model pieces in accordance with base ten) of the model pieces in order to solve structured problems occurs only after children have demonstrated proficiency in physically solving the structured problems.
4. The first crude records that are kept to derive operational rules and procedures should include every move made with the model pieces used to illustrate structured problems.
5. Crude record-keeping procedures are organized and simplified to the common styles of the computational operation.
6. Practice of the computational operations is with childlike activities and games (instead of rote drill) having the goals of improved performance and accuracy.
7. Abstract computational exercises and examples are used for practice and evaluative devices only after children have demonstrated proficiency with record keeping in real or structured problems and in childlike learning activities and games.

Division with Whole Numbers

Early efforts to introduce and develop the division operation or algorithm should be closely related to the acquisition and mastery of the multiplication facts. Those efforts can be followed closely by structured problems in which a larger number or quantity is to be separated into less than ten equal groups. The number to be separated should be represented by pieces of a base-ten block model for number and the separation can be performed to determine the amount in each equal-size subgroup. Larger numerical units may need to be exchanged for smaller units in order to perform the separations. When children can physically solve the structured problems, record keeping that resembles the division operation should be initiated. Consider a structured problem in which 527 is to be separated into 3 equal parts. The first record of the separation solution may look like the following:

In each group

```
            1 hundreds   7 tens   5 ones
        3 ⟌ 5 hundreds   2 tens   7 ones
  groups   3 hundreds
            2 hundreds  20 tens
                        22 tens
                        21 tens
                         1 ten   10 ones
                                 17 ones
                                 15 ones
                                  2 Remainder
```

Classroom teachers may have particular preferences for a style and form of recording the operation. In any case, records can be shortened as quickly as children understand the recording procedure, and that understanding depends on giving attention to the sizes of the numerical units represented by digits in the original number, the concepts of base ten and positional value.

```
      175                    5                   175
  3 ⟌ 527                   70               3 ⟌ 527
   -3 hundreds             100                  3
    22 tens          3 ⟌ 527                   22
   -21 tens             -300 = 3 × 100         21
    17 ones             227                    17
   -15 ones            -210 = 3 × 70           15
     2 R                 17                     2 R
                       -15 = 3 × 5
                         2 R
```

Children's attention should be drawn to the uses that could be made of the multiplication facts or multiplication ideas. "What number multiplied by 3 is almost 500?" "What number multiplied by 3 is almost 22 tens?" "What number multiplied by 3 is almost 17?" After sufficient activities resulting in correct recording procedures like these with structured problems, children may be given the tasks of solving several such problems without actually manipulating the models for number. They are to use what they know about multiplication and subtraction. Identical reasoning is to be applied to problems that involve a greater number to be separated into more than ten equal groups. The skills of multiplication and subtraction that must be applied are of a higher level. For example, if a problem required 4609 to be separated or divided into 28 equal groups (or into groups of 28—the division operation is the same), children may be guided to use reasoning and procedures similar to the following (assume that children are involved in the simulated "discussion" and refer to the examples):

"4 thousands cannot be separated into 28 equal parts. However, 4 thousands can be thought of as 40 hundreds, and 40 hundreds with the 6 hundreds are 46 hundreds. 46 hundreds is greater than 28 and, thus, can be separated into 28 equal parts. What number multiplied by 28 is almost 46 hundreds? Or, if 46 hundreds are put into 28 equal groups, how large will each group be? How many hundreds will be left over? What can be done with those hundreds? Those 18 hundreds can be thought of as 180 tens, and 180 tens with 0 tens are 180 tens. How many tens should go into each group? What number multiplied by 28 is almost 180 tens? . . ."

```
         Th  H T O
              1 6 4
      2 8 ) 4 6 0 9
              . . . .
              2 8
              1 8 0
              . . . . .
              1 6 8
                1 2 9
                . . . .
                1 1 2
                  1 7  R
```

The inverse operation, multiplication, can be used to verify both of the preceding examples: 3 × 175 is almost 527 and 28 × 164 is almost 4609.

```
   175          164
 ×   3        ×  28
    15         1312
   210         3280
   300         4592
   525       +   17  R
 +   2         4609
   527
```

Multiplication and subtraction facts and ideas are employed in the same manner when the division involves decimal-fraction numerals or mixed decimal-fraction numerals. The only new or different idea pertains to naming the numerical units in the result or quotient, and there are two mathematically meaningful procedures for helping children understand and acquire this operational technique. Both procedures should be utilized to strengthen proficiencies with the operation. The conventional arithmetical procedure is similar to division with common fractions and involves renaming the quantitative expression indicating division. Children should already know how to divide by a whole number (the divisor is a whole number), but division by a decimal fraction or a mixed decimal-fraction numeral arithmetically is virtually impossible. Therefore, the division expression must be renamed so that the divisor becomes a whole number. That renaming procedure makes use of the major ideas that $1 \times N = N$ and that there are many, many names for 1. For example:

$$4.34\overline{)27.095} \qquad \frac{27.095}{4.34} \qquad \frac{27.095}{4.34} \times 1 = \frac{27.095}{4.34}$$

$$\frac{27.095}{4.34} \times \frac{100}{100} = \frac{2709.5}{434} \qquad 434\overline{)2709.5}$$

The other procedure utilizes estimation. The whole-number part of the mixed decimal-fraction numeral that is to be divided (the dividend) is 27, and the whole-number part of the mixed decimal-fraction divisor is 4. Therefore, the whole-number part of the result (quotient) should be about 6.

Division with Decimal Fractions

In classroom instructional procedures, multiplication and division with decimal fractions are sometimes related to multiplication and division with common fractions. Other than to develop ideas such as $3 \times 1/10 = 3/10$; $N \times 1/100 = N/100$; $1/10$ of $1/10 = 1/100$; $1/10$ of $1/100 = 1/1000$; and $1/100$ of $1/100 = 1/10,000$ with physical object models and drawings, this instructional emphasis is impractical. Addition and subtraction of decimal-fraction numerals is generally not related to addition and subtraction of common fractions, so the stressed relationship is not consistent. Also, the difficulties that some children have with the operations of multiplication and division with common fractions may make the instructional procedures that attempt to relate the two procedures untenable.

Examples of Learning Experiences

Several of the learning experiences presented as examples were selected because of their multiple uses or because of the modifications or extensions that are possible. Selected examples primarily are directed toward practice and reinforcement-type learning experiences because specific examples and general procedures for introductory and developmental learning experiences have been described previously.

Compare Sums Two or three children. A deck of numeral cards with one of the digits 0, 1, 2, 3, 4, 5, 6, 7, 8, or 9 on each of the cards and four cards with each digit. A physical object model (chips, counters, cubes, or sticks) may be kept available for children to verify responses. The purpose of the game is to help children practice the addition facts. The numeral cards are mixed and placed face down on the table. Each child, in two rotation turns, draws one card and then another card, placing the cards in front of himself or herself. After all children have two cards, the sums of each child's cards are compared, and the child with the greatest sum wins or takes all of the other cards. Ties are resolved by having each child who is tied draw another card and add that amount to the existing sums. When all of the cards have been used, the winner is the child with the most cards. This game can be extended to "Compare Differences" (the order in which the cards are drawn does not matter), "Compare Products," or "Compare Ratios."

Par 3 Two to four children. A deck of numeral cards with one of the digits 0, 1, 2, 3, 4, 5, 6, 7, 8, or 9 on each of the cards and four cards with each digit. The purposes of the game are to help children practice the basic arithmetical facts and operations, including division; the ideas of renaming numbers; and developing, reading, and writing quantitative expressions. The length of the game can be predetermined by stating the number of plays or "deals" that are to be made. Each child, in turn, deals or distributes the cards for one play. While a child is dealing the cards to the other players, he or she says: "I'm going to deal you each three cards. You can add, subtract, multiply, or divide with the numerals on these cards in any way you know how, as long as you get this answer." At the completion of the statement and after each player has received three cards, the next card from the top of the undealt deck is placed face up on the table. The remaining undealt cards are placed face down on the table. The children do their mental calculations simultaneously and when they have arrived at a way to obtain the answer (the number on the card placed face up on the table), they place the cards they have used face up in the order and ways they have used the cards and wait for the other players to finish. When all players are finished, each, in turn, must explain how he or she arrived at the answer. The object is to use all of the cards. If a player cannot arrive at the answer with the cards he or she has been dealt, that child is allowed to draw up to two more cards, one at a time, from the undealt cards. Single-numeral cards may be used in any manner, as addends, factors, divisors, parts or fractions, exponents, and so on, depending on the children's abilities. Major ideas such as the distributive property of multiplication over addition may be used (not necessarily named or defined). The numeral cards that are not used by a player are placed face down in front of him or her. After each child has explained his or her calculations, that child's individual score for the round is determined by the number of cards that were not used. An incorrect expression indicates that none of the cards were used and all must be counted. Each score is entered on a score-keeping sheet and at the end of the game, the player with the lowest score is the winner. After each round, all of the cards are gathered, remixed, and redealt by another child who repeats the statements of instruction. (An additional requirement for successful plays may be added at a later time. That rule would require that players write the quantitative expression, number sentence or equation, that they have made.) This game is appropriate for many ability levels. Younger children may use only the addition and subtraction ideas. Older and more capable children will also use multiplication, division, fractions, properties of number, exponents, and so on, depending on their proficiencies.

Make an Example (Subtraction) Three or four children. A deck of numeral cards with one of the digits 0, 1, 2, 3, 4, 5, 6, 7, 8, or 9 on each of the cards and four cards with each digit, and a grid or pocket chart in which the cards can be placed. The purpose of the activity or game is to help children practice subtraction

Geometry

Geometry as a particular content area with specific objectives and directed learning activities is of relatively recent concern in elementary mathematics programs. Although some mathematicians and mathematics educators were advocating that simple geometric concepts and skills be included in elementary programs more than twenty-five years ago, the advent of content directed specifically toward geometric entities, the relationships between and among them, and performance skills related to geometric concepts can be traced to the 1950s. Prior to that time, all of the geometric ideas in the elementary school program that went beyond identifying and naming simple plane figures and solids generally were introduced and developed in measurement problems and examples. It was in the decade following 1950 that elementary programs came to be called elementary mathematics programs instead of arithmetic. *Arithmetic*, the most elementary field of mathematics dealing with the procedures for performing computations with numerals, had been virtually the entire elementary program. The inclusion of geometry as a content area and the inclusion of other mathematical ideas pertaining to number and operations were influential in altering the description of modern or contemporary programs to elementary mathematics. Unfortunately, the term *arithmetic* might well be used to describe the content and instructional efforts in many contemporary elementary classrooms.

ideas. The object of the activity or game is for the participants to make a subtraction example, and the size of the example is predetermined. For example, no numeral in the subtraction example to be made can be "longer" than five digits. The grid or pocket chart is placed on the table. One child mixes the cards and deals seven cards to each participant. Each participant, in turn, tries to place one of his or her numeral cards in the grid in order to make a correct subtraction example or exercise complete with minuend, subtrahend, and difference (Figure 9.10). Only the cards that children have been dealt are to be used, but a variation in the game may require that when a play cannot be made, one card must be taken from the undealt cards. If possible, that card can be played at that turn. The intent is for each child to play as many cards as possible, leaving as few in his or her hand as possible. When no child can play a card, the activity or game is ended. The number of cards each child has remaining is counted, and the activity is repeated. Participants may be asked to copy the example or exercise and complete it if it is unfinished. Keeping score of the cards that children have remaining after each example is made will make the activity more gamelike. This activity can be extended to making addition, multiplication, and division examples with whole numbers and with decimal fractions.

What You Roll Is What You Do (Multiplication and Division) Two to four children. Play money in powers of 10 ($1, $10, $100, $1000), a numeral cube with the digits 2, 3, 4, 5, 6, and 7 on the six faces, and an operational cube with three multiplication signs and three division signs on the six faces. The purpose of the activity or game is to help children practice multiplication and division by a one-digit numeral as well as addition and subtraction. One child is the "banker" and arranges the denominations of bills in appropriate piles. Each other participant is given two $100 bills. Each participant, in turn, rolls both the numeral cube and the sign cube. The sign and the numeral describe the "negotiation" that is to be conducted with the banker. For example, if a ⊠ and a ③ are rolled, that child's money is to be tripled, $3 \times N = \square$. The needed money is to be obtained from the banker. If a ④ and a ⊡ are rolled, the child is to divide his or her money into four equal parts, keep one part, and give the other three parts to the banker. Figure 9.11 shows how each child should record his or her operations. (When dividing, any remainder is also to be returned to

Figure 9.10

Figure 9.11

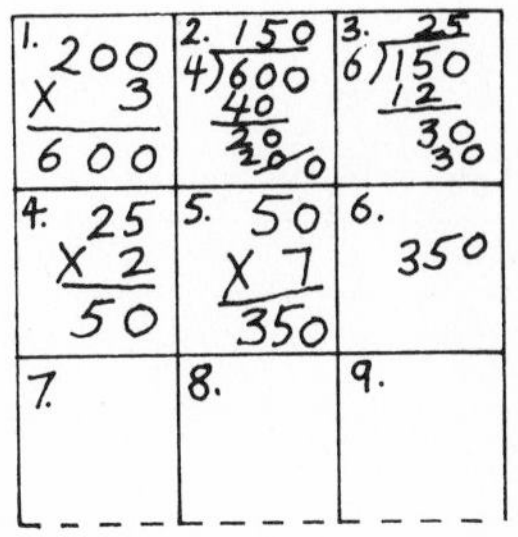

the banker.) The banker should also keep a record of each transaction indicating the total amount of money in the bank. A predetermined number of plays for each participant can determine the length of the activity or game. At the end of that number of plays, the participant with the most money wins the game, and amounts of money must be in accord with the records.

Find Part of a Part (Common Fractions)   One or more children. Sheets of paper to be folded and two fractional numeral cubes with numerals such as 1/2, 1/3, 2/3, 1/4, 3/4, 1/6, 5/6, 1/8, 3/8, and 5/8 on the faces of the cubes. One of the fraction-numeral cubes is rolled and a sheet of paper is folded to show the part or parts named on the cube. That amount is then shaded or colored in one way. The piece of paper is then unfolded. Then the second fraction numeral cube is rolled and the paper is again folded (preferably perpendicular to the first foldings) to show the second amount named. That amount is shaded or colored in another way over the first shading or coloring. Then the piece of paper is unfolded to find the amount of the part of a part. Figure 9.12 pictures a situation in which the fraction numerals 2/3 and 3/4 were rolled. (The order of rolling will not change the picture.) The task is to name the part of a part with a common-fraction numeral. If the piece of paper is considered 1, how large is each small folded part? How many of these small parts have been shaded twice? The activity can be repeated by using a new sheet of paper each time. If an organized record of a series of such activities is kept, a procedure can be developed for solving such problems without folding paper. A similar type of activity, in which children make drawings on squared paper, can be used to find a fractional part of a fractional part with decimal fractions.

Figure 9.12

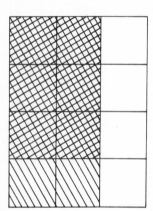

Suggested Activities

1. Examine a commercially produced elementary mathematics textbook series and/or the accompanying teachers' manuals to ascertain the following information:
   a. How are the basic arithmetical facts to be introduced, developed, and practiced with children in that particular program?
   b. At what levels and how are the operations of addition, subtraction, multiplication, and division with whole numbers sequenced throughout the program?
   c. At what levels and how are the computational operations with common fractions sequenced in the program?
   d. At what levels and how are the computational operations with decimal-fraction numerals sequenced in the program?
   e. How are pictured, structured, and word problems utilized in regard to the computational operations?
   f. When, how, and what verification procedures for the computational operations are suggested and used?
2. Examine the rules and procedures for one or more commercially produced children's table games for their possible uses in practicing the arithmetical facts and the computational operations.
3. Construct a ring toss game having more than one peg and more than one ring. Consider assigning (and attaching) different numerical values to each of the pegs and different numerical values to each of the rings. Devise rules and procedures for ring toss games to practice addition, subtraction, multiplication, and division.
4. Teach a small group of adults one of the games described in "Examples of Learning Experiences." ("Par 3" is the most challenging.)

Chap

ideas. The object of the activity or game is for the participants to make a subtraction example, and the size of the example is predetermined. For example, no numeral in the subtraction example to be made can be "longer" than five digits. The grid or pocket chart is placed on the table. One child mixes the cards and deals seven cards to each participant. Each participant, in turn, tries to place one of his or her numeral cards in the grid in order to make a correct subtraction example or exercise complete with minuend, subtrahend, and difference (Figure 9.10). Only the cards that children have been dealt are to be used, but a variation in the game may require that when a play cannot be made, one card must be taken from the undealt cards. If possible, that card can be played at that turn. The intent is for each child to play as many cards as possible, leaving as few in his or her hand as possible. When no child can play a card, the activity or game is ended. The number of cards each child has remaining is counted, and the activity is repeated. Participants may be asked to copy the example or exercise and complete it if it is unfinished. Keeping score of the cards that children have remaining after each example is made will make the activity more gamelike. This activity can be extended to making addition, multiplication, and division examples with whole numbers and with decimal fractions.

Figure 9.10

What You Roll Is What You Do (Multiplication and Division) Two to four children. Play money in powers of 10 ($1, $10, $100, $1000), a numeral cube with the digits 2, 3, 4, 5, 6, and 7 on the six faces, and an operational cube with three multiplication signs and three division signs on the six faces. The purpose of the activity or game is to help children practice multiplication and division by a one-digit numeral as well as addition and subtraction. One child is the "banker" and arranges the denominations of bills in appropriate piles. Each other participant is given two $100 bills. Each participant, in turn, rolls both the numeral cube and the sign cube. The sign and the numeral describe the "negotiation" that is to be conducted with the banker. For example, if a $\boxed{\times}$ and a $\boxed{3}$ are rolled, that child's money is to be tripled, $3 \times N = \square$. The needed money is to be obtained from the banker. If a $\boxed{4}$ and a $\boxed{\div}$ are rolled, the child is to divide his or her money into four equal parts, keep one part, and give the other three parts to the banker. Figure 9.11 shows how each child should record his or her operations. (When dividing, any remainder is also to be returned to

Figure 9.11

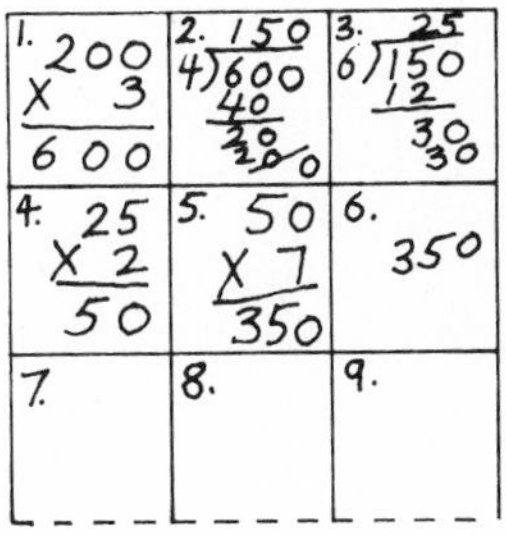

the banker.) The banker should also keep a record of each transaction indicating the total amount of money in the bank. A predetermined number of plays for each participant can determine the length of the activity or game. At the end of that number of plays, the participant with the most money wins the game, and amounts of money must be in accord with the records.

Find Part of a Part (Common Fractions) One or more children. Sheets of paper to be folded and two fractional numeral cubes with numerals such as 1/2, 1/3, 2/3, 1/4, 3/4, 1/6, 5/6, 1/8, 3/8, and 5/8 on the faces of the cubes. One of the fraction-numeral cubes is rolled and a sheet of paper is folded to show the part or parts named on the cube. That amount is then shaded or colored in one way. The piece of paper is then unfolded. Then the second fraction numeral cube is rolled and the paper is again folded (preferably perpendicular to the first foldings) to show the second amount named. That amount is shaded or colored in another way over the first shading or coloring. Then the piece of paper is unfolded to find the amount of the part of a part. Figure 9.12 pictures a situation in which the fraction numerals 2/3 and 3/4 were rolled. (The order of rolling will not change the picture.) The task is to name the part of a part with a common-fraction numeral. If the piece of paper is considered 1, how large is each small folded part? How many of these small parts have been shaded twice? The activity can be repeated by using a new sheet of paper each time. If an organized record of a series of such activities is kept, a procedure can be developed for solving such problems without folding paper. A similar type of activity, in which children make drawings on squared paper, can be used to find a fractional part of a fractional part with decimal fractions.

Figure 9.12

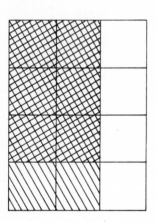

Suggested Activities

1. Examine a commercially produced elementary mathematics textbook series and/or the accompanying teachers' manuals to ascertain the following information:
   a. How are the basic arithmetical facts to be introduced, developed, and practiced with children in that particular program?

b. At what levels and how are the operations of addition, sub-traction, multiplication, and division with whole numbers sequenced throughout the program?

c. At what levels and how are the computational operations with common fractions sequenced in the program?

d. At what levels and how are the computational operations with decimal-fraction numerals sequenced in the program?

e. How are pictured, structured, and word problems utilized in regard to the computational operations?

f. When, how, and what verification procedures for the com-putational operations are suggested and used?

2. Examine the rules and procedures for one or more commer-cially produced children's table games for their possible uses in practicing the arithmetical facts and the computational operations.

3. Construct a ring toss game having more than one peg and more than one ring. Consider assigning (and attaching) different numerical values to each of the pegs and different numerical values to each of the rings. Devise rules and procedures for ring toss games to practice addition, subtraction, multiplica-tion, and division.

4. Teach a small group of adults one of the games described in "Examples of Learning Experiences." ("Par 3" is the most challenging.)

Chapter 10

Geometry

Geometry as a particular content area with specific objectives and directed learning activities is of relatively recent concern in elementary mathematics programs. Although some mathematicians and mathematics educators were advocating that simple geometric concepts and skills be included in elementary programs more than twenty-five years ago, the advent of content directed specifically toward geometric entities, the relationships between and among them, and performance skills related to geometric concepts can be traced to the 1950s. Prior to that time, all of the geometric ideas in the elementary school program that went beyond identifying and naming simple plane figures and solids generally were introduced and developed in measurement problems and examples. It was in the decade following 1950 that elementary programs came to be called elementary mathematics programs instead of arithmetic. *Arithmetic*, the most elementary field of mathematics dealing with the procedures for performing computations with numerals, had been virtually the entire elementary program. The inclusion of geometry as a content area and the inclusion of other mathematical ideas pertaining to number and operations were influential in altering the description of modern or contemporary programs to elementary mathematics. Unfortunately, the term *arithmetic* might well be used to describe the content and instructional efforts in many contemporary elementary classrooms.

Importance of the Area

Several reasons for including geometric concepts and performance skill activities in the elementary mathematics program have appeared in the professional literature of mathematics educators. Most of those arguments continue to be valid. In the late 1950s, there was a great concern that the schools of this country were not producing a sufficient number of well-prepared mathematicians and scientists. This criticism was based on the scientific achievements of other countries, and evidence from studies indicating superior performances in mathematics achievement tests by students in other countries was used then and later to support the allegation. Suggestions for alleviating the deficiencies recommended better mathematical preparation of children in the elementary and secondary schools to allow for more intensive and exhaustive studies of mathematics at higher levels. Those suggestions called for the addition of new content to both elementary and secondary mathematics programs and the earlier introduction and development of concepts and skills. The allegation that an insufficient number of well-prepared mathematicians and scientists are emerging from colleges and universities might be repudiated today, but the arguments are still being made for including content of geometry and other major mathematical ideas and for introducing concepts and performance skills earlier in the program.

Rationale for Inclusion

Evidence from research studies and the actual performances of children in elementary mathematics programs have indicated that children can acquire and use geometric concepts and skills. However, the revelation that children are capable of assimilating or acquiring mathematical concepts or skills (or concepts and skills in other areas) is not sufficient reason to incorporate that content into the elementary program. To be an appropriate part of the instructional program, concepts and skills should be applicable by children to problem situations immediately and in the future, should be the foundations or prerequisites for later studies of importance, and should be an integral part of the structure of mathematical ideas that children are to develop. Elementary geometric concepts and skills can and should meet these criteria. Many of the problems that children encounter in the world outside of school involve geometric structures or entities with and without dimension descriptions. The ideas and skills of geometry to be introduced and spirally developed in the elementary program are foundations and prerequisites for mathematical concepts to be studied at higher levels, and elementary geometric concepts and skills can be related to and associated with other mathematical ideas as children develop their own structures of mathematical ideas.

Other evidence from research studies and observations of children in early classroom activities dealing with geometric ideas suggest another reason for including geometry as a content area in the elementary mathematics program. Preschool experiences, backgrounds, socioeconomic conditions, language development, and the like, appear to be more highly related to young children's in-school achievements with concepts and skills pertaining to number and operations on number than they are to the acquisition of elementary geometric ideas. Young children can acquire and use introductory ideas and skills of geometry even though they are having difficulties with the concepts and skills of number and operations on number. Success in the acquisition and use of simple geometric ideas may help children develop better or more desirable self-concepts, attitudes toward school in general, and attitudes toward the study of elementary mathematics. Children's successes with the study of simple geometric ideas can be redirected toward the study of other mathematical concepts and skills.

Differing Directions

Over the past several decades, geometry as a content area in elementary mathematics programs has evolved in several directions. Differences in objectives or goals, content, instructional materials, and instructional approaches and procedures have been and continue to be evident or implied in the differences in form and substance of the content materials that were and that continue to be published. As with other curricular modifications and developments in elementary mathematics, there was an early emphasis on precision in the use of language and exactness in children's learning experiences dealing with geometric ideas. In later developments, attention to preciseness in language and exactness was redirected toward emphasis on major ideas as they might be expressed or described in the language of children. Some earlier efforts treated geometry as a supplementary topic for "enrichment" to be interjected into the program activities if time and other conditions permitted. The "other conditions" sometimes included previous adequate achievement by children with the arithmetical aspects of the program. The treatment of geometry as a supplementary or enrichment topic, in which geometric activities were attached to units or chapters in printed materials dealing with other mathematical concepts and skills or as isolated experiences, suggested to classroom teachers and children that geometry was not an integral part of the elementary mathematics program. *Integral aspects* of a program are intended for all children in accordance with their individual capabilities and with regard to their development of an integrated, accurate, and as complete as possible structure of mathematical ideas and skills. As indicated by printed materials and other approaches, more recent program developments consider and treat elementary geometric concepts and skills as an integral part of the elementary mathematics program.

Content directed toward geometric ideas, instructional materials, and instructional approaches and procedures in contemporary elementary mathematics programs continues to vary. Obviously, those variations suggest different achievement objectives for children. Some programs are limited, for the most part, to the introduction and development of vocabulary and to identification and definition of geometric entities in an abstract manner. Other programs extend the development of vocabulary, identification, and definition to paper-and-pencil drawings and constructions. Learning experiences and activities in some programs are primarily based on measurement problems involving geometric entities. In many instances, children's seeing, understanding, and doing is restricted to using two-dimensional pictures and drawings. In another approach, concepts and skills of geometry are built on the teacher's and children's use of physical object models and the way they see the characteristics of those models in the real world. If the content area of geometry is to be an integral part of the elementary mathematics program, the introduction and development of geometric concepts and performance skills should fit in with the educational principles that guide and direct the entire program.

Nature of Elementary Geometry

Geometry in the elementary school program is not the geometry that was formerly taught at the upper or secondary school levels. That geometry was the formal study of primarily abstract definitions, axioms, theorems, and proofs, including paper-and-pencil constructions. *Formal geometry* may be defined as the study of points in space and the subsets of points in space or the study of spacial relationships. It may also be defined as the branch or field of mathematics in which the properties of figures in space are deduced from their defining conditions by means of assumed properties of space. Thus, the elements to be dealt with in the formal study of geometry are abstract entities or things. The elements to be dealt with and studied by children in the field of arithmetic are numbers and numerals, which can be represented with physical object models for number. The characteristics of numbers and numerals, the relationships that exist within and between numbers and numerals, and the operations that can be performed on numbers and numerals can be introduced and developed for study by children with physical object models. Similarly, the elements of geometry to be dealt with and studied by children are abstract entities, which can be represented by physical object models for those entities. Names, attributes, and characteristics of those entities; the relationships that exist within and among them; and the operations that can be performed in regard to those entities—all can be introduced and developed for children's study at the elementary level with physical object models. Also, the applications of arithmetical ideas to descriptions of geometric entities and to quantitative problems involving geometric entities can be illustrated with models and pictures of models for those entities.

Classification of Entities

The entities of geometry may be classified in regard to the characteristic of dimension. The basic element of arithmetic might be described as a single object or "one." All of the other elements,

Figure 10.1

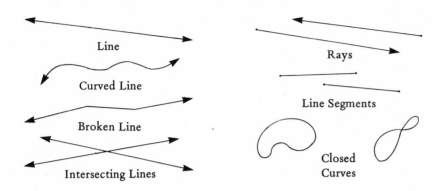

numbers and numerals, are described, defined, and utilized in relation to the basic element, *one*. The basic element of geometry is a *point*, and all of the other elements, geometric configurations, are made up of points and are described and defined in relation to that basic element. A *point* has no (0) dimensions. Single points have no length, no width, no depth or height, only describable positions. A *line* may be thought of as the union of a set of points in which each point "touches" only two other points. Lines and portions of lines, as illustrated and named in Figure 10.1, have only one dimension—length. Remember that the illustrations are not abstract geometric lines, only drawings. Each drawing shows a line within one plane of points, which can be thought of as a flat surface of points. Since points have no dimensions, each line or portion of a line (a ray or a line segment) may be considered to contain an infinite number of points. Also, since geometric points cannot be seen, geometric lines cannot be seen. Therefore, it is important that young children see drawings and models used to illustrate points, lines, and other geometric configurations, which are made up of or defined by points and line segments.

Common two-dimensional or plane figures are illustrated in Figure 10.2. Those figures may be thought of as having two dimensions: length or height, and width. Each of the figures is comprised of portions of lines or line segments, and only the line segments or those points in the line segments are a part of the figures. The points in the space bounded by the line segments are not a part of the figure. The points in the line segments of

Figure 10.2

Figure 10.3

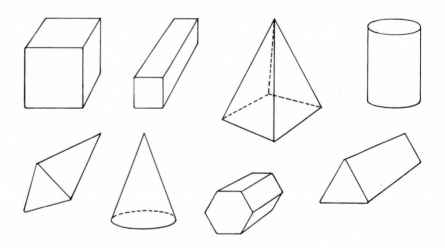

each figure are in one plane of points, thus, *plane figures*.

Geometric *solids* have three dimensions. Those three dimensions can be given various names, but they can generally be thought of as length, width, and height. The solid is made up of all of the points within the space bounded by portions of planes that are defined by line segments and points. Other than spheres, cylinders, and cones, virtually all of the geometric solids that children encounter in the elementary mathematics program have edges that can be described as line segments and faces or surfaces that can be defined as regions or portions of planes. For example, a rectangular solid has surfaces that are all rectangular regions. Since geometric solids are made up of points, the "solids" cannot be seen or touched. However, as with plane figures, there are many real-life models that can be used to help children see and understand the characteristics of geometric solids and the relationships that exist within and among those geometric configurations (see Figure 10.3).

Basic Needs
It may be difficult to convince some critics of elementary mathematics programs, whether they be laypersons or professional educators, that elementary geometric concepts and performance skills should be basic elements of the elementary mathematics program. Yet, those same critics will be quick to point out that many children emerging from the elementary program are poorly prepared both for later studies and for solving problems in the real world or for entry into semiskilled or skilled vocations or professions. Many of those requirements or performance skills are related to geometric concepts and problems involving geometric configurations. If the term *basic* is used to refer to fundamental ideas and skills, foundations on which necessary problem-solving concepts and skills are to be built, then the rudiments of geometry should be basic elements of the elementary mathematics program.

The content area of geometry in an active laboratory-type elementary mathematics program involves the study of real things, their characteristics, their internal relationships, and their relationships to other things. The things are models or representations of geometric configurations, real objects that have the characteristics of abstract geometric entities. The general goal of elementary mathematics programs pertaining to developing children's familiarity with the main ideas of geometry implies that children learn to communicate meaningfully about geometric elements or entities, use geometric ideas in the performance skills of construction, and apply those ideas and skills in problem-solving situations. Some of those problems will not require the use of numerical information or computational operations for solution. Solving quantitative problems that involve geometric entities and concepts will call for the use of arithmetical and measurement concepts and performance skills.

Communication Skills

In an active laboratory approach, children's communication skills—both oral and written, including the language needed to name, describe, and compare geometric entities—are developed through references to physical object models. Drawings are employed only after children can realize that those drawings represent real situations. Early utilization of models for geometric entities and continued reference to them throughout the program provide children with a solid foundation on which to build concepts pertaining to the major ideas or themes of the content area. Their acquisition and utilization of performance skills through participation in learning activities and games and in construction projects can be meaningfully associated with attributes and characteristics visible in the models. If a unit-of-content approach is employed in the instructional procedures, each unit of study should include opportunities for children to acquire and discuss ideas and skills in introductory and developmental activities involving the uses of models, in construction of two- and three-dimensional projects, in paper-and-pencil drawings or constructions, in structured or contrived problems, in problems derived from the in-school and out-of-school environments, and in games involving geometric ideas and skills. Providing a wide variety of learning activities, projects, and games with a wide range of performance expectations will allow individual children to participate at their own ability levels. The variety and range of learning experiences being conducted at the same time with individuals or small groups of children also will allow children to recognize the extent of performance expectations.

Major Ideas or Content Themes

The major ideas or themes of the content area of geometry are not built on or directly related to the major ideas or themes of the previously described content areas. Concepts, ideas, and performance skills of those areas are not prerequisites for the introduction and development of the major ideas or themes and the associated performance skills of geometry. Simple numerical ideas may be used to describe the characteristics of geometric entities (triangles have only *three* angles or "corners"; quadrilaterals have *four* sides; and so on), but the number ideas are quite simple. Operations, either with objects or with numerals, are applied only to quantitative problem situations involving geometric entities, and these primarily pertain to *measurement* situations. Simple counting and crude comparisons of measurement will be used by children when they are dealing with the following major ideas.

The major ideas or content themes of *geometry* pertain to the relationships that may exist between two or more component parts *within* one geometric entity, to the relationships that may exist *between* two or more component parts of two or more geometric entities, and to the relationships that may exist *between* two or more geometric entities. Using the language of children to express or describe these relationships when they are being introduced and developed is of utmost importance if they are to have meaning for children. Teachers can use—and should accept—phrases such as "the same shape and the same size" for congruence; "the same shape but different sizes" for similarity; "the same on both sides" for symmetry; "run into each other" for intersect; "never run into each other" for parallel; "corner" for angle and "square corner" for right angle; and a "make square corners" for perpendicular. Precise terminology and definitions can and should be introduced in context or in the actions of learning experiences by the teacher. Children will then begin to use the words and definitions they hear with meaning and understanding. Descriptions of the following major ideas or themes in the content area of geometry attempt to integrate the language of children and technical terms.

Some geometric entities are exactly the same size and the same shape as other geometric entities (congruence).

Although the first geometric entities to be introduced in some elementary mathematics programs may be points and lines, and although all geometric points are the "same size and shape" as all other geometric points and all straight lines are the same size and shape as all other straight lines, this major idea might be better introduced with models of two-dimensional plane figures or with three-dimensional geometric solids. A brief description of three introductory learning activities directed toward this idea or theme follows:

1. A pegboard, pegs or golf tees, and loops of rubber string are used as parts of a model for two-dimensional plane figures. The teacher or a child "builds" several different triangles, quadrilaterals, or other figures on the pegboard using the pegs or tees for points (vertices) and the rubber string for sides. Another child or small group of children is then directed to construct figures that are the same size and the same shape. The task can be made more difficult by suggesting that the constructed figures be "turned in different directions."

2. A small group of children is given a collection of figures cut from heavy paper or cardboard. The cut-out shapes are of a single variety (triangles, quadrilaterals, or pentagons, for example). Some of the figures are different shapes. Some of the figures are exactly the same size and the same shape; some of the figures are proportionately the same shape but different sizes; and some of the figures are the same sizes but different shapes. The children are directed to put those figures that have exactly the same shape and the same size into groups.

3. A small group of children is given a collection of three-dimensional solids or models for geometric solids. The collection is composed of objects similar to those in the preceding activity and the children are given a similar direction.

In each of the activities, techniques for making the physical comparisons should be developed and discussed by children. The major idea can then be spirally developed through similar activities with other geometric entities. Developmental and practice learning experiences will involve games and construction projects. Construction projects will include both physical representations and paper-and-pencil drawings. In addition to constructions on the pegboard, physical representations can be made from soda straws, sticks, strips of plastic, or heavy paper along with appropriate construction materials and tools. With young children, templates and cutouts should be among the first tools used to measure and make congruent cut-out shapes and three-dimensional solids. The uses of a straightedge and a compass for constructions should be delayed until children have the psychomotor skills to handle those tools. As the major idea is being developed, children should be encouraged to generalize the minimum and maximum criteria for establishing the relationship of congruence with different types of geometric configurations. As with the terms and phrases to be used with the other major ideas or themes of geometry, vocabulary is expanded and extended during the learning experiences within one classroom and throughout the program. There are many "new" terms to be dealt with in the area of geometry, including names of the entities, names of the parts of entities, and phrases indicating relationships. However, many children are eager to learn the terminology because it is new and different. When the new vocabulary is introduced and used with real objects and activities, it is not difficult for children to acquire. Good judgment on the part of the teacher should be applied to selecting and emphasizing the terminology that children will be encouraged to learn and use.

Some geometric entities are different sizes, but proportionately the same shape as other geometric entities (similarity).

Congruence between two or more geometric entities can be considered a unique circumstance of similarity in that the relational proportions are all one-to-one. The introduction of similarity to young children is similar in manner to the introduction of the idea of congruence. The same three types of activities can be employed, and only the direction of the task will be changed. For this major idea or theme, children will be asked to construct or find figures or shapes that are the same shape but different sizes. However, ascertaining similarity with three-dimensional shapes is more difficult for children (and adults) than determining whether similarity exists between two-dimensional figures. Therefore, it would be appropriate for activities pertaining to possible similarity between geometric solids to follow activities involving similarity with two-dimensional figures. The idea of proportionality is not emphasized or discussed in the introductory activities. To handle the idea of proportionality, children must be familiar with the concepts and associated skills of equivalent fractions or equivalent ratios. *Proportionality* of similar two-dimensional figures or shapes pertains to the relationships between corresponding sides or ascertaining proportionality between corresponding sides of geometric entities. Instead, children should be helped to employ a procedure in which the corners or angles of the plane figures are compared. With the exception of rectangles, when two plane figures have the same number of angles (or vertices) and the corresponding angles of the two figures are the same size, the two figures are similar. To find out if two corresponding angles are equal, young children may place one of the angles adjacent to or on top of the other, employ a template or cut-out angle or figure, or utilize a sheet of paper folded to the size of one of the angles. At later levels, they will be taught to use the common and familiar tools of geometry—the compass and protractor—to perform these comparisons. Spiral development of this major idea or theme is also similar to that of the idea of congruence and to the following major ideas and themes. Continued activities, games, and construction projects are directed toward seeing and understanding similarity in a full range of geometric entities. Constructions begin with simple tools and materials and proceed to the use of tools and materials requiring greater dexterity. As children acquire other mathematical concepts and skills in areas of numeration and notation, measurement, and operations on number using numerals, those concepts and skills are to be utilized, related to, and integrated with the concepts and skills of geometry in problem situations. For example, making scale drawings can be introduced to children as an application of similarity after the ideas of similarity have been developed in other learning activities and after children have acquired some basic measurement ideas and skills. Ascertaining the relationship of similarity through determining the equal proportionality of sides should occur after children have demonstrated proficiency with the idea of similarity using angles as the elements of the entities to be compared, after they have acquired simple measurement ideas and skills, and after they have dealt with equivalent fractions and equivalent ratios. At each level of development, children should attempt to ascertain the minimum and maximum conditions for establishing the relationship of similarity with different types of geometric configurations. At later levels, those conditions should also be directed toward the relationships between corresponding sides and surfaces.

A geometric entity may have characteristics such that there is a correspondence in size, form, and arrangement of parts on opposite sides of a point, line, or plane (symmetry).

This idea might best be introduced with activities and procedures that do not involve specific geometric entities or models for geometric entities. Correspondence of parts of geometric entities in size, form, or arrangement (symmetry) on opposite sides of a point is not the easiest of these three related ideas for children to see and understand. The only two-dimensional or plane figure in which the parts are symmetrical around a point is a circle. In children's earliest experiences with circles, that point may be difficult for them to locate even though it is the center of the circle. Of course, the location of the point that is the same distance from all of the points in a circle can be approximated when drawings of circles are used. Initially, the drawings of circles will be made by using templates or cutouts of circles. When those tools are employed, the centers of the circles are not located. When children are capable of using a compass to draw pictures of circles, the centers of the circles are evident and the relationship of the center to all points in the circles can be more precisely established. When either models or drawings of three-dimensional shapes are used, the location of a point of symmetry must be imagined. Spheres are the only three-dimensional shapes in which there is a correspondence of parts in size, form, and arrangement on opposite sides of a point. Of course, children can discuss, imagine, and predict where the point of symmetry for spheres will be, but those activities are abstract in nature. For those reasons, the idea of symmetry around a point might best be delayed until after the ideas of symmetry on opposite sides of a straight line and symmetry on opposite sides of a plane are introduced and developed.

The idea of symmetry on opposite sides of a line can be introduced with activities utilizing folded sheets of paper. By making one straight fold in a sheet of paper and then opening the folded sheet, children can see that the crease represents part of a straight line. Construction activities can then follow with the directions that the "pictures" to be drawn or made must be the same on opposite sides of the crease. The sheets of paper are then refolded on the same crease and part of a picture is drawn with the crease as one edge as in Figure 10.4. After children have made drawings of "one-half" of their pictures, they may be directed to keep the sheet of paper folded and cut out their pictures. (The teacher may actually do this by folding a sheet of paper, drawing, and cutting with a scissors.) Children may then show their pictures and point out the line of symmetry. That line may be made more evident by marking over the crease using a straightedge and a marking device. Lines of symmetry can then be extended in

Figure 10.4

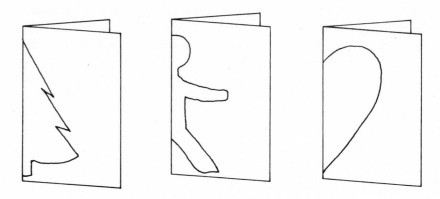

Figure 10.5

activities that require children to draw those lines on various pictures, including pictures of two-dimensional geometric entities (see Figure 10.5). The same picture may have several different lines of symmetry. After those activities, children may be involved in project activities in which they construct or draw two-dimensional geometric entities and indicate the lines of symmetry.

Symmetry on opposite sides of a plane may be introduced with real items such as oranges, candy bars, or pieces of clay that resemble three-dimensional geometric entities, as long as one realizes that these items are not very precise models. The idea is to "slice" the items with a sheet of points (the cutting edge of a knife) so that the size and form of the two pieces are as identical as possible on opposite sides of the slice. The idea may then be extended to determining the imagined plane of points that would separate models for three-dimensional geometric entities into two symmetrical parts. As with the other major ideas, each level of development should involve children in establishing the minimum and maximum conditions for finding the points, lines, and planes of symmetry.

Two geometric entities may share a common element or elements (intersection).

Lines in the same plane of points may intersect, and the common shared element is a point. Two-dimensional figures in the same plane of points may share or have a common point or have a common line segment as a side or as part of a side. Two-dimensional figures in the same plane of points may also intersect and share two or more common points. When those common points are joined with line segments, other two-dimensional figures are constructed. Of course, two-dimensional figures that lie in different planes of points may also intersect in the same manner. Two different planes of points may intersect, and the common shared element is a line of points. Two three-dimensional geometric entities may intersect so that they share either a common point, a common line segment, a common plane surface of points, or a common "solid" set of points. The drawings in Figure 10.6 illustrate some of these possible intersections. This major idea is prerequisite to the two following major ideas or themes, which pertain to nonintersection and a specific case of intersection, respectively. The spiral development of this theme or idea should be related to the complexity of the geometric entities that intersect to share a common element or elements. Introduction of the idea should utilize activities with models, constructions, and drawings of the intersections of one-dimensional geometric entities (lines, rays, and line segments). These activities should provide opportunities for children to see and

Figure 10.6 *Possible Intersections*

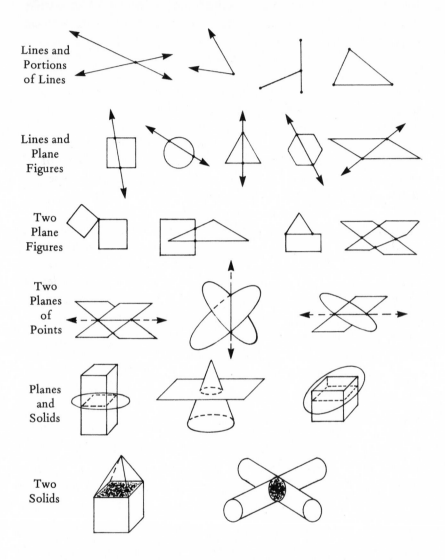

discuss the nature of the intersections and the corners or angles that are formed by the intersections. The extent to which these ideas (opposite angles and adjacent angles, for example) are developed depends on the interests and capabilities of the children and the specific goals of the program. Study of the nature of intersections of a two-dimensional entity (plane figures) with a one dimensional entity (lines); intersections of two-dimensional entities with two-dimensional entities; and intersections of a one-dimensional, two-dimensional, and three-dimensional entities with three-dimensional entities (geometric solids) should follow in a logical sequential manner.

Two geometric entities that lie in the same plane of points, two planes of points, or two geometric entities that lie in different planes of points may never intersect (parallelism).

As with the major idea of intersection, the spiral development of this content theme should be related to the complexity of the geometric entities involved. Physical object models (rope and string), constructions, and drawings of lines in the same plane of points that would never intersect no matter how far they are extended can be used in introductory activities. As with other geometric configurations, a search for parallel lines or line segments can be made within the classroom in an effort to help children see geometric ideas in the real world. The idea of parallelism can then be extended to application in two-dimensional plane figures in looking at the relationships between opposite sides of those figures. Again, models, constructions, and drawings may be used in learning experiences. After concepts and skills pertaining to parallelism of the line segments that form opposite sides of two-dimensional plane figures have been developed with children, the idea may be extended to opposite plane surfaces or regions of geometric solids.

Two geometric entities that lie in the same plane of points, two planes of points, or two geometric entities that lie in different planes of points may intersect such that square corners (right angles) are formed (perpendicularity).

A prerequisite to the development of this major idea or theme is the concept of a square corner or right angle. The term *right angle* may be introduced and utilized if the term *angle* has been used in previous geometric learning experiences or activities. The concept of right angle either may be introduced, developed, and practiced prior to the introduction of the idea of perpendicularity or simultaneously with its introduction. The nature of a square corner or right angle may be introduced prior to the idea of perpendicularity of interesting geometric entities by references to the types of corners that exist in the classroom and objects in the classroom. The majority of those corners probably will be square corners or "rounded" square corners. Children can use the corners of a sheet of paper or a book as models of a square corner to ascertain whether other corners or angles are square corners or right angles. Children might also use a simple carpenter's square or learn how to make a model for a square corner by folding a piece of paper, which need not have an existing square corner. The model can be made by folding any sheet of paper to make a crease or straight edge and then folding that straight edge back on itself. The result will be a folded square corner, which can be used as a model with which to compare other corners or angles. (Later that model can be used in crude measurements of angles to ascertain whether the measurements of angles are less than or greater than a right angle. Also, by folding the model into two equal parts, then four equal parts, then eight equal parts, a crude type of protractor is developed; angles can be crudely measured, and the idea of *degree* as the unit for measuring angles might be more meaningfully developed.)

The spiral development of the idea of perpendicularity is similar in stages of complexity to spiral development of the idea of parallelism. Physical object models, constructions, and drawings of lines, plane figures, and geometric solids are used sequentially. As each type of geometric entity is considered, attention is given to the possibilities of intersections of the various parts or components being perpendicular. Attributes and characteristics of intersecting lines and line segments, plane figures, and geometric solids are described in terms of perpendicularity (and parallelism) when possible. Later, attention should be given to the combinations of corners or to the sums of angles. Initially, those combinations or sums need not involve numerical information, merely references to the types of corners or angles that are formed by the combinations or sums.

In an active laboratory-type elementary mathematics program, concepts and skills are to be introduced to and developed with children in a unified, related structure of mathematical ideas by emphasizing the preceding major ideas or content themes and the relationships of those ideas to each other. The instructional procedures are informal in nature and based on the use of models and other representations in common classroom learning experiences and activities. The major ideas are introduced to children early in the school program and developed in a spiral manner. Spiral development in complexity involves dealing with the ideas sequentially in relation to one type of geometric entity and then applying the ideas to other geometric entities. Children become more powerful with each idea as it is woven into increasingly difficult or complex tasks and as it is related to concepts and skills in other content areas. In every instance, children have acquired the concepts of the major ideas and the associated skills only to the extent that they can perform or demonstrate those concepts and skills in directed tasks. Mere repetition of names, definitions, and relationships orally or in writing is not a true indication of strength in the area.

Performance Skills

The performance expectations for children in this content area may be categorized as vocabulary or communication skills, classification skills, comparison skills, and construction skills. The classifications or categories of skills are not unrelated to each other and may need to be applied in the same learning experiences or activities. Vocabulary or communication skills are necessary when tasks involve classification, comparison, or construction of geometric entities. Construction skills will be applied to instructional activities or tasks that pertain to classifications of geometric entities and to learning activities that involve making comparisons between geometric entities. Classification skills will be involved initially in comparison activities because the comparisons to be made generally will entail geometric entities from the same classification.

Communication Skills

In their study of geometry in the elementary mathematics program, children will encounter a large number of "new" terms or words, which they may or may not have heard used correctly in their previous in-school and out-of-school experiences. Those terms, words, or phrases include not only the names for geometric entities but also words or phrases used to describe relationships between geometric entities. The extent to which terminology is introduced and applied depends on the learning opportunities that are presented to children, the nature of the communication utilized in those learning experiences, and the individual interests and capabilities of children. As emphasized earlier, the development of communication skills should not be restricted to reading and writing symbols. Oral—listening and speaking—skills are developed first. A listing of the possible terms to be introduced and utilized in a spirally developed program follows. The order of the listing does not imply an order for their introduction and use.

Point	Triangle	Pentagon
Line	Right triangle	Hexagon
Ray	Isosceles triangle	Octagon
Line segment	Equilateral triangle	Polygon
Broken line	Obtuse triangle	Regular
Curved line	Scalene triangle	
Open curve		Cube
Closed curve	Quadrilateral	Rectangular solid
	Rectangle	Prism
Angle	Square	Triangular prism
Right angle	Parallelogram	Pyramid
Acute angle	Irregular	Cylinder
Obtuse angle		Cone
Straight angle	Circle	Sphere
Vertex	Circumference	
	Diameter	Intersect
	Radius	Congruent
	Chord	Similar
	Arc	Symmetrical
		Parallel
		Perpendicular

Classification Skills

Although one-dimensional geometric entities may be classified (straight lines may be classified as horizontal, vertical, or oblique), in most elementary mathematics programs they are merely named in accordance with their attributes or characteristics. Similarly, angles are named and not really classified in accordance with their sizes: angles that are less than a right angle (acute), right angles, angles that are larger than a right angle (obtuse), and straight angles. In the elementary program, very little is done with classification of three-dimensional geometric entities. General names are associated with those forms in accordance with their attributes and characteristics. The achievement expectations for children in regard to classification skills primarily pertain to two-dimensional entities or plane figures. Initially, collections of a variety of plane figures are classified according to one attribute or characteristic—either the number of sides or the number of angles in each plane figure. Plane figures may also be classified in regard to whether all of the sides of each figure are equal, regular, or irregular. A collection or display of plane figures of one general type (particularly triangles or rectangles) can be further classified according to one characteristic or attribute. Consider the tasks of classifying a collection of modeled or pictured triangles and the number of subgroups that would emerge with each of the following questions:

1. Does the triangle have a right angle?
2. What is the size or name of the largest angle in each triangle?
3. How many equal angles does each triangle have?
4. How many equal sides does each triangle have?

Now, consider the tasks of classifying a collection of modeled or pictured quadrilaterals and the number of subgroups that would emerge with each of the following questions:

1. How many right angles does each quadrilateral have?
2. Which quadrilaterals have all sides equal in length?
3. Which quadrilaterals have all angles equal in size?
4. How many sides of equal length does each quadrilateral have?
5. How many pairs of opposite parallel sides does each quadrilateral have?

In the preceding questions, one attribute, either the nature of angles or the nature of sides, was given as the classification characteristic. Also, the figures in each subgroup could be given a descriptive name. Triangles or quadrilaterals may also be classified according to two stated or given characteristics or attributes. In relation to each appropriate collection, consider these classification task questions:

1. Which triangles have a right angle and two equal sides?
2. Which triangles have all equal-length sides and all equal-size angles?
3. Which triangles have two equal-length sides and two equal-size angles?
4. Which quadrilaterals have opposite sides equal and opposite angles equal?

As classification skills are developed, children should be helped to see and discuss the minimum characteristics that are needed to establish the name or classification for various plane figures and geometric solids.

Comparison Skills
The comparison skills to be developed and acquired by children pertain to ascertaining relationships that exist between the component parts within one geometric entity and to ascertaining relationships that exist between two geometric entities. These skills were described in the section on major ideas or content themes. It is not unreasonable to expect children in an active laboratory-type elementary mathematics program to ascertain and describe in their own words the relationships of intersection, congruence, similarity, symmetry, parallelism, and perpendicularity. Of course, general terms of comparison, such as *longer, shorter, higher, bigger, smaller, thicker,* and *thinner*, will also be used. In later learning activities involving measurement, children will be expected to become adept at being more precise and specific in comparison of the size, distance between points, summations of lengths of sides, amounts of surfaces contained in bounded regions, and amounts of capacity or volume. Those expectations will also involve skills with the computational operations.

Construction Skills
Expectations for performance skills of construction include both physical model constructions and paper-and-pencil constructions. Projects that provide opportunities for children to practice and develop these skills are an integral part of the geometry content area. Initial constructions may not require the use of special tools or the preparation of material parts by children. Constructing models of plane figures on a pegboard with golf tees or pegs and loops of rubber string or on a geoboard with rubber bands are

examples of such activities. If heavy paper is precut to the shapes of surfaces by an adult, children can use glue or tape to construct geometric solids. In later constructions of physical models, children will be expected to use a straightedge, templates or cutouts of shapes, scissors, and appropriate construction materials. Initial paper-and-pencil constructions or drawings may require only a straightedge and templates or cutout figures along with the pencil and paper. Later, children may be helped to use the compass as a construction and drawing tool. In all instances, the tools and the materials of construction to be used must be appropriate to the capabilities of children. Construction projects, projects in which the skills can be practiced, need not be limited to products that are distinct models of geometric entities. Geometric pictures, pinwheels, snowflakes, games, and scale models are suitable projects. Quality and standards for projects should be maintained through attention to minimum requirements in accuracy and appearance. (A pinwheel is not a pinwheel unless it turns in the wind.) However, standards should not be so high as to discourage children in their construction endeavors.

Materials for Instruction

A great many of the materials that can be used for instruction in the area of geometry are already available in most elementary classrooms. Other useful materials can be obtained at little or no cost by encouraging children in the classroom and friends to save and collect items from out-of-school situations. Some materials that can be used repeatedly in activities and games may be constructed by teachers and children in the course of program activities. Such projects can be purposeful learning activities and an integral part of the instructional program. Materials that are considered for purchase should be carefully studied and evaluated in regard to the following:

1. Their possible multiple uses in a variety of learning activities directed toward different purposes or objectives
2. The possibilities of using other materials that are more readily available for the same purposes

3. The difficulty, time, and effort involved in constructing similar materials or materials that will accomplish the same purposes
4. The importance of the materials in relation to other materials that are needed for the elementary mathematics program
5. Whether the contemplated materials are designed for use by the teacher or for use by children
6. The durability of the materials in regard to their projected continued use by children

Most of the instructional materials to be utilized for geometric learning experiences in an active laboratory-type elementary mathematics program are similar in form to but different in nature from instructional materials used in the other content areas. Construction materials and tools allow children to build or make projects that require geometric concepts and skills in the building process or that display geometric ideas. The same construction materials and tools may be used by children to make projects for other content areas, and some of those projects may require the application of geometric ideas and skills. The familiar types or categories of instructional aids include physical object models, pictorial manipulative materials, and abstract practice materials.

Physical Object Models

Physical object models should be available or should be capable of being constructed readily for all of the types of geometric entities to be introduced and developed: zero dimensions (points); one dimension (lines and portions of lines); two dimensions (plane figures); and three dimensions (geometric solids). As with models for other mathematical ideas, each model should illustrate or be capable of demonstrating the mathematical idea that it represents. Since the entities of geometry are abstract and cannot be seen, the models for those entities cannot be exact or precise as models for number can be. However, children will be able to see and understand the ideas of those entities if models such as the following are used in introductory and developmental learning experiences.

Points or vertices: Tips and heads of pencils, pins, tacks, golf tees, pegs; and "points" of intersection seen in "lines" on classroom walls and other objects.

Lines and segments of lines: Rope, string, wire, soda straws, loops of rubber string, rubber bands; and "lines" of intersection of "planes" in the classroom.

Plane figures: "Figures" made by children holding rope or string; "figures" made with soda straws or wire; "figures" made with golf tees or pegs and loops of rubber string on a pegboard; "figures" made with rubber bands on a geoboard; thin, flat cutouts of "figures"; thin, flat plastic shapes; and "plane figures" seen on objects in the classroom.

Geometric solids: Boxes, cans, balls, and other small objects; "solids" constructed from heavy paper; points in space bounded by ropes or string held by children to form the edges of "solids"; and objects or parts of objects in the school environment.

The nature of the items in the preceding list calls for a minimal monetary investment for the physical objects that can be used as models for geometric ideas. These suggestions are based on personal observations of and experiences with children in elementary mathematics laboratory activities and the observations and experiences of other classroom teachers. Those observations and experiences have indicated that young children can see and understand geometric ideas and acquire geometric performance skills as well with these common materials as they can with expensive polished wooden or plastic objects.

Pictorial Manipulative Materials

Pictorial manipulative materials that can be used for developmental and practice purposes include geometry picture cards, geometry word cards, geometry dominoes, and pictures of geometric entities. Geometry picture cards are merely durable cards (of regular playing-card size) with a picture of a geometric entity drawn on each card (see Figure 10.7). Different sets or decks of cards may be made. For example, one deck may contain only

Figure 10.7

pictures of various lines and portions of lines; one deck may contain only pictures of angles; and one deck may contain only pictures of plane figures. Each deck should be planned and constructed so that (1) the cards can be used to randomly assign or direct children to find, draw, or construct the geometric entity shown on the card and (2) rules for a variety of card games (which might involve either matching, classifying, or comparing the pictures on the cards) can be devised. For example, a deck of cards containing pictures of plane figures can be planned and constructed so that games of "Congruence" and "Similarity" can be played. Planning involves selecting various triangles, quadrilaterals, and other plane figures to be drawn on the cards. Selection of one figure implies that another similar figure (same proportional shape, different size) will also be used on the cards. Each figure is drawn on four separate cards, perhaps in different positions. The deck is kept to a usable size by restricting the number of different pictures to be drawn. The completed deck can be used in games involving the ideas of congruence and similarity. Rules for the games require matching on the basis of some established criteria. One of those games is described in the section "Examples of Learning Experiences."

Geometry word cards are similar to geometry picture cards except that words or phrases instead of pictures appear on the cards. The words or phrases to be used include names for geometric entities and/or phrases describing attributes or characteristics

Figure 10.8

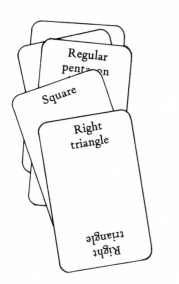

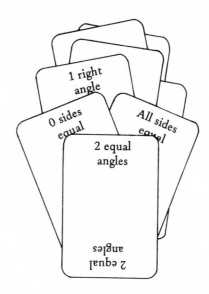

of geometric entities (see Figure 10.8). One name or one descriptive phrase will appear on each card. Descriptive phrases pertaining to plane figures will refer either to the nature of angles or to the nature of sides. Each set or deck of word cards should be planned and constructed so that (1) the cards can be used to randomly assign or direct children to find, draw, or construct the geometric entity named on the card or to find, draw, or construct a geometric entity with the characteristic described on the card (when a set or deck of word cards containing descriptive phrases about plane figures is being used, children may draw two of the cards and then attempt to draw or construct one plane figure that has both characteristics) and (2) the cards may be used in conjunction with related geometry picture cards in naming and classification activities. For example, the descriptive phrase cards pertaining to plane figures can be used with the plane-figure cards in an activity that requires children to classify the pictures according to the descriptive phrases.

Geometry dominoes may be constructed from heavy tagboard. Each domino will contain two pictures of geometric entities.

Figure 10.9

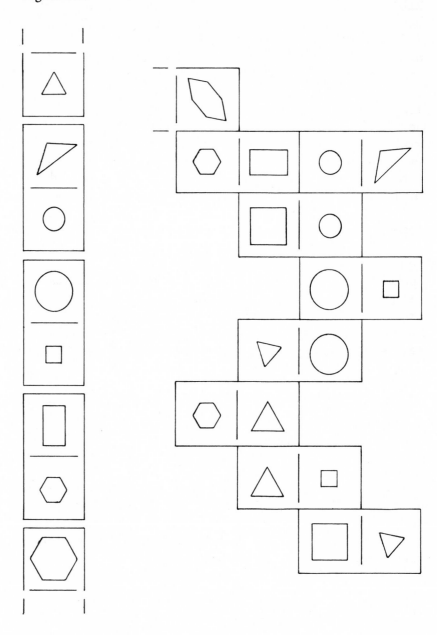

The dominoes in Figure 10.9 contain pictures of plane figures. The set is planned and drawn so that classification skills and/or relationships can be applied in the domino games to be played. Each domino has a large picture of one figure in one general classification (triangles, quadrilaterals, pentagons, and so forth) of plane figures on one end and a small picture of another figure from a different general classification on the other end. For each picture, there is a "congruent" picture and a "similar" picture on other dominoes. Figure 10.9 shows two games that may be played. One of the games is a regular domino train game in which the "match" requires only pictures of the same general classification. Each child playing must describe the nature of the match when it is made. The other game is directed toward "exactness" in the matches that are made through the scoring procedure. One point is given for a match of only the same general classification; two points are given for a match of "similarity," the same proportional shape but different sizes; and three points are given for a match of "congruence," the same shape and the same size. (White, red, and blue poker chips may be used to keep score quickly and easily.) Note that in this game, the dominoes are played side by side instead of end to end. In both games, the participants start with the same number of dominoes, one domino is taken from the unused pile to start the game, children draw an additional domino when they cannot play from their group, and the game ends when one child has played all of his or her dominoes.

Activity Cards

Activity cards with and without pictures can be used to initiate activities through statements of directions or questions. Directions may indicate that the activity cards are to be used with either physical object models or pictorial manipulatives. The activity card illustrated in Figure 10.10 directs children to use a physical object model and make scale drawings.

Abstract Printed Materials

Abstract practice materials include textbook pages, workbook pages, worksheets, and dittoed pages. These materials should not be used by children until the ideas and skills have been introduced

Figure 10.10

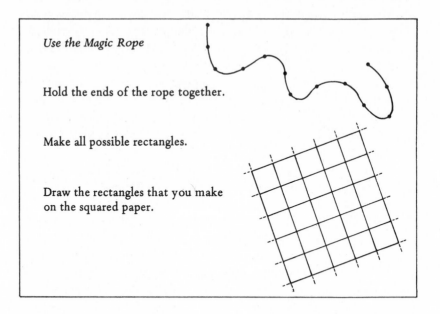

Use the Magic Rope

Hold the ends of the rope together.

Make all possible rectangles.

Draw the rectangles that you make on the squared paper.

and developed through the use of physical object models. Some may be constructed for multiple use and contain nothing more than pictures of geometric entities. Different directions for using the pages can be given for different tasks. For example, consider the illustration of a page filled with pictures of triangles in Figure 10.11. One direction might be to place an A inside the acute triangles, an R inside all of the right triangles, and an O inside all of the obtuse triangles. Other directions for different practice tasks might be given for the same page.

Figure 10.11

Name_____

Directions:_____

_____

Common Strategies or General Procedures

Classroom teachers must plan and arrange program activities and learning opportunities so that specific time and efforts are allowed for pupil achievement of the objectives, concepts, and performance skills of the content area of geometry. Children will not attain the achievement expectations associated with geometric ideas if the content materials and suggested activities are merely made available at interest centers, which children can attend if and when they complete their other tasks in elementary mathematics or in other subject areas. Also, pupil objectives will not be well met if geometric activities are incidentally attached to or sporadically interjected within or between learning experiences specifically pertaining to the introduction and development of the concepts and skills of other content areas.

Unit Approach

A more appropriate procedure is to utilize an instructional-unit approach in which geometric concepts or major ideas are the themes in units of study that recur in the spiral development of the curriculum. In those units of study, involving adequate periods of time and concentrated efforts, all of the learning opportunities for children involve the discussion and application of geometric concepts and skills. The length of time devoted to an instructional unit and the nature of learning opportunities for children in an instructional unit will vary according to objectives that are established for individual children. The learning opportunities or experiences provided in any one instructional unit need not be limited to dealing with only one type of geometric entity—points, lines, plane figures, or geometric solids. In addition, the learning experiences selected for one instructional unit need not be restricted to one general type of learning experience—introductory or developmental activities with physical object models, developmental and practice activities with pictorial manipulatives and models, practice activities with games, practice exercises on abstract printed materials, or pupil-made projects or constructions. A good instructional unit will provide a number of appropriate learning opportunities for each child in the classroom involving different types of geometric entities and different kinds of learning experiences. Mere participation in a learning experience does not indicate satisfactory achievement. The teacher must ascertain that children have achieved the learning purposes of the activities, and applied performance skills are the indicators.

Sequencing Activities

It is not necessary for geometric concepts and skills to be introduced to and developed with children in a specific sequence of geometric entities—from points to lines, from lines to plane figures, from plane figures to geometric solids. Physical object models of any of the four kinds of geometric entities can and should be used in introductory and developmental learning activities. In each instance, children and teachers must use their imaginations because the models represent abstract geometric ideas. Discussions should be directed toward the real nature of the entities and the need to use models and drawings. Whether early or initial learning activities employ models for points, for lines or line segments, for plane figures, or for geometric solids, the general procedures or common strategies of introduction and development will be similar. Those procedures will involve general vocabulary terms, discussions and descriptions of the attributes or characteristics of the entities, and determination of the relationships that exist within and between geometric entities.

Regardless of the type of geometric entity, common strategies and general procedures follow a logical sequence from the introduction and development of ideas with physical object models to development and practice of those ideas and their associated skills in other activities and in games before applications of those ideas and skills in model or drawing constructions, in abstract practice exercises, or in word-problem situations. In some instances, constructions of physical models can be considered developmental and practice activities.

Communication Skills

The initial communication skills to be developed should be oral—listening and speaking—skills, involving the vocabulary needed to name entities and to describe attributes and characteristics and leading to discussions of the relationships that may exist within and between the component elements of geometric entities. The extent to which printed or written symbols are introduced and utilized depends on the individual capabilities of children and the goals of the program. However, the words of geometry are no more difficult for children to learn to read than the words from other content areas in the elementary school program, and the short symbols for geometric entities and the relationships that may exist within or between them are often miniature drawings of those entities or relationships. The printed or written symbols to be introduced and developed with children should be associated with and derived from the contexts of learning experiences involving models and drawings. Some of the short symbols or signs that may be introduced and utilized to facilitate communication include the use of capital letters to name points and vertices; extending the naming of points with letters to naming and identifying lines and portions of lines, plane figures, and solids; using miniature drawings as abbreviations for names of geometric entities; and the common relational symbols (see Figure 10.12). As children are introduced to these symbols, they should be given opportunities to use those symbols on their own drawings or on prepared drawings to name elements of geometric entities and to describe relationships.

Examples of Learning Experiences

A number of learning activities have been suggested or implied in preceding sections of this chapter. Those suggestions may be reviewed in regard to purposes and procedures. The following examples are intended to illustrate further varieties and approaches suitable for an active laboratory-type elementary mathematics program.

Different-in-One-Way Train Two to four children. A collection of construction-paper cutouts of circle, square, equilateral triangle, and possible other regular shapes. The collection should consist of different shapes, two different sizes of each of the shapes, and different colors of each shape and size. Pieces in the collection should differ in at least three attributes—shape, size (large and small), and color. If wooden or plastic blocks are available, a fourth attribute, thickness (thick and thin), can be added. Before participating in this activity or game, children should become familiar with the attributes of the pieces in the collection. This can be accomplished by giving the children the pieces and asking them to place them in groups so that one word can be used to describe each group. An easy way to initiate this preliminary

Figure 10.12

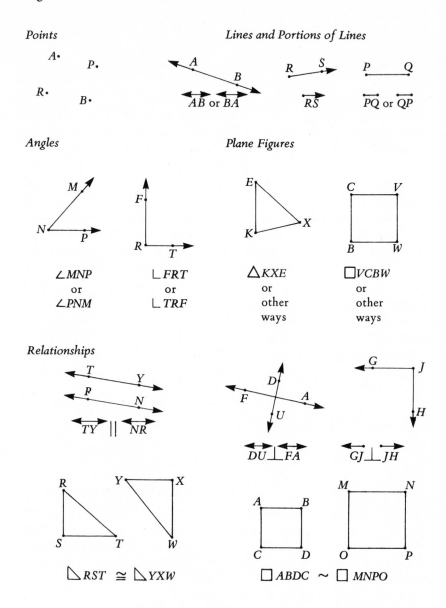

activity is to hold up one piece and give the direction to "say one word about this piece." These preliminaries can be repeated three or four times until the participating children have established the attributes. This understanding and skill can be ascertained by asking a child (and others) to "show me the big, red, thick triangle." To start the different-in-one-way activity or game, all of the pieces are placed on the table or floor. The children are told that they are going to make a train in which each piece in the train must be different from the piece next to it in only one way. One piece is taken from the collection to start the train. The train can be built around the collection in the middle so that all participants can see the pieces that have been played and the pieces that remain. The teacher, or a child who knows the game, can then start by taking one of the pieces from the collection and placing it beside the starting piece. Each child will play in turn, selecting a piece and placing it in the train. Each time a piece is "played," the child must name the one way in which it is different from the adjacent piece. Plays are allowed on either end of the train. Participants should watch each play to be sure that the play is correct. The activity can be made more gamelike if a piece put down improperly must be taken back and kept by the person who played that piece. The game or play continues until no child can find a piece in the left-over collection that could be played on either end of the train. The winner of the game is the child who has had to keep the fewest number of pieces. When children become proficient at the activity, it can be extended to "different in two ways" and/or "different in three ways."

Congruence Three or four children. A deck of plane-figure picture cards (as briefly described in "Materials for Instruction"). The size of the deck of cards used is adjusted to the number of children participating in the game. Each picture card in the deck to be used should have three other congruent-shape picture cards and four related similar-shape cards. For example, if an equilateral triangle is selected as one of the pictured shapes to be used, there should be four cards with large congruent equilateral triangles and four cards with smaller equilateral triangles (congruent to each other). The cards are sorted into groups of four congruent pictures and the pictures to be used in the game are selected—for beginners, perhaps larger and smaller squares, equilateral triangles, rectangles, and parallelograms. If three children are to participate, six groups of four cards each (24 cards) might be used so that each child starts with eight cards. For four participants, eight groups of four cards each could be used. *One additional unmatching card is then added to the deck*. The deck of cards is mixed and dealt one at a time, in turn, to each of the players using all of the cards. The player to the left (direction of dealing) will have one more card than the other players. Each child looks for pairs of congruent cards in his or her hand and lays those pairs on the table. Then the child to the left of the dealer draws one card from the dealer and ascertains whether that card is a congruent match for one of the cards left in his or her hand. Matched pairs are laid on the table as they are made. Each child then takes turns drawing one card from the player on the right, playing in turn, and looking for a congruent match. The cards in the participants' hands will diminish as matches are made. When a player has no cards left, he or she is out of the game. The loser is the player who is left with the unmatching card. Other types of matching games can be played with the same deck of cards. Those games may involve either congruence or similarity.

Squares Two children. Twenty-four chips or counters of one color and 24 chips or counters of another color (24 chips of one color for each player) and a grid of large squares (see Figure 10.13). The grid may be drawn on a large sheet of cardboard, on a sheet of plastic, or on a table top. The children are reminded that 4 chips of one color on the intersections of the lines on the grid can determine a square. Each child is to place one chip at a time, taking turns, on one of the intersections trying to make a square with four of his or her chips and at the same time trying to prevent the other player from making squares. When a player makes a square, he or she can take one of the other player's chips from the board or grid. That chip cannot be a part of a square. If there are no chips on the grid that are not in a square, the opposing player must give the square maker a chip from the chips that have not been played. A square may be larger than one unit on the grid. Initially, children will only make squares that follow the lines of the grid. Later, they should see that squares can also be made in a "diagonal" manner. It is possible to place one chip so that the chip is a vertex or corner for more than one square. One of the opponent's chips is to be taken for each square that is made. After each player has played 24 times, once for each chip, the player who has taken the greatest number of the opponent's chips wins the game. The game can be made a bit more complex by altering the scoring procedures. One point can be given for each of the unit squares that is enclosed by the four corners or

Figure 10.13

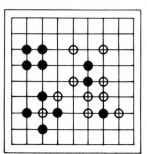

vertices of each square that is made. Notice that in the illustration there is a square that would receive one point, a square that would receive two points, and a square that would receive four points.

Make All Possible Triangles One to four children. Soda straws, thin plastic or paper strips cut to lengths of 3, 4, 5, and 6 inches (other planned lengths could be used). At least eight or ten pieces of each length. Material such as glue, pins, brads, or short strips of pipe cleaners with which to join the pieces. The children are given the strips or straws of different lengths and the appropriate material to join the pieces, and told to make as many different triangles as possible by joining the pieces at their ends. Children are expected to construct equilateral, isosceles, and scalene triangles of different sizes. With 3-, 4-, and 5-inch straws, they can construct a right triangle. After the triangles are constructed, the children can be asked to sort or classify the triangles. "Put the triangles that are alike in some way in the same group." Either angles or sides can be used as the classification criteria.

Make Models of Geometric Solids Children working individually or in pairs. Construction paper, templates, straightedges, scissors, glue or tape, and physical object models of geometric solids. Children are given the models and the construction materials and tools. Each child is to select one geometric model, study it, and attempt to draw on and cut one piece of construction paper so that the one piece can be folded and glued or taped to make a geometric solid like the one selected. The construction does not have to be the same size as the model. Children's first attempts should be directed toward cubes, rectangular solids, triangular prisms, pyramids with square bases, and pyramids with triangular bases. The object is to help children see the surfaces of geometric solids. Successful constructions should be displayed. One appropriate display might be a mobile of hanging geometric solids.

Geometric Entity Search Small groups of children. The environment of the classroom or the school. The object of this activity is to help children see geometric configurations in the real world. The activity can be initiated in several ways. Small groups of children are formed and each small group is given paper and pencil and directed to search for geometric entities or shapes in the room. As they find the shapes or configurations, they are to write the location, name, or place of that configuration on the paper. The shapes to be searched for may be assigned in several ways. Each group might draw a card that will contain the name of the shape they are to seek, or each group can be given a sheet of paper with column headings for different shapes—circles, squares, and so forth. In some instances, teachers and children might want to glue or pin colored yarn around some of the shapes that are found.

Make a Map of the Room   Individual children or small groups of children working together. Squared paper, straightedge, and pencil. This project can be best conducted in rooms that have either ceilings or floors of square tiles. The activity may be a child's first attempts at drawing to scale. The children are given the squared paper, straightedge, and pencil and told to draw a map of the room. Each square on the paper is to represent one square on the floor or ceiling. No use of measuring instruments is required, only counting. Details to be included in the map depend on the capabilities of the children participating. After the wall boundary lines are established, perhaps doors and windows should be located on the map. Other significant details can be added as desired. Children might compare their maps or take their maps to other rooms to compare room shapes and sizes. If maps of each of the rooms in the school are drawn to the same scale, those maps may be joined to make one map or scale drawing of the school.

Suggested Activities

1. Select one elementary grade level (K-6) pupil textbook or teacher's manual from a commercially published textbook program. Use the table of contents and index to locate the content dealing with geometry. Study the presentation of that content to ascertain or determine the following:
   a. Geometric entities that are to be dealt with
   b. General nature of the suggested approach; that is, formal versus informal, uses of physical object models, drawings, constructions, practice exercises
   c. Vocabulary and symbolism to be introduced to children

    d. Achievement expectations in terms of concepts to be understood and performance skills to be mastered by children

2. For the level selected in activity 1, plan and develop an instructional unit (preferably using an active laboratory approach) that involves several types of geometric entities and different kinds of learning experiences (activities, games, and projects).

3. Begin a collection of models of geometric entities.

4. Make a list of the geometric entities and vocabulary that are involved in children's indoor and outdoor games.

5. Prepare the materials for and teach one of the games suggested in this chapter to a small group of children or adults. Evaluate the success of the game in regard to participants' involvement in thinking, uses of concepts, and uses of performance skills and in regard to interest and motivation.

Chapter 11   **Measurement**

In reality, the ideas of measurement are the ideas of numeration and notation; the acts of measuring are applications of the ideas of numeration and notation or applications of performance skills associated with those ideas; and quantitative problems involving measurements are similar to other problems that involve combining, separating, or comparing physical quantities and selecting and performing the fundamental operations on numbers using numerals as solution procedures. Designating measurement as a specific content area and planning and directing specific learning experiences or activities toward the nature of measurement and the applications of these ideas and performance skills are efforts to help children master ideas and skills that are necessary both in the further study of mathematics, science, and other academic and prevocational areas and in solving problems encountered in the world outside of school. Measurement problems, along with problems involving money, are prevalent in both in-school and out-of-school environments. Helping children to learn to deal with those problems should be a basic endeavor of the elementary mathematics program.

Importance of the Area

Treating measurement as a particular content area with instructional time and effort specifically planned for and directed toward introducing, developing, and practicing the applications of measurement ideas and skills is an attempt to alleviate the problems and difficulties with the ideas and skills of measuring that many children encounter and to respond to criticisms from educators and laypersons. Simply stated, those criticisms are that children are not learning how to measure various quantities or amounts and are not learning how to apply measurement ideas and skills to quantitative problem situations. Instructional programs that treat measuring and measurement problems incidentally along with the content ideas and skills of numeration and notation and/or the computational operations are less likely to attain the desired achievement expectations than are programs that are organized and planned to handle measurement learning experiences and activities as distinct instructional units in a content area. The integration of measurement ideas and performance skills with other content ideas and skills is highly desirable, but that integration is better achieved after measurement ideas and skills have received specific attention.

Differences in Approach

Instructional units directed toward measurement learning experiences and activities for children in an active laboratory-type elementary mathematics program may differ in several ways from the prevailing practices and approaches in conventional or traditional programs. In conventional programs, or programs that are dominated by textual or printed materials, types of measurement (linear, surface, volume, and so on) are often dealt with as isolated topics at different times. The involvement of children with the content ideas and expected performance skills may be passive rather than active. In each topic or unit, there are generally tables of equivalent measures to be memorized, often in a rote manner with few real measuring activities on the parts of children, who, thus, have little understanding of the units of measurement being introduced and developed. Each topic on different types of measurement usually includes quantitative problems requiring addition, subtraction, multiplication, or division. In some of those problems values are substituted in formulas that have not been meaningfully established. In some instances, emphasis is placed on converting units from one system of measurement to units in another system of measurement. Quite often children are treated as if they had identical abilities and could acquire and achieve the same ideas and skills at the same time.

Telling Time

In some elementary mathematics programs, inordinate amounts of time and effort are spent dealing with topics that do not involve major ideas of measurement or associated performance skills of measuring. Yet these topics are considered by some program materials and teachers to be topics of measurement. Those topics include naming and ordering the days of the week and the months of the year, "telling time" (reading a clock or watch face might be more descriptive), and naming and using the money values of coins. The intent here is not to suggest that these topics should not be covered at the elementary school level. The point is that these topics do not involve the major ideas of measurement or the acts of measuring. Several of these topics (days of the week and months of the year) might as well be a part of the language arts program or the general program of the elementary school. "Telling time" or reading a clock or watch face does require the use of numerical ideas and information. However, if the emphasis is merely on reading a clock face, that topic can be dealt with as a reading task or as a part of the reading program. (As described in a later section, it is possible to introduce and develop ideas that pertain to measuring time. Establishing units, developing relationships between units, and actually measuring time can be meaningfully introduced and developed.) Children can be "taught" to read a clock face without really understanding the units of time that are named by adhering to given rules, such as "the short hand is the hour hand; the long hand is the minute hand; and there are 60 minutes in one hour." If the instructional goal is to have children acquire competencies to read the clock, activities can be directed toward helping children associate related elements of the clock face and reading those relationships. (Of course, digital clocks and watches

are another matter, easy to read, but perhaps more difficult for
children to understand.) Two pairs of related elements appear
or are implied on every regular clock or watch face. As indicated
in the illustrations in Figure 11.1, those pairs of elements are
(1) the hour marks with numerals and the short—or hour—hand,
and (2) the minute marks and the long—or minute—hand. Some
clocks and watches have a sweep-second hand. The movements
of that hand can be used to help children obtain a general idea of
the length of a minute and of the relationship between the movements of the minute hand and the sweep-second hand. The
instructional procedures can give attention to the two pairs of
elements individually and then put the pairs together. Children
can first learn to read a clock face that has only the hour marks
with numerals and the hour hand. When the hour hand points
directly at an hour mark, it is the hour of the numeral. The idea
that the minute hand will be pointing to 12 is irrelevant. When
the hour hand points between two hour numerals, it is after one
of the hours and before the other. Comments such as "a little
after _____ o'clock, almost _____ o'clock, half way between _____
and _____ o'clock, or _____ o'clock" may be used. For example,
the first illustration in Figure 11.1 indicates "a little after two
o'clock." When children can read a clock face with only the hour
marks and the hour hand, a clock face with only the minute marks
and the minute hand may be used to help children ascertain "How
much after _____ o'clock, or how much before _____ o'clock."
The second illustration in Figure 11.1 shows 21 minutes after
some hour. The two pairs of related elements can then be combined on one clock face.

Money Values

Identifying, naming, and working with the exchange values of
coins is better developed in relation to the content area of numeration and notation than as an aspect of measurement. The exchange
value of coins is similar to the broader concept of base. Unfortunately, the exchange values of coins in the monetary system of
this country and in the systems of most other countries are multibased. Most early problems involving coins require children to
understand the concept of base as it applies to coin values and to
be able to count in multiples of the coins used. More complex
problems require that children be able to add, subtract, multiply,
and divide coin values. Learning experiences and activities in

Figure 11.1

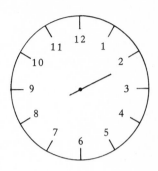

which coin values are associated with physical object models for whole numbers will help children remember those values. Early learning activities might also involve the exchanges of chips or counters of different colors in regard to values in games or activities similar to those used to develop ideas of base ten and positional value. For example, in games of "What You Roll Is What You Get" with three different colors of chips and a numeral cube, ten white chips can be exchanged for one red chip, and ten red chips can be exchanged for one blue chip (or five white chips can be exchanged for one red chip and five red chips can be exchanged for one blue chip). The monetary values of single coins and the amounts of money represented by groups of coins are not measured. Those quantitative values are determined by other means.

Nature of Activities

Learning experiences intended to help children in an active laboratory-type elementary mathematics program acquire measurement concepts and skills should be consistent with principles or beliefs about children and how they learn and with desirable characteristics of a good elementary mathematics program. Consistency with beliefs or principles can be maintained by continued adherence to a basic premise about the nature of measurement and measuring and a basic belief about how children can learn best about measurements and the acts of measuring.

Every measurement activity is the comparison of one quantity to another quantity, and one of those quantities is the referent unit. In numeration and notation learning activities when children are attempting to describe numerically a quantity of single objects by counting or by some other operation, the referent unit is one of those single objects. The ability to determine an exact number of objects by counting the single objects, using one object as the counting referent unit, is a prerequisite to learning activities that require ascertaining amounts or quantities in measuring situations in which the referent unit is not as real or obvious. When young children are using real objects as referent units in early measurement activities, they will be able to see and handle the referent units, but they will not be able to see those same objects or referent units in the quantity that is to be measured. For example, when children are measuring the length

Figure 11.2

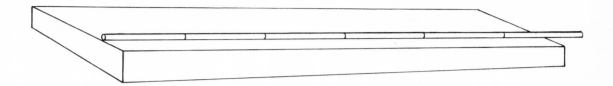

of a table or desk using ice cream sticks or soda straws as the units or measurement, they will be able to see and count the straws or sticks that they place along the edge or length of the table (see Figure 11.2). However, the table will not be distinctly marked in lengths of ice cream sticks and when the sticks are removed, the relationship between the length of the table and the length of one ice cream stick will not be visible.

In every measurement or measuring situation, the quantity to be measured and the referent unit by which the measurement of that quantity is to be described must be established. If referent units are made real and meaningful for children, the measurement comparisons between the quantities or amounts to be measured and the referent units can be seen and understood. Also, descriptions of the measured amounts in terms of the referent units can be made more easily.

Children learn by doing, by participating in an active manner. If children are to learn about the nature of measurement and to perform the acts of measuring, they must measure or compare quantities or amounts with referent units. Instructional activities that are limited to passive observations of and references to quantities to be measured, measurement units to be used, tables of measurement equivalents, and measuring instruments and tools can not be expected to achieve the same results in terms of children's understanding of concepts and acquisition of performance skills as learning experiences that require active participation in measuring situations.

Crude Comparisons

The earliest measurement activities for young children might be called *crude* comparisons, in which two objects or amounts can be visually compared in regard to one quantitative characteristic. For examples, two pieces of rope or string can be compared in regard to their lengths; two pieces of paper can be compared in regard to their amounts of surface; and two objects can be compared in regard to their weights. By merely placing the two objects or amounts side by side or by holding them, some conclusion can be reached in regard to their relative sizes. Neither the amount of size of either object nor the amount of difference between the two objects is specified in terms of units of measurement. Either of the two objects or amounts can be the referent, in that one of the object amounts is to be compared to the other. As a result of that comparison, some general comparative term, such as *longer, shorter, taller, bigger, smaller, heavier,* or *lighter,* can be used to describe the comparison situation. In a specific instance, such as Figure 11.3 in which the lengths of string A and string B are to be compared, the general comparative term to be used depends on which of the strings is the referent. The referent is established either by the question that is asked—"Which string is longer?" (*than the shorter string*) implies that the shorter string is the referent—or by the statement that results—"String A is shorter" (*than string B*) implies that the longer string is the referent. Two different statements can be made about each comparison, and in these early activities, children should be encouraged either to make both statements for each comparative situation or to alternately use larger amounts and smaller amounts as the referent units. In these early activities, one quantity or amount is being crudely measured in reference to another quantity or amount.

Figure 11.3

Referent Units

In subsequent measurement activities, yet early in the school program, a characteristic such as the length or the weight of a physical object or thing will be established as a referent unit, and the amount or quantity to be measured will be compared to that characteristic referent unit as it is displayed in or by a number of the objects or things. The referent units employed in these early learning experiences need not be those commonly used by adults. Using the length of ice cream sticks, the amount of surface of square pieces of plastic or cardboard, the space taken up by a wooden block or cube, and the weights of same-size objects will be more meaningful to children than an early development of such ideas as inch, centimeter, square inch, square centimeter, cubic inch, cubic centimeter, ounce, and gram. In any case, those terms and units are not common or standard to young children. When those referent units are introduced and used, they should first be treated as physical referent units (sticks, rods, blocks, cubes) then named and commonly used. In an active laboratory-type elementary mathematics program, physical object referent units are established and used as models for attributes or characteristics that are to be measured. The attributes or characteristics of other objects or things can be quantitatively described in relation to the modeled referent units.

Performance Expectations

Distance

Children in the elementary school will be expected to be able to find and describe measured quantitative attributes of distance, amounts of weight, amounts of surface, amounts of capacity, and perhaps amounts of time. A variety of terms are used in the elementary mathematics program and outside of school that are descriptively specific but that pertain to the measurement of *distance* or linear measurement. A list of some of those terms includes *length, width, height, altitude, perimeter, circumference,* and other words that would fit into the direction "Measure the _____ ," and imply that a distance is to be measured.

Adults and children who are unsure of the uses of the terms *perimeter* and *area* and the measurements implied by those terms may not have had sufficient learning opportunities in which those terms were associated respectively with measuring the amounts of distance around shapes and the amounts of surface contained within regions. If development of the ideas of perimeter and area is restricted to the uses of drawings and formulas, and to the substitutions of numerals into formulas so that computations can be performed, some confusion should be expected. The drawings appear to be alike in pictured problems of both types and the formulas for area and perimeter have similar variables. Children will have fewer difficulties if the quantities to be measured are physically represented so that what is to be measured can be seen and described and if real referent units are used in the comparisons (see Figure 11.4). For example, when plane figures are constructed with string or rope, the perimeter can be seen as the length of the rope or string around the figure. In other activities, shapes can be made with wires, rods, or straws.

Figure 11.4

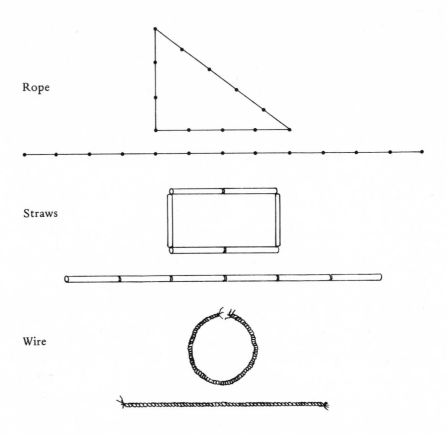

Rope

Straws

Wire

In either type of activity, procedures involving addition of the lengths of the sides of the figures will be meaningful to children and appropriate formulas can be developed.

Surface
Similarly, if cut-out regions bounded by plane figures are used when amounts of *surface* are to be measured, the surfaces of those regions can actually be covered with referent units, preferably small squares and halves of small squares as in Figure 11.5. (Small cut-out rectangles, equilateral triangles, or other regular shapes can also be used as referent units.) Children will be able to see that the surface of the cut-out region is to be covered, that the amount of surface is to be named or described in terms of the referent unit, and that a procedure can be established for

Figure 11.5

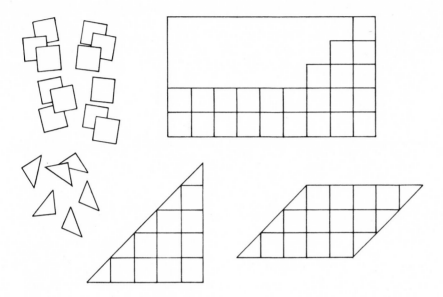

finding out the amount of surface in other regions. The general sequence of finding the amounts of surface in regions bounded by plane figures should proceed from simple to more complex regions. For example, children should initially find the amount of surface in rectangular regions. Then they might be asked to find the amount of surface in regions bounded by other parallelograms. With the background of those experiences, they can be helped to see that all triangles are one-half of a parallelogram. (Two congruent triangular regions can be placed next to each other so that a region shaped like a parallelogram is formed.) The procedures of placing referent units on the regions should lead to the development of appropriate formulas for finding the amount of surface or area without the use of physical referent units. For all parallelograms, including rectangles, that formula will involve multiplying the number of referent units in each row and the number of rows. For triangular regions, the formula will involve finding one-half of the amount of surface of the parallelogram that could be made by two such triangles. Procedures for finding the amounts of surface contained in more complex or irregular regions are derived from partitioning those regions into triangular shapes.

Figure 11.6

Weight

When children begin comparing the *weights* of objects that are not so greatly different that the heavier and lighter objects can be discerned by lifting, a pan balance becomes necessary. When a pan balance is introduced, children should be given opportunities to experiment by placing objects in the pans and to discover that for the instrument to work properly, the empty pans must be in balance before objects are placed in them. (See Figure 11.6.) The first use of a pan balance will be to compare the weights of two objects: Which is heavier? Which is lighter? A number of objects can be ordered in regard to heaviness by successive comparisons of two of the objects at a time. When children understand how a pan balance works, and after they have compared the weights of many different objects, they are ready to begin comparing the weights of objects to the weights of referent units. The referent units should be relatively small and as equal in weight to each other as possible (small cubes or washers, for example) so that the heaviness of the object to be weighed can be described in terms of the number of referent units needed to balance the object. Successful experiences with such measuring activities will help children to understand standard weights or referent units named in grams, ounces, or pounds when those weight units are used with a balance. Using the standard weight referent units with a pan balance should precede weighing objects with spring scales in which the manner and process of weighing cannot be observed.

Figure 11.7

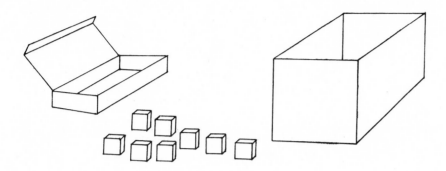

Capacity

Children's first experiences and activities with measuring *capacity* should involve the traditional idea of volume and should make use of small empty boxes and small cubes to put into those boxes (see Figure 11.7). The questions to be answered will pertain to the number of cubes that can be put into each box. Specifically, how many cubes can be put into each row, how many rows can be made in the bottom layer, and how many layers of cubes will the box hold? Another type of activity involves constructing rectangular solids with small cubes. This activity is described in the section "Examples of Learning Experiences." Cubes or cubic units are the referents for volume measures. Although children in the elementary school may not be expected to find the volume of more complex geometric solids, as measured in cubic units, procedures for deriving those volume measures should be related to finding the volume of rectangular solids.

Children in the elementary mathematics program are also expected to deal with problems involving *liquid capacity* measures. In the metric system of measurement, liquid capacity measures utilize cubic units (cubic centimeters; 1 liter = 1000 cubic centimeters). However, common English standard measurements of liquid capacity utilize other distinct units (teaspoon, tablespoon, cup, pint, quart, gallon). In order to introduce, develop, and practice using those common units with children, containers to hold liquids are needed. Initially, the containers may be the bottles and jars in which household products are sold. One can compare the capacities of those containers by pouring sand, water, or some other material from one container to another. Children should be helped to note the relative capacities of these non-standard containers and to see that containers of varying shapes and sizes can have the same capacity. When the fluid-ounce capacity of containers is shown on the bottle or jar, the relationship of fluid ounces to common liquid measures can be developed. Eventually, however, measuring devices for the common liquid measures should be used to develop the relationships of equivalent measures and to measure amounts. Equivalents and relationships can be established by pouring from one measuring device to another. The measurement of an amount of liquid simply requires the repeated use of the appropriate measuring device.

Time

Measuring *time* may or may not be a topic in the elementary mathematics program. If learning activities are directed toward measuring time, several approaches may be used. One approach utilizes the sweep-second hand and minute hand of a watch or clock as the measurement device. In that approach, attention is given to the movements of the sweep-second hand and/or the minute hand of a watch or clock, and events are measured in terms of the number of seconds or minutes it takes for them to occur. In another approach, devices are constructed for the purposes of measuring time. They may include devices that drip water, pour sand, or burn candles. The time length of events can then be measured in regard to the amounts of water that is dripped, sand that is poured, or candle that is burned. A third approach utilizes the relationships between time amounts that are measured by a clock or watch and time amounts that are shown by other devices. The other devices might be sand timers or glasses or sun dials. The amount of time that it takes for the sand in various sand timers to run from one side to the other can be measured by the second and minute hands of a clock or watch. Shadows on a sun dial can be observed, or sun dials can be constructed in relation to the hours shown on a clock. A comprehensive approach to measuring time would involve children in learning experiences and activities integrating all of these approaches. A minimal instructional treatment of time in the content area of measurement will merely help children learn to read the faces of clocks and watches to "tell time."

Two Systems of Measurement

In modern or contemporary elementary mathematics programs, children are expected to utilize both the common English or U.S. standard system of measurement and the metric system of measurement. Basic concepts and skills are to be applied in problems that require naming or describing measurements; problems that require combining, separating, or comparing measurements; and problems that require the computational operations of addition, subtraction, multiplication, or division of measurements in both common U.S. units and the metric units. The common U.S. system of measurement is multibased and children as well as adults may have difficulties remembering and using all of the units and equivalents of the system in problem situations. The metric system of measurement is a simpler, interrelated system with a consistent use of base ten and unit names that have descriptive prefixes denoting powers of 10 (ten, one hundred, one thousand, one-tenth, one-hundredth, one-thousandth, and so on). Because of the base-ten characteristic, children's study and use of the metric system of measurement can be closely related to and integrated with their study and use of the decimal system of numeration. Regardless of these obvious differences, there is a great deal of similarity in the processes of developing ideas and skills of measuring with nonstandard units, with the system of common U.S. standard units, and with units in the metric system in an active laboratory-type elementary mathematics program.

Major Ideas or Content Themes

The major ideas or themes of the content area of measurement do not involve the sizes and names of units; the numeration and notation skills that are used to determine the number of units in a measurement; the tables of measurement equivalents; the combining, separating, or comparison problems that might involve measurements; or the possibilities of performing the computational operations of addition, subtraction, multiplication, or division with numerals describing measurements. *Measurement* is a content area in which concepts and skills from other areas are to be applied, and, conversely, measurement and the acts of measuring are opportunities to apply other mathematical concepts and skills. The performance skills that children are expected to acquire involve the application of concepts and skills from the content areas of numeration and notation, operations on collections of objects, operations on number using numerals, and geometry. The following major ideas or themes of the content area of measurement should be spirally developed throughout the elementary mathematics program in accordance with the concepts of measurement and the types of measurement that are to be introduced, developed, and practiced, with the prerequisite concepts and skills which are to be applied.

Altering or changing the shape or configuration of a quantity does not affect the total amount of that quantity.

This idea refers to conservation of amount of length, amount of surface, amount of volume, and so on. Coiling or looping a straightened length of rope or string, and vice versa, does not shorten or lengthen the amount of rope. Since the rope or string serves as a physical model for portions of lines, the same idea pertains to the linear measurements of line segments and to combining the linear measurements of several line segments. The original amount of surface does not change by rearranging the positions of the model or the referent units used to measure the amount of surface, by cutting or folding the region of surface and repositioning the pieces, or by drawing lines to partition the region and combining the parts in a new or differently shaped region (see Figure 11.8). Similarly, when cubes are used as referent units to introduce and develop the concept of volume, rearranging them to a new configuration does not affect the original measured volume of a geometric solid, and pouring an amount of liquid from a container of one shape to a container of another shape does not change the amount of liquid. This idea should be emphasized as each type of measurement (distance, surface, capacity, weight) is introduced and developed and re-emphasized when those topics reappear in more complex tasks and problems later in the program. As indicated in the section "Common Strategies or General Procedures," it is not necessary to introduce and develop this idea sequentially from linear measurements to measurements of surface to measurements of capacity or volume.

Figure 11.8

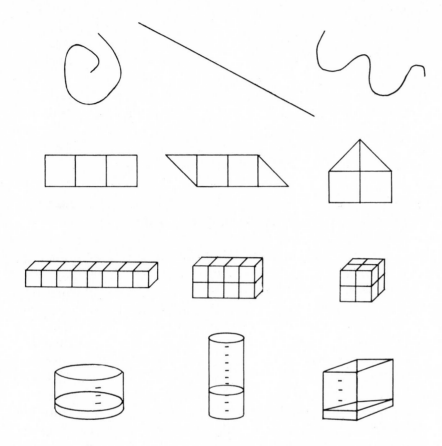

In an active laboratory-type elementary mathematics program utilizing physical object referent units, children can see this concept or idea as readily with one type of measurement as they can with another. When children have acquired and applied the idea with one type of measurement, the idea can be extended to other types of measurement and applied to more difficult or more complex tasks and problems.

Common or standard units of measurement are used by societies or cultures to communicate about amounts or quantities.

Common or standard units are necessary in everyday affairs, business, and industry. If a person were living or working completely alone, he or she might use any units of measurement that would satisfy the needs of encountered problems or tasks. Small, isolated societies or cultures in the world may still use measurement units that were developed for their own particular limited situations. Large societal and cultural segments of the world (countries) adopt and mandate a standard system of measurement. That legally adopted system of measurement suffices for the conduct of everyday affairs, business, and industry within the country or cultural segment. However, in order for those countries or cultural segments to participate in international business or industry, they must deal with several systems of measurement. Because products must be redesigned or repackaged for sale in areas using a different system of measurement, there are national and international efforts to adopt a worldwide system of standard measurements. Young children in the early years of the elementary mathematics program may be aware of the names, sizes, and uses of some of the common standard units of measurement. However, introductory measurement activities should treat all referent units of measurement as if they were not common or standard in societal use. The meanings and basic concepts of the various types of measurement can be introduced and developed with nonstandard referent units. Even when the referent units selected and made available by the teacher are commonly used by the adult population, children's earliest measurement activities with those referent units should not be based on or emphasize the standard names and sizes of those units. After measurement concepts and ideas have been introduced and developed with children using nonstandard referent units and common units employed as nonstandard units, specific names and sizes of common standard units can be introduced. The need for using common standard referent units in order to communicate with each other, in order to share and understand quantitative ideas, can then be meaningfully developed.

All numerals derived from acts of measuring are approximate numbers.

Exact numbers are derived only from situations in which distinct single objects can be counted. The ability to count an exact number of distinct single objects is a prerequisite to performing acts of measuring. In children's earliest measurement activities, they will count numbers of referent units. Later, they will use tools and instruments on which the referent units are represented by marks and numerals. The numerals that children derive from counting referent units in their early measuring experiences will appear to be exact numbers. However, while using nonstandard units and common units as nonstandard units to measure the same quantities or amounts, children probably will arrive at slightly different results, especially if some of those quantities or amounts are selected carefully by the teacher so that the result does not appear to be an "exact" number of the referent units and involves a fractional part of the referent unit. The minor differences in children's responses can then be attributed to the slight differences in the referent units that were used ("Were the units all exactly the same size?"); the procedures that were used ("Were there any spaces between the referent units? Were the referent units all placed in the same way?"); and the judgments that were made about the fractional part. Children should be helped to understand that exact comparison ratios in measurements are impossible because of the natures of the quantities measured, the referent units used, and the possibilities of minor errors. Each measurement task requires that the measurer try to be as precise as possible in describing the measured quantity. The quantitative description or numeral can only be approximate. Even in early measurements, the statements of description can be similar to "The measurement of this quantity is closer to _____ (units) than it is to _____ (units)." Later, when smaller referent units are being used and when children are learning to use measuring instruments and devices they should learn how to minimize measurement errors by utilizing smaller units and by acquiring proficiency in the uses of the devices and instruments. While measurements in quantitative problem situations are often discussed and treated as if they were exact numbers, the term *exactly* and its synonyms should be discouraged when either the measurements involved or the response to the problem is being described.

The precision of a measurement depends on the instrument or procedure employed in the measurement, the size of the smallest referent unit, and the proficiency of the measurer in using the measuring instrument and procedure.

The precision of a measurement is generally described in terms of the smallest referent unit used. For example, a measurement is "correct to the nearest _____." A *tolerance*, or allowable measurement error, of one-half of that smallest referent unit is thus established by the rounding-off procedure, which is the basis for the idea that all numerals derived from acts of measuring are approximate numbers. There are three criteria pertaining to precision in this major idea or theme, and the precision of a measurement depends solely on one criterion only when the elements of the other two criteria are identical for two or more separate measurements of the same amount or quantity. For example, if a quantity or amount is to be measured by two measurers who will utilize the same instrument and procedure and who are equally proficient, then the sole criterion for precision of the measurement will be the size of the smallest referent unit to be used. However, if two equally proficient measurers agree on the smallest referent unit to be used, but employ different instruments in the measurement procedure, the sole criterion for the precision of the resulting measurement will be the process involving the instruments. Consider two persons measuring the thickness or diameter of a cylindrical rod, one using a micrometer and the other using a tape measure or ruler. One of the measurements will be more precise than the other. Similarly, if two persons are to measure the same quantity or amount with the same instrument and procedure and agree on the size of the smallest referent unit, the sole criterion for the precision of the measurements will be the proficiencies of the measurers.

In regard to measurements, precision and accuracy are not synonyms. Questions pertaining to measurements either suggest, state, or imply the referent units to be used in responses. Those given or implied referent units may not be small units. Thus, a measurement response may be accurate or correct in regard to the given or implied unit but not very precise. For example, consider the responses that are given in pounds, kilograms, or stones (in Great Britain) when the weights of people are to be ascertained. Those responses may be accurate or correct insofar as the units used, but the weights would be more precise if the smaller units of ounces and grams were also used. The idea or theme of precision can be introduced in children's early measurement experiences by describing measurements as "correct to the nearest (referent unit)." As children learn to use smaller and smaller standard units, utilizing appropriate instruments and procedures, they should be helped to understand that they are becoming more proficient and more precise in their measurements. Teachers should be aware of the fact that children cannot measure in or use fractional parts of a unit until they have acquired meanings for and understanding of common and decimal fractions. It is unreasonable to expect children to measure drawings of lines to the nearest one-fourth inch before they understand and can use the concept of one-fourth.

These major ideas or content themes apply to all of the types of measurement situations and problems that children will encounter in the elementary mathematics program. Each idea can and should be spirally developed throughout the program as children deal with new and more difficult or complex measuring tasks and measurement problems. When performance skills are being introduced, developed, and practiced, children's attention should be drawn to these major ideas, which consist of the central themes of measurements, and the acts of measuring.

Performance Skills

Children completing the elementary mathematics program are expected to be able to measure amounts of distance, surface, capacity, and weight with degrees of precision that are appropriate for further study in academic and prevocational areas and for application to out-of-school problems and occupations. In addition, they are expected to be able to deal with units of time. The ability to recall measurement unit names, definitions, and measurement equivalents is not sufficient for those purposes. The major criterion is the application of concepts and facts in the performance of measurement tasks and in the solution of problems involving measurements. Currently, and for a long time in the future, children will be expected to perform those skills with two systems of measurement—the common U.S. and English system and the metric system.

Communication Skills
In order to communicate with others about measurements, it will be necessary for children to acquire the vocabulary of measurement. This skill goes beyond memorizing terms or names of referent units and definitions of those terms or units. Vocabulary terms are used to communicate meaning, and that type of

use requires that children understand and use the concepts named by those terms. To use referent unit names with meaning, children must acquire ideas about the nature and approximate size of each referent unit to be used. In contemporary programs, referent units from both the common U.S. system and the metric system of measurements must be included. In addition to oral and written names for the referent units, children will also be expected to read and write abbreviations and descriptive symbols for those terms. Many measuring instruments utilize some type of scaled number line. Children are expected to develop skills in reading scaled and numbered referent units on rules, tape measures, scales, protractors, liquid measuring containers, and other devices that they will use in measuring activities. They will also be expected to obtain measurement information from devices such as watches or clocks and thermometers, which they may not actually use in acts of measuring. In an active laboratory-type elementary mathematics program, children should acquire listening, speaking, reading, and writing vocabularies as the terms and symbols are introduced and developed in real measuring situations.

Problem Solving

In order to solve problems involving measurements, children must understand the nature and size of the referent units that are named in the measurements. They must also be able to ascertain the nature of each problem, whether it involves combining, separating, or comparing the quantities described by the given measurements. Some of the problems that children will encounter merely require adding, subtracting, multiplying, or dividing numerical quantities described in measurement units. Those problems with approximate numbers are solved in the same manner as problems with exact numbers, with particular attention given to the necessity of exchanging or regrouping referent units in accordance with the specific equivalents. The approximate numbers of measurement are treated as exact counting numbers. Many of the problems that children will be expected to solve require the substitution of numerical information into formulas that were established for finding amounts of distance, surface, volume, or capacity in regard to geometric entities. If the formulas are developed and established by children in the processes of introductory laboratory-type experiences, those children will be much more likely to understand the nature of the measurement that is required, the symbols in the formulas, and the utilization of formulas in the solutions or problems.

Estimation

Helping children to develop skills of making reasonable estimates of quantities or amounts that might be measured should be an integral part of the learning experiences pertaining to measurement. Estimations may be used to ascertain the reasonableness of solutions to problems, in situations where it is impossible to actually perform the measuring act, or in situations where a reasonable estimate would be sufficient to communicate an idea about the quantity or amount. After children have acquired meaning and understanding of the referent units utilized in each of the types of measurement (distance, surface, and capacity) through the uses of physical object referent units and the common measuring instruments, they should be given opportunities to estimate amounts or quantities and to compare those estimations with the real measurements. An estimation of quantity is not just a guess. Estimations are based on knowledge and understanding. For example, children cannot make reasonable estimates of a distance such as the height of a room unless they are familiar with the units of measurement that might be used in the actual measurement of that distance.

Drawing to Scale

Children emerging from the elementary mathematics program might reasonably be expected to construct simple scale drawings. The construction of scale drawings involves measurement concepts and skills and is related to the major geometric idea of similarity. A shape, figure, or configuration is represented by a drawing that is the same shape but proportionately a different size. The shape or figure may be something from the real world, or it may be a drawing or picture. In most instances, a larger shape or configuration is to be represented by a smaller drawing. However, it is also possible to make a drawing to scale that is larger than the original shape or object. Children should be given opportunities to make scale drawings of both types. Children's first experiences with making scale drawings might deal with simple two-dimensional geometric entities such as rectangles, parallelograms, or triangles or with making simple maps. Later activities can involve more complex configurations and, perhaps, three-dimensional models. Helping children learn to construct scale drawings also implies that they learn to read and interpret scale drawings and models that were constructed or prepared by others. Such drawings appear in a variety of reading and study materials. In addition, many children's toys have been constructed to scale—dolls, doll houses and furniture, and model planes and ships, for example. An interesting activity for children is to determine the real measurements of the pictured objects in scale drawings or the real measurements of a modeled object. The goal of directing learning experiences or activities toward scale drawings and models should be to help children acquire greater proficiency with measurement concepts and skills.

Reading Graphs and Graphing

The abilities to obtain information from graphs or pictorial representations and to construct similar graphs or pictorial representations to present numerical information about some topic or subject are achievement expectations for children in most elementary mathematics programs. Basically, these are reading, writing, and drawing skills and might be appropriately placed in another content area or in a separate content area. These important topics are included here because of their relationships to scale drawings, plottings of points and distances, and the measurement concepts and skills that are utilized in the constructions. The first graphs and pictorial representations that children are asked to read and interpret or to construct will probably contain numerical information about exact or counted numbers. Therefore, ideas and skills related to those graphs and pictorial representations could be introduced and developed as aspects of numeration and notation. Although reading and interpreting the first simple graphic representations to be introduced may not require children to apply measurement concepts and skills, the construction or drawing of "readable" simple graphs does require some proficiency with the ideas and skills of measuring. Topics that help children develop abilities to read and interpret graphs and to construct graphs should be closely related when learning experiences are being planned and selected. Children should be given opportunities to interpret and to construct graphs of each type in a most simple to most complex sequence. The complexity of graphs depends on the nature of the graph, the types of data that are to be presented, and the number of variables that are to be shown. A logical sequence might be from pictographs to bar graphs to line graphs to region graphs (rectangular or circular). Within that sequence, graphs can become more complex by including additional variables or combinations of data. Before each type of graph is introduced, either to be interpreted or to be constructed, consideration should be given to the concepts and skills of numeration and notation, geometry, and measurement that are prerequisites for understanding the graph and completing the instructional tasks.

Materials for Instruction

The basic materials needed to provide opportunities for children to participate in measuring activities are of two types: things to be measured and things with which to measure. Elementary classrooms are filled with things to measure and they should be utilized, but for some specific introductory and developmental activities the things to be measured should be selected and prepared.

1. To introduce and develop concepts and procedures for measuring amounts of surface, cutouts of plane-figure regions (rectangles, squares, parallelograms, triangles) to be covered with physical object units such as small squares and parts of small squares, rectangles and parts of rectangles, and small equilateral triangles should be available.
2. To introduce and develop concepts and procedures for measuring capacity or volume in cubic units, small empty boxes to be filled with small cubes should be collected and used.
3. To introduce and develop concepts and procedures for measuring liquid capacity, empty containers of commercial products as well as liquid measuring devices will be helpful.

Careful selection or preparation of things to be measured will help children see and understand the nature of the types of measurement and the development of special measurement formulas.

Physical Objects

Things for children to measure with are of two kinds: physical object units or models of units, and the commonly used measuring instruments and devices. Physical object measurement units or models for units should have as one of their major characteristics or attributes the characteristic or attribute that is to be measured. For example:

1. Physical object units to be used to measure distances should have length as one of their primary attributes.
2. Physical object units to be used to measure amounts of surface should have as one of their major characteristics the capability of covering surface.
3. Physical object units to be used to measure amounts of volume should take up space.

The physical object units to be used in any one measuring activity should be either congruent or recognizable fractional parts of the units. Although some of the physical object units used in introductory and developmental measuring activities actually may be standard units, initial learning experiences will treat all measurement units as if they were nonstandard units. Later, the obviously nonstandard physical object units will be discarded or stored away and emphasis will be placed on the names, sizes, and relationships of standard units. Physical object units for both the common U.S. system and the metric system should be available and used.

Measuring Devices

After concepts and procedures of measuring have been introduced and developed with physical object units, children can begin using common measuring instruments and devices. For some types of measurement, particularly distance, children can construct their own measuring devices by using the standard physical object units. Measuring instruments and devices for both systems of measurement are to be used. The following chart lists examples of measuring materials and instruments that can be used at varying levels of development. The lists are not intended to be complete; other physical object units and measuring instruments could also be employed.

Type of Measurement	Physical Object Units	Measuring Instruments or Devices
Distance	String Rope Rods Straws Pencils	Rulers Tape Measures Micrometers Calipers
Surface	Small squares and parts of small squares Small rectangles and parts of small rectangles Small equilateral triangles	Rulers Tape measures
Volume (cubic measurements)	Small cubes	Rulers Tape measures
Capacity (liquid)	Cups Glasses Bottles Jars Centimeter cubes	Liquid measuring devices
Weight	Paper clips Coins Small cubes Washers Miscellaneous objects	Pan balances Spring scales

Note that the common measuring instruments used in the formal measuring procedures for finding amounts of surface and volume or capacity are linear measuring devices. However, those devices are utilized to find the number of square or cubic units in a row, the number of rows, and the number of layers—not merely amounts of linear measures. Formulas for finding amounts of surface and capacity are meaningfully developed only through the uses of appropriate physical referent units, not through linear measures.

In some instances, objects that appear to be models or units for one type of measurement can be used in other types of measurement. For example, centimeter cubes and decimeter rods can be used effectively by children to measure distances. The centimeter cubes and decimeter rods can also be used as units of weight and as units of volume or capacity. When the same physical materials are used as referent units for different types of measurement, care must be taken to make certain that children understand the nature of the measurement being made and how the physical referent units are being used.

Drawing and Construction Tools

The drawing and construction tools and materials utilized for drawing and making models of geometric entities will also be employed in making drawings and models involving measurements. In addition, appropriate measuring instruments and devices will be needed to make drawings and models of specific sizes. Abstract printed materials dealing with measurements are needed only for evaluating the extent to which children have acquired measurement ideas, concepts, and skills. Such materials can be used to ascertain whether children (1) have memorized measurement unit equivalents; (2) can measure lines to a nearest unit or fractional part of a unit; (3) can read the face of a clock, a thermometer, or some other measurement device; (4) can perform the operations of addition, subtraction, multiplication, and division in examples or exercises containing measurements; and (5) can solve problems by applying formulas for finding amount of distance, surface, volume, or capacity.

Common Strategies or General Procedures

The basic common strategy for helping children to acquire the ideas and facts of measurement and the skills of measuring is to provide opportunities for children to be actively involved in laboratory-type measuring experiences and activities. Children's understanding of the ideas and facts of measurement and their proficiencies with acts of measuring are developed through applications in real situations. The measurements to be made should be purposeful and realistic for the participating children.

Sequencing Activities

The general sequence of measuring activities for each type of measurement to be conducted proceeds from the uses of measuring materials that are most concrete to those that are most abstract. Initially, physical object referent units are employed and the amount or quantity to be measured is compared to and described in terms of those physical referent units. The physical referent units are then used with common measuring devices to measure the same attributes or characteristics of the same thing or object. The physical referent units are discarded or discontinued in use only when children understand the acts of measuring with physical referent units and the relationships of the physical referent units to the common measuring devices. Finally, children will employ only the appropriate common measuring devices or instruments to ascertain the measurements necessary to describe quantities or amounts and to solve problems involving measurements.

Use of Referent Units

In an active laboratory approach to measurement, all of the physical object referent units that are used by children in early measurement activities are dealt with as if they were nonstandard or uncommon units. The object units for each type of measurement are regular in shape, and the units used in any one measurement should be congruent to each other. All of the referent units used should be available for use by all children. The uses of items, such as children's fingers or hands, that might vary in size or shape as they are used should be avoided. In the earliest measuring activities, quantities or amounts are measured to the nearest whole number of physical object referent units. In later activities after children have acquired understandings of and skills with fractions, particularly equal parts of a unit, quantities or amounts can be measured to the preciseness of a nearest fractional part of a physical referent unit. Those named or described fractional parts thus become smaller referent units. As children begin to understanding the types of measurement that are being made and gain proficiency with the procedures for making those measurements with physical object referent units, the strategy for teachers is to begin to use only physical referent units that represent common standard units in the U.S. and metric systems of measurement. In brief, the general procedure is to begin children's measuring experiences with nonstandard physical referent units and to proceed to standard units of both the metric system and the common U.S. system. The standard physical referent units are then to be used in conjunction with the appropriate common measuring instruments or devices. In that relationship, the markings that indicate a unit and fractional parts of a unit on the measuring devices are more easily understood. This combined use of the two kinds of measuring materials also facilitates the development and application of formulas to measurement situations. Similarly, children's vocabularies (listening, speaking, reading, and writing) are developed in the context of actual measuring experiences and references to the types of units that are used.

Major Ideas or Themes

As children encounter and participate in making various kinds of measurements (distance, surface, capacity, weight), emphasis should be given to the major ideas or themes of the content area as well as to developing specific skills. Children's attention should be drawn to the fact that for several reasons their measurements are not exact, that it is possible to be exact only when single distinct objects are being counted, and that it is impossible to be exact when using numerals to describe the measurement of a quantity or amount. Measurements can only be as precise as the measurer's proficiency with the measuring instruments and the smallness of the referent units being used allow. The communication of measurements and solutions to problems involving measurements to other people requires the use of standard measurement referent units. Children should be helped to see that the same quantity or amount can exist in different shapes, forms, or configurations. Each of these ideas or themes can be introduced with early measuring activities and spirally developed throughout the elementary mathematics program as more difficult and complex measuring situations and problems arise.

Dealing with Two Systems of Measurement

Exercises and examples that involve converting measurements in units of one system of measurements to units in the other system need not and should not be a part of children's study of measurement in an active elementary mathematics program. Such exercises and examples require computational procedures with approximate, not exact, equivalents between the common U.S. system and the metric system of measurements. Since the original measurements are approximate numbers and the between-systems equivalents are approximations, the results of the computational conversions are not very precise descriptions of measurements. The only real purpose for having children convert measurements is to practice the computational operations of multiplication and division with mixed common fractions or decimal fractions. Converting from measurements in units of one system to units of measurement in the other system does not help children understand the major ideas of measurement or acquire proficiencies with the processes of measuring. When such conversions are included as topics in the elementary mathematics program, the stated purposes usually pertain to helping children understand the relationships between measurements and the units of measurement in the two systems. However, there are more appropriate instructional procedures for achieving those purposes. The major ideas of measurement, the types of measurement, and the procedures for measuring with the referent units of both systems are identical. Only the sizes of the referent units, the names of the units, and the exchange bases for equivalent amounts within each system are different. It is also worth noting that new measuring devices and tools are now marked in both systems of measurement, thus eliminating the need for conversion from one system to another. There should be a great deal of similarity in the processes of developing ideas and skills of measuring with the system of U.S. common standard units and with the metric system.

Children who are unfamiliar with both systems of measurement might actually find measurement with the metric system easier

Figure 11.9

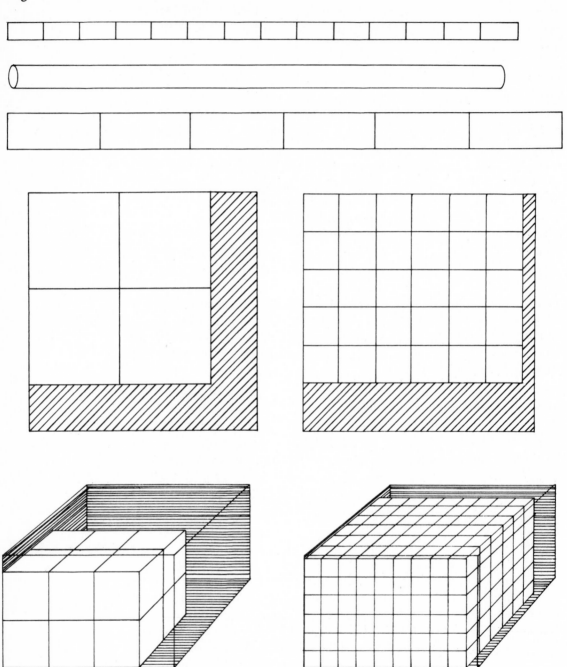

because of the consistent use of base ten and their previous uses of base ten in numeration and notation learning experiences and activities. Initially, children should measure amounts or quantities with referent units from either one system of measurement or the other. Then, if children are allowed to measure the same amounts or quantities with physical referent units and measuring devices of both systems at the same time, they will see the sameness of the measuring procedures as well as the differences in the sizes of the referent units used in the two systems, and they will get a general idea of the comparative relationships between the sizes of the referent units of the two systems that are used to make the same type of measurement. Another natural observation will be that the same quantity or amount can be described in terms of different units. For example, children should be allowed to measure the same distance between objects or lengths of things with units of the common U.S. system and with units of the metric system. The physical object referent units of the two systems can be placed beside, on, or in things to make the same measurement (see Figure 11.9). The referent units of the two systems should not be intermixed to make a measurement. The goals are to help children learn to measure and describe amounts or quantities with both systems of measurement and to acquire general ideas about the comparative relationships of referent units used for the same types of measurement in the two systems. For example, 1 inch is a little bit longer than 2 centimeters, 1 square centimeter is a little bit less than 1 square half-inch, and so on.

Organizing for Instruction

Organizing the elementary classroom for an active approach to measurement involves the following:

1. Plan and select the types of measurement that are to be dealt with in one instructional unit or in one period of learning experiences and activities.
2. Provide the appropriate kinds and sufficient numbers of measuring materials so that all children can be actively involved in measuring as individuals or in small groups.

3. Predetermine and provide a sufficient number of things that are to be measured so that children will not have to wait to participate in a measuring activity.

For some measurement tasks or activities, individuals or small groups of children will remain at one location in the classroom. For other activities, individuals and small groups may move from place to place in the room. A visitor to an elementary mathematics class involved in an active approach to measurement would see individuals and small groups of children busily engaged in measurement activities and a teacher moving from place to place guiding and directing activities and observing children's procedures and progress.

Some teachers might wish to utilize an organizational approach in which only one type of measurement is dealt with during one instructional period or unit of study. All children in the classroom would be engaged in some type of learning experience or activity directed toward understanding the ideas, units, and measuring procedures of the same kind of quantity or amount. In such an approach, the sequence of instructional units generally proceeds from linear measurement to surface or area to volume to liquid capacity. In spite of the fact that the referent units for these types of measurement are distinctly different, the attitudes or dispositions of educators supporting this approach appear to be that competencies in measuring length are prerequisites to measuring area and that competencies in measuring or determining amounts of length and surface are prerequisites for measuring amounts of cubic volume and liquid capacity. These attitudes and dispositions are more relevant to programs that approach measurement in a more abstract manner through formulas and the applications of formulas than they are to an active laboratory approach. Instructional units dealing with "telling time" or reading the clock and weighing objects do not fit in the sequence and are interjected into the program at the discretion of the teacher or the printed instructional materials used. When this organizational approach is used, children often are left on their own to discern differences between the types of measurement and the referent units employed in each type of measurement. When the program is dominated by printed instructional materials and children's participation in the teaching-learning process is relatively passive, misconceptions about the natures of measuring different types of quantities or amounts and confusions about the differences between measuring amounts of distance, surface, and volume are likely to occur.

For active laboratory-type elementary mathematics programs, the recommendations are that different types of measurement should be dealt with in the same instructional periods or units, and that during any one instructional unit, each child in the classroom should participate in measuring activities dealing with different types of measurement. If that participation involves the use of physical referent units for the different types of measurement, children will be much more likely to see and understand the nature of each type of measurement, the kinds of referent units that are used, and the procedures for measuring.

Levels of development in terms of difficulty and complexity will evolve naturally and can be similar for any one child with the various types of measurement during any one instructional unit. Procedures employing physical referent units will lead children to the meaningful development of formulas and the utilization of linear measurements to ascertain the numerical values to be substituted in formulas. Utilizing this organizational approach for instruction in measurement implies that teachers and/or children will keep records and gather information pertaining to individual progress and participation in learning experiences and activities. By using the data that are collected, teachers can guide and direct individual children to and through appropriate sequences of measurement learning experiences and activities for introducing, developing, and practicing performance skills associated with major ideas or themes and achievement expectations.

Examples of Learning Experiences

There is no scarcity of things or objects to be measured in an elementary classroom. The instructional procedure should not allow children to attempt to measure those things indiscriminately or at random. Instead, the quantities or amounts to be measured by individuals and small groups of children should be carefully selected and listed so that individual measurements of the same things or objects can be compared and discussed with references to procedures and precision. Individuals and small groups of children should compare the measurements they make with the measurements made by other children. It will be easier for children to compare and discuss measurements if they are encouraged or required to keep records, including drawings of the measurements that they make. In some instances, teacher-prepared record-keeping sheets will help children organize and present pertinent information and measurement results. If things or objects to be measured are listed on the record-keeping sheets, children should be informed that the things or objects need not be measured in the order in which they are listed. Most of the following examples of measuring activities involve some form of record keeping by children. However, record keeping should not be required until children have demonstrated their understanding of the nature of the measurements to be made and of the general procedures for making those measurements.

Figure 11.10

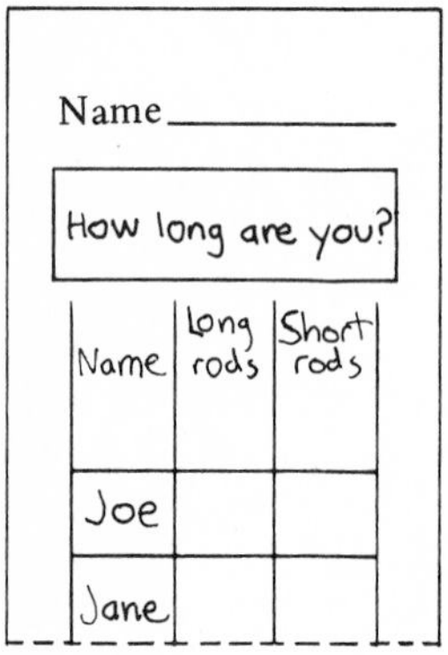

How Long Are You? A small group of young children working together. A quantity of centimeter cubes and decimeter rods and a record-keeping sheet similar to the one shown in Figure 11.10. A large cardboard box will also be helpful. The children are given the centimeter cubes and decimeter rods and the box and are provided a working space next to an open wall. The object is for the participating children to measure one another's lengths (heights) using the decimeter rods and the centimeter cubes as referent units. The procedure is for each child, in turn, to lie on the floor with his or her feet flat against the wall, making himself or herself as long as possible. The box is then placed square against the top of that person's head by another child and held there while the child who is being measured gets up. Then the task is to find the shortest distance from the base of the wall to the box by placing the decimeter rods and the centimeter cubes in a straight line. The numerical information about the measurement of each child is placed on the record-keeping sheet. Teachers may use their own judgment about the vocabulary that is to be introduced and references to units of the metric system.

Make Figures with the Same Amounts of Surface Individual children. Squared paper, straightedge, and pencil. Each child is given the materials and is told to draw as many figures as possible that enclose *N* squares (the number of squares is given). The lines of the squares on the paper are to be followed except that diagonal lines to make half-squares can be drawn. Figure 11.11 shows figures that might be drawn to enclose 12 square units. After each child thinks that he or she has made all of the possible drawings, comparisons with the drawings constructed by other children can be made. The generalization should be reached that different shapes or figures can enclose the same amounts of surface. The activity can be extended by removing the restrictions about how the boundary lines can be drawn. The same activity can also involve finding the distance around (the perimeter) each shape or figure. The generalization can then be extended to the idea that different regions containing the same amount of surface may have different perimeters.

Figure 11.11

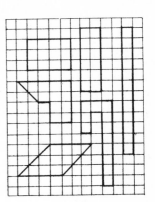

Make Rectangular Solids Children working as individuals or in small groups. Small cubes and a record-keeping sheet. Numeral cubes might also be used. Two different approaches might be used, or the two approaches might be treated as separate activities. In one approach, the children are given a definite number of small cubes and told to make as many different rectangular solids as possible. The number of cubes used might best be a multiple of 12 (12, 24, 36, 48) so that a variety of constructions is possible (see Figure 11.12). As each solid is made, the numerical information about that solid should be entered on a record-keeping sheet indicating how long, how wide, how high, and how many cubes altogether. This activity may serve as the introductory foundation for developing the formula for finding the volume of a box or other rectangular solids. In the second approach, three numeral cubes are rolled and the numerals shown on the cubes describe the length, width, and height of the rectangular solid to be constructed. With each roll of the three numeral cubes, several different rectangular solids can be built as each numeral could be used to describe either the length, width, or height. The ideas of both the associative property of multiplication and conservation of quantity or mass can be further developed with this activity.

Which Bottle Holds More Liquid? A large-group activity with children participating individually at different times. No special materials are necessary, but shelf space for the bottles that will be collected should be available. Children are invited or encouraged to bring an empty plastic bottle from home. For reasons of safety, the bottle should be plastic, not glass, and should be

Figure 11.12

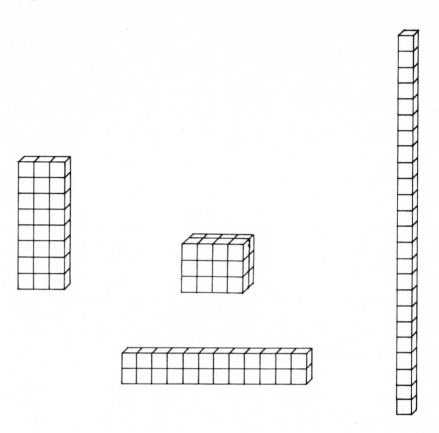

washed thoroughly before it is brought to school. Only one bottle of each kind will be needed so a rule might be established that the first bottle of one kind that is brought will be the one that is used. Each bottle will be tagged with the name of the child who brought it. As each child brings a bottle, he or she places that bottle on the shelf in its appropriate place so that the bottles are arranged in order from the bottle that holds least to the bottle that holds most. When there is a question or challenge about the capacity of particular bottles, the children whose names are on the bottles and the questioner or challenger should be allowed to fill and pour water (or some other material such as sand) from one bottle to the other. Later, liquid measuring devices can be used to find out how much liquid each bottle will hold.

Figure 11.13

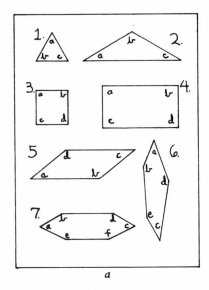

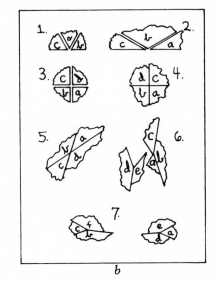

a   b

When the activity is completed, all of the bottles will be arranged in order of capacity on the shelf.

Find The Total Amount of the Corners (Angles) in Plane Figures Individuals or small groups of children working together. Plain white paper, straightedge, pencil, scissors, glue or paste, and sheets of colored construction paper. The children are given the plain white paper, straightedge, and pencil and told to draw different kinds of plane figures (triangles, quadrilaterals, pentagons, and hexagons, for example) large enough so that they can be cut out easily and the corners or angles torn off. Each corner or angle of each figure should be named (inside the figure) with a small letter. Figure 11.13a shows some of the figures that might be drawn. After several figures have been drawn, the scissors are used to cut out the shapes. Then, one by one, the corners of each figure are torn off, placed adjacent to one another on a sheet of construction paper, and pasted to it. Figure 11.13b shows how the figures drawn on the first part might be placed and pasted. Some teachers may want children to cut out two congruent shapes for each drawing, have children tear the corners off one of the congruent shapes, and paste one of the original shapes and the

Figure 11.14

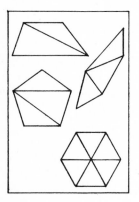

combination of the torn-off corners of the other cut-out shape on one sheet of construction paper in a "before and after" manner. The nature of the generalizations that are made about the sums of the angles or corners of different kinds of plane figures will depend on the mathematical maturities of the children participating. Sums in terms of degrees should not be dealt with until children are capable of using a protractor to measure angles. Until that time, children can be helped to describe the total amount of the corners or angles in plane figures in terms of the amount of turn that a hand or ray with its end point at the common vertex would make—one-half turn, one full turn, one and one-half turns, and so on. When children are placing and pasting the corners of plane figures that total more than one full turn, they may either cut, place, and paste the amounts greater than one full turn or draw lines to clarify the total. Variations in this activity would include cutting or partitioning all of the plane-figure regions into triangular regions and then determining the total amount of turn or degrees on the basis of one-half turn (or 180 degrees) per triangle (Figure 11.14) and making a chart to show the names of the plane figures, the number of angles in each plane figure, and the total amount of turn or degrees in the angles (Figure 11.15).

Figure 11.15

Figure 11.16

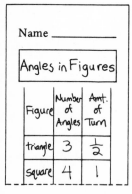

Name _____

Angles in Figures		
Figure	Number of Angles	Amt. of Turn
triangle	3	$\frac{1}{2}$
square	4	1

Name _____

Things That Are Round

Name of Thing	Distance around A	Distance across B	A + B	A − B	A × B	B) A

Things That Are Round Two or three children working together. A cloth or plastic dressmaker's measuring tape, a chart similar to the one shown in Figure 11.16, paper on which to perform computations, and circular things in the room. The small group of children is given the pliable tape measure (the tape may be marked in units of inches or centimeters) and the prepared chart and told to find circular or round objects in the classroom. The tape is to be used to measure the distance around and the distance across the approximate center of each circular object. Those measurements are to be entered on the chart and the indicated operations for each pair of measurements is to be performed. The results of those operations are entered in the appropriate columns of the chart. After a small group of children has measured a sufficient number (more than eight) of circular objects and performed the indicated operations, they can study the chart they have made in order to make some generalizations about the results of their computations. The object of the activity is to help children understand the relationship between the circumference and diameter of all circles. However, the conclusions or generalizations reached may be as simple as "The larger the circle, the greater the sum of the distance around and the distance across." But, "Regardless of the sizes of the circles, when the distance around is divided by the distance across, the answers (quotients) are about the same." Naturally, children should be encouraged to be as precise as possible in their measurements. However, teachers should be aware that ability to perform the computational operations with mixed common and decimal numbers is a prerequisite and that more precise measurements involving smaller units require greater proficiencies with the operations. The extent to which the generalization about the result of dividing the distance around a circle by the distance across that circle is extended or utilized in other problem situations involving *pi* or the relationships between the circumference and diameter is up to the classroom teacher, whose judgment should be based on the goals of the program and the varying capabilities of children.

Suggested Activities

1. Review an elementary mathematics textbook series and the promotional and supplementary materials (scope and sequence

chart, workbooks, and the like) that accompany it for purposes of

a. determining the types of measurement that are dealt with at various levels.

b. ascertaining the extent to which attention is given to the concepts or ideas of standard units, conservation of quantity, measurements as approximate numbers, and precision in measurements.

c. analyzing the general approach that is suggested for helping children learn about the nature of measurement and how to measure. Consider the referent units and measuring materials and devices that are to be used at different levels and the procedures for involving children with the uses of those materials.

d. determining whether appropriate attention is given to both the common U.S. system and the metric system of measurement.

e. ascertaining what kinds of quantitative problems and examples or exercises are presented for solutions by children. How are formulas dealt with?

2. Refer to the chart on page 341 dealing with types of measurement, physical object units, and measuring instruments or devices in the section "Materials for Instruction." Extend that chart to include "Measuring Activities" and "Projects of Application" and list some activities and projects for each type of measurement.

3. Select one general age or grade level in the elementary school. Develop an instructional unit for measurement that will include learning experiences and activities in measuring amounts of distance, surface, cubic volume, liquid capacity, and weight for that general age or grade level.

4. Devise a record of participation and progress sheet that might be used for each child participating in the instructional unit developed for activity 3.

5. Begin a collection of physical objects that might be used as nonstandard referent units by children who are learning to measure.

Mathematical Learning Aids for Classroom Construction

Following are some examples of materials or construction projects described in the companion volume to this text, *Active Learning Experiences for Teaching Elementary School Mathematics*. Additional suggestions for instructional aids that teachers and/or children can make are included in references cited in Appendix B.

Models for Number

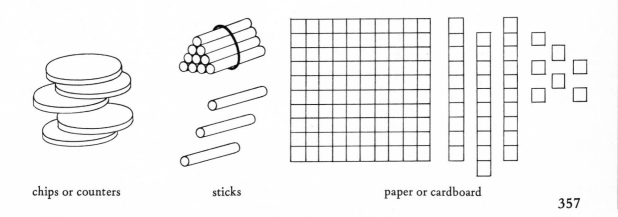

chips or counters   sticks   paper or cardboard

357

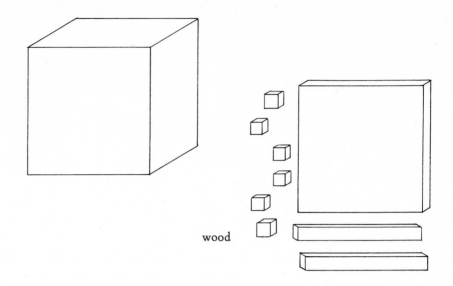

wood

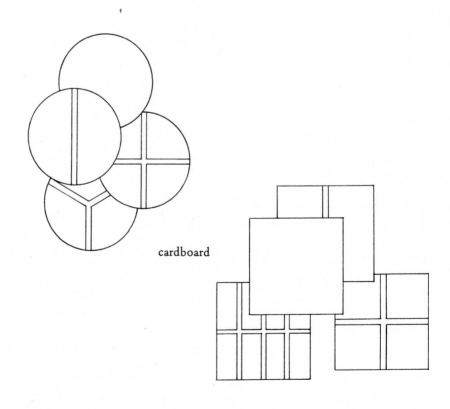

cardboard

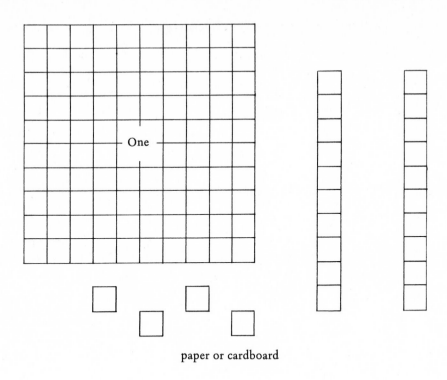

paper or cardboard

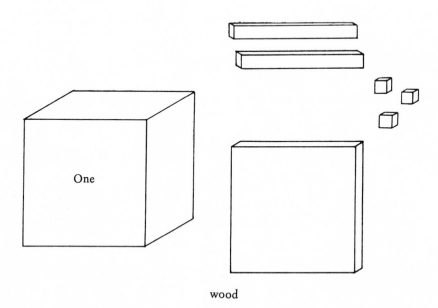

wood

Hundred Boards and Related Materials

Hundred Squares Board

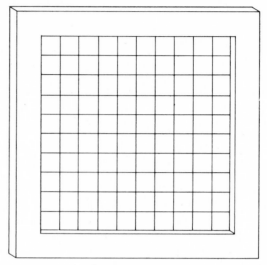

heavy cardboard

Strips of Squares

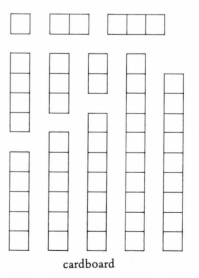

cardboard

Hundred Board (with Nails or Hooks)

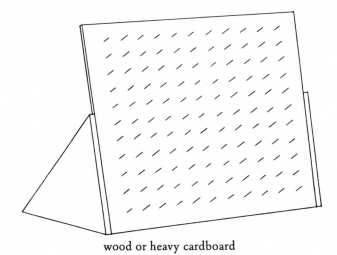

wood or heavy cardboard

Numeral Tags

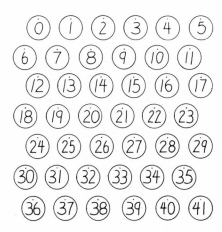

. . . and so on to 100

(Randomly selected three-digit numerals may be written on the back of the tags.)

Learning Aids for Place Value

Place-Value Flip Chart

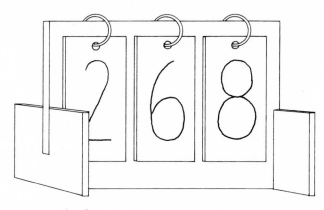

notebook rings
3- by 5-inch cards
heavy cardboard

Place-Value Odometer

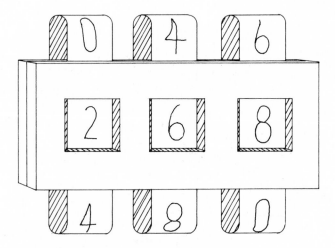

loops made of strips of paper
two layers of heavy cardboard

Place-Value Tray

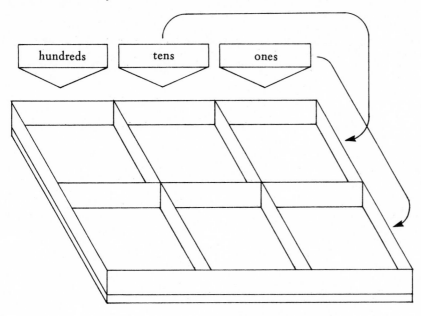

wood or cardboard

Cubes

Cubes can be made of wood or plastic. Numerals can either be written directly on the cube with durable ink, written on gummed labels and then pasted on the cube, or written on masking tape covering the cube.

Numeral Cubes—Whole Numbers

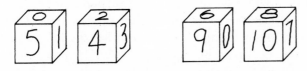

(0, 1, 2, 3, 4, 5)   (0, 6, 7, 8, 9, 10)
(To generate larger numerals, two, three, four, or more cubes may be rolled.)

Fraction Numeral Cubes

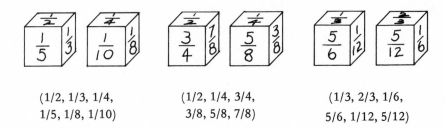

(1/2, 1/3, 1/4,   (1/2, 1/4, 3/4,   (1/3, 2/3, 1/6,
1/5, 1/8, 1/10)   3/8, 5/8, 7/8)   5/6, 1/12, 5/12)

Operational or Sign Cubes

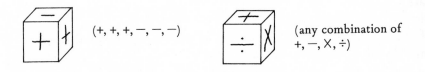

(+, +, +, −, −, −)   (any combination of
                                                +, −, ×, ÷)

Cards

Some of the commercially produced children's card games available in toy departments can be used in elementary mathematics learning activities. However, decks of cards commonly used by adults are not recommended for use in classrooms. Teachers would not want children to leave school counting "ace, deuce, trey, . . . , jack, queen, king." The matching or sequencing ideas that are involved in both children's games and common card decks can be employed to construct similar decks of cards.

The constructed decks should be as durable and attractive as possible. To avoid thick, unwieldy, unattractive materials, the pictures, numerals, or words should be drawn directly on blank cards rather than first drawn on other paper and pasted on the card. Blank cards may be purchased or prepared. Test drawing instruments before using to make sure that the ink does not smear after drying or soak through the card. Templates or cardboard cutouts will be helpful in making the cards more attractive and the drawings more precise. The composition of elements in each deck of cards should be carefully planned before construction

small whole numbers

or drawing begins. Prior to constructing any set of cards, several precise and defined uses of the deck in terms of children's learning activities and games should be determined.

Number Picture Cards

Separate decks of number picture cards may be constructed for small whole numbers, whole numbers greater than 10, common fractions, and decimal fractions. Each deck of cards should be prepared so that it can be used by itself or with an associated deck of numeral cards.

Picture cards for small whole numbers are made by drawing small distinct single objects on cards. The numbers of pictures of objects on cards should not exceed ten. Cards should be prepared to have 0, 1, 2, 3, 4, 5, 6, 7, 8, and 9 pictures of objects. The deck should contain at least three cards of each number of pictures. The pictures may be arranged in configurations so that children can easily recognize the number of objects pictured on the card without counting. The pictures on different cards may be of different objects or forms, but the pictures on any one card should be the same.

Number picture cards for whole numbers greater than 10 should contain pictures of appropriate models for number, preferably ice-cream sticks and bundles of ten ice-cream sticks or pieces from a base-ten block model. Naturally, every number cannot be represented in one deck. Each deck of cards should be planned and constructed so that (1) the same pictured number appears on at least two different cards and (2) some of the cards picture the sums of two other cards and/or some of the cards picture multiples of other cards.

A set of number picture cards for decimal fractions can be constructed in much the same manner as a set of picture cards for whole numbers greater than 10. In fact, the picture cards for whole numbers greater than 10 can be used as decimal fraction picture cards *if* a referent model or picture of *one* is distinctly specified and referred to before and during any activity or game utilizing the cards.

As with other number picture cards, each card in a deck of common fraction picture cards will contain a picture of one number. The following chart indicates the common fractions that might be pictured and the number of cards for each picture in one usable set or deck. The same region or referent for *one*

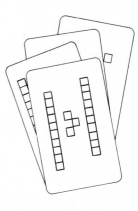

whole numbers greater than 10

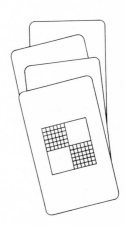

common fractions

should be used for all the pictures in one set of cards. However, it is recommended that the region for *one* be partitioned in different ways on different cards to show the same fractional quantity or number (see illustration in margin).

Fraction	Number of Cards	Fraction	Number of Cards
1/2	3	6/8	3
1/4	3	7/8	2
2/4	3	1/3	3
3/4	3	2/3	3
1/8	2	1/6	2
2/8	3	2/6	3
3/8	2	3/6	3
4/8	3	4/6	3
5/8	2	5/6	2

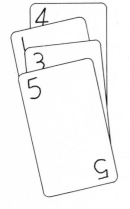

small whole numbers

Numeral Cards

Separate decks of numeral cards also may be constructed for small whole numbers, larger whole numbers, common fractions, and decimal fractions. As previously implied, decks of numeral cards can be used in conjunction with corresponding number picture cards.

A set of numeral cards for small whole numbers should include the ideas of both matching and ordering. Sequences of numerals can be printed or drawn on cards with different colors so that one deck may have the same numeral on three or four different cards in different colors. Numerals on the cards probably should not exceed 20. However, for any particular activity or game, a deck can be separated for use by color or to contain only certain numerals.

Color	Numerals
Black	0, 1, 2, 3, 4, 5, 6, 7, 8, 9, 10, . . .
Red	0, 1, 2, 3, 4, 5, 6, 7, 8, 9, 10, . . .
Blue	0, 1, 2, 3, 4, 5, 6, 7, 8, 9, 10, . . .
Other	0, 1, 2, 3, 4, 5, 6, 7, 8, 9, 10, . . .

larger whole numbers

Numerals cards for larger whole numbers are not necessary for every numeral in any particular sequence. For example, certain numerals between 100 and 1000 can be selected and drawn on cards. Those cards can be used by children to practice showing and comparing quantities or numbers with models, comparing numerals, and ordering numerals.

Decimal fraction numerals and mixed decimal fraction numerals can be selected, drawn on cards, and the cards used in the same manner.

A deck of common fraction numeral cards can be constructed to correspond with the common fraction number picture cards. Such a deck would contain the same number of cards as the number picture cards. At one level of development, children might use these cards with a physical object model, such as a fraction pie. At another level the cards could be used with the common fraction number picture cards. At a later level, the cards could be used by themselves in a variety of activities and games.

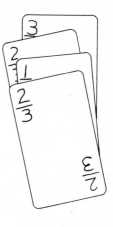

common fractions

Geometry Cards

Two types of cards pertaining to geometric concepts might be prepared. Geometry word cards can contain phrases that describe an attribute or characteristic of a geometric entity. Geometry picture cards can contain pictures of geometric entities. The two types of cards can be prepared so that they can be used separately or together. Also, the word cards might be used with physical object models.

Examples of phrases:
  0 sides equal
  2 sides equal
  All sides equal
  2 opposite sides parallel
  All opposite sides parallel
  0 angles equal
  2 angles equal
  All angles equal
  0 right angles
  1 right angle
  2 right angles
  All right angles

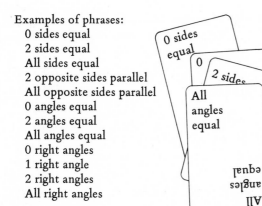

Types of pictures in different sets:
  One-dimensional: lines and parts of lines; angles
  Two-dimensional: plane figures—deck is constructed to include pictures that are of the same general classification; some pictures are congruent, some pictures are similar

Dominoes

Sets of dominoes may be purchased in any toy department. In the smallest set of dominoes, 6 is the largest number. Sets with 9 as the largest number and 12 as the largest number are also made and sold. The following chart illustrates the numerical arrangement of dots on a set of dominoes in which 6 is the largest number. Note that every possible combination of the numbers appears and that each combination appears only once.

A variety of games, each with different rules and game objectives, which are mathematical in nature, can be played with regular sets of dominoes to practice arithmetical ideas and skills.

Sets of dominoes with mathematical representations other than whole numbers (dots) can be constructed. Games that are similar in rules and approaches to those played with regular dominoes can be played with the constructed dominoes to develop and practice other mathematical ideas.

Domino games primarily involve matching. With representations of number values, the matching generally pertains to matching equivalent values. If dominoes are made for the areas of geometry or measurement, the nature of the matching to be done should be carefully considered and planned prior to construction.

Fraction Dominoes

A set of fraction dominoes can be constructed in the following manner.

1. Decide which pictures of fractions are to be used: 1/2, 1/3, 2/3, 1/4, 2/4, 3/4, . . .
2. Ascertain the possible combinations in the set.
3. Decide what type of drawings (circular or square, for example) are going to be used, and whether different drawings for the same fraction will be utilized. Sample drawings for 1/4 are shown in the margin.

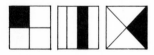

4. Cut the domino pieces from heavy tagboard or fiberboard, each domino approximately 1 1/2 inches by 3 inches.
5. Make one domino for each of the combinations either (a) by drawing the fraction pictures on the dominoes or (b) by drawing the desired fraction pictures on a sheet of paper, reproducing the pictures to avoid the tasks of repetition in drawing, and cutting and pasting the pictures on the dominoes.

6/6	6/5	6/4	6/3	6/2	6/1	6/0

	5/5	5/4	5/3	5/2	5/1	5/0

		4/4	4/3	4/2	4/1	4/0

			3/3	3/2	3/1	3/0

				2/2	2/1	2/0

					1/1	1/0

						0/0

The following chart can be used with reference to the chart on page 369 that illustrates a set of regular dominoes to ascertain the possible combinations and the dominoes to be made.

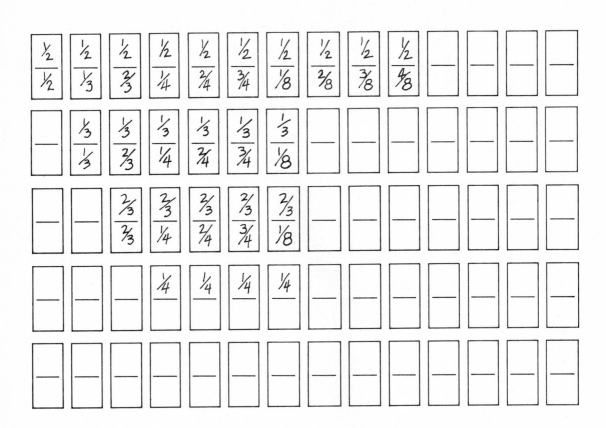

Geometry Dominoes

A different procedure may be used to make a set of geometry dominoes, which can be used to practice ideas of classification, similarity, and congruence. The procedure does not involve making all the possible combinations of two of the pictures of the geometric shapes that are to be used. Obviously, if one wished to include all the figures in the following chart, the number of possible combinations would be too large and cumbersome for one set of dominoes.

However, a usable game set can be made by including each figure twice with no figure appearing on a domino with itself, with a drawing that is similar (same shape, but different size), and if possible, not with a figure in the same general classification (triangles, quadrilaterals, pentagons, hexagons, octagons). Also, each domino should contain one larger drawing and one smaller drawing.

The number of dominoes in the set will depend on the number of figures selected for inclusion. The following chart suggests some of the figures that might be included in a set of dominoes pertaining to plane figures. The dominoes must be large enough (perhaps 2 inches by 4 inches) so that the drawings of the figures can be easily made and so that differences in the drawings can be easily seen. Templates and/or small cardboard cutouts will be helpful in drawing the pictures of figures. The two large pictures of each figure should be congruent; the two small pictures of each figure should be similar to the large picture of the same figure and congruent to each other.

Figures	*Number of Pictures*	
Scalene triangle	2 large	2 small
Scalene right triangle	2 large	2 small
Isosceles triangle	2 large	2 small
Isosceles right triangle	2 large	2 small
Equilateral triangle	2 large	2 small
Irregular quadrilateral	2 large	2 small
Parallelogram	2 large	2 small
Rectangle	2 large	2 small
Square	2 large	2 small
Circle	2 large	2 small
Irregular pentagon	2 large	2 small
Regular pentagon	2 large	2 small
Irregular hexagon	2 large	2 small
Regular hexagon	2 large	2 small
Irregular octagon	2 large	2 small
Regular octagon	2 large	2 small

Geometry Attribute Shapes and Solids

Construction-paper shapes can be made with three characteristics or attributes (shape, size, and color) for use in comparison and classification activities and games. A minimum set of shapes would include three different shapes, two different sizes of each shape, and four different colors of each shape and size. If circles, squares, and equilateral triangles are selected for the shapes, the set should include four large circles of four different colors, four small circles of the same four different colors, four large squares of the same four different colors, four small squares of the same four different colors, four large equilateral triangles of the same four different colors, and four small equilateral triangles of the same four different colors. The length of the sides of the large squares, the diameters of the large circles, and the heights of the large equilateral triangles should be equal. Similarly, those measurements of the small figures should be equal to each other.

The construction or acquisition of wooden solids can add another attribute—thickness—to the set. A minimum set of wooden attribute solids would include four different colors of three different shapes of two different sizes of two different thicknesses.

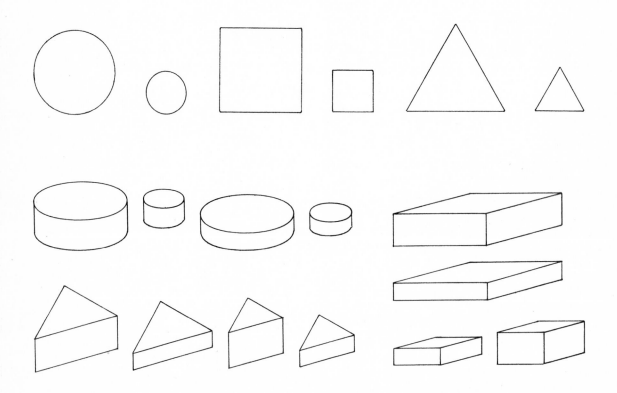

Puzzles

Addition Number Puzzles
Following are only several examples of the many puzzles that can
be made. Each puzzle can be drawn on a separate piece of cardboard. Solutions for each of the following puzzles are to be found
by arranging numeral disks on the puzzles that sums are the same
along all lines. Different sequences of numerals can be used
to find solutions.

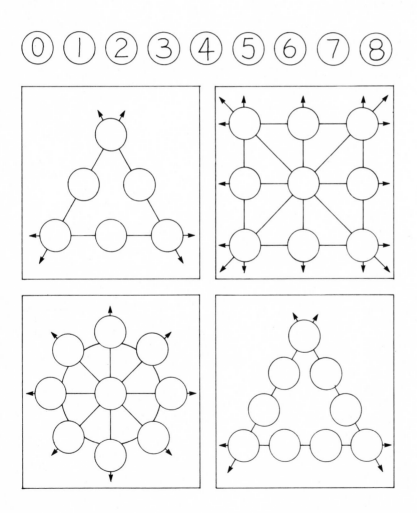

Tangram Puzzle
Some activities for tangram puzzles:

1. Associate plane figure names and attributes with the pieces.
2. Cover the larger pieces with smaller pieces. Which pieces have the same amounts of surface?
3. Make all possible squares. Make different size squares as many different ways as possible. Keep a record by making drawings.
4. Make all possible triangles. Make different size triangles as many different ways as possible. Keep a record by making drawings.
5. Use all of the pieces to make one large _____: square, triangle, rectangle, or parallelogram.

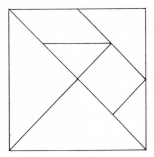

Can be cut from one square of cardboard. The intersections are midpoints of line segments.

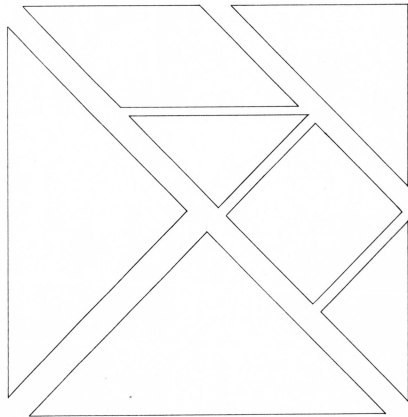

6. Make a tangram puzzle for others to solve. Use the pieces to make a picture. Draw the outside outline of the picture to make the puzzle.
7. Solve a tangram puzzle made by someone else.

Miscellaneous Materials

Spinner

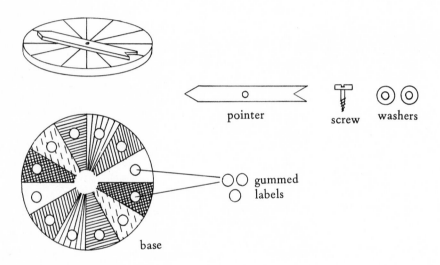

pointer   screw   washers

gummed labels

base

Number Lines

| 0 | 1 | 2 | 3 | 4 | 5 | 6 | 7 | 8 | 9 | 10 | 11 | 12 | 13 | 14 | 15 | 16 | 17 | 18 |

$^-8$ $^-7$ $^-6$ $^-5$ $^-4$ $^-3$ $^-2$ $^-1$ 0 $^+1$ $^+2$ $^+3$ $^+4$ $^+5$ $^+6$ $^+7$

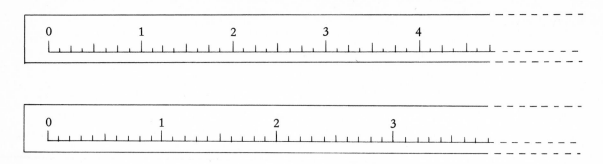

Measuring Rope

Knots are tied at equal intervals. Length of rope is 12 units. Prior to tying knots, rope must be longer than 12 units to allow for rope used in knotting.

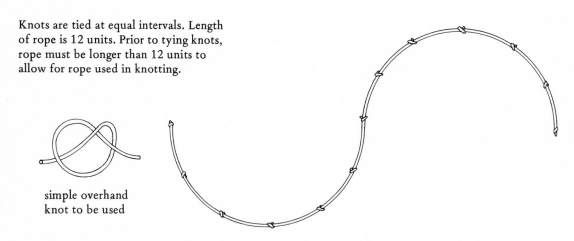

simple overhand
knot to be used

Pan Balance

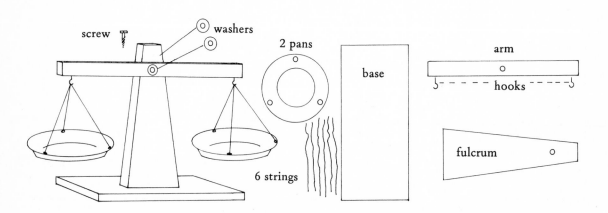

Surface Figures

small squares and diagonal halves of squares

Pegboard and Ring Toss Game

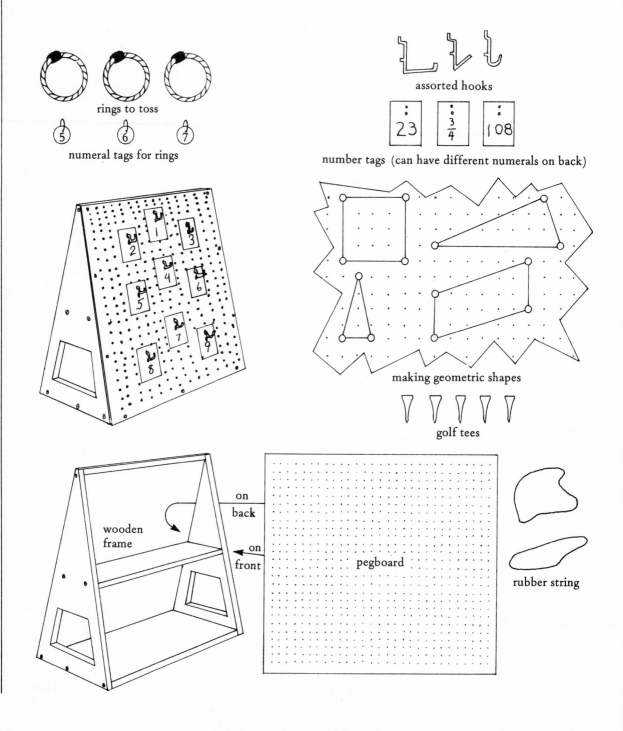

rings to toss

numeral tags for rings

assorted hooks

number tags (can have different numerals on back)

making geometric shapes

golf tees

wooden frame

on back

on front

pegboard

rubber string

Suggested Sources of Ideas for Active Elementary Mathematics Programs

Appendix B

With the exception of *Active Learning Experiences for Teaching Elementary School Mathematics*, which is the companion volume to this text and therefore is completely compatible with the principles contained herein, the inclusion of a source in the following lists does not indicate that the ideas, materials, and procedures described in the source are in *total* accord with the approach advocated in this text. Furthermore, the appearance of a source in the lists does not constitute an endorsement by this author. The lists of suggested sources are not intended to be exhaustive. The sources are suggested merely to extend the reader's possibilities for finding learning experience that he or she may wish to include in an active elementary mathematics program. The ideas, materials, and procedures in any source should be carefully studied and evaluated by elementary mathematics program planners and developers—including classroom teachers, program directors, and administrators—prior to purchase and/or adoption.

NCTM Publications

The following publications are available from the National Council of Teachers of Mathematics (NCTM), 1906 Association Drive, Reston, Virginia 22091.

Bidwell, J.K., ed. *Metric Measurement Activity Cards*. 1974.
> Ninety-four activity cards on forty-seven pages removable for duplication. K-6 metric activities in linear, area, and volume measurement.

Cathcart, W.G., ed. *The Mathematics Laboratory: Readings from "The Arithmetic Teacher."* 1977.
> Forty articles on the what, why, when, and how of mathematics laboratories in elementary schools.

NCTM. *Instructional Aids in Mathematics: 34th Yearbook*. 1973.
> An illustrated guide to instructional aids, including ideas on evaluating quality and utility, suggestions for use, and ways of constructing materials.

NCTM. *Mathematics Learning in Early Childhood: 37th Yearbook*. 1976.
> Ideas and activities for instruction are included in chapters on cognition, curriculum, research, and teaching procedures. Presents a developmental-learning point of view with emphasis on problem solving and relating mathematics to the child's real world.

Olson, Alton T. *Mathematics Through Paper Folding*. 1975.
> Illustrated paper-folding activities directed toward discovering and demonstrating mathematical relationships.

Smith, S.E., Jr., and Backman, C.A., eds. *Games and Puzzles for Elementary and Middle School Mathematics: Readings from "The Arithmetic Teacher."* 1975.
> More than 100 articles dealing with the uses of games and puzzles pertaining to whole numbers, numeration, integers, rational numbers, number theory and patterns, geometry and measurement, reasoning, and logic.

Suydam, Marilyn, ed. *Developing Computational Skills: 1978 Yearbook*. 1978.

A variety of authors present views on teaching the basic facts, algorithms, and mental arithmetic. Also ideas on teaching learning disabled children, motivating junior high school students, and using a calculator.

Walter, Marion I. *Boxes, Squares, and Other Things: A Teacher's Guide for a Unit in Informal Geometry*. 1970.

Intended to help children visualize two- and three-dimensional objects. Introduces geometric transformations, symmetry, and group theory.

Additional References

Association of Teachers of Mathematics. *Notes on Mathematics in Primary Schools*. Cambridge: Cambridge University Press.

Bitter, G.; Mikesell, U.L.; and Maurdeff, K.G. *Activities Handbook for Teaching the Metric System*. Boston: Allyn and Bacon.

Buckeye, Donald A., et al. *Cheap Math Lab Equipment*. Troy, Mich.: Midwest Publications, 1972.

Charbonneau, Manon P. *Learning to Think in a Math Lab*. Boston: National Association of Independent Schools, 1971.

Dumas, Enoch, and Schminke, C.W. *Math Activities for Child Involvement*. 2nd ed. Boston: Allyn and Bacon, 1977.

Educational Teaching Aids. *Holiday Math Activity Books (Primary and Intermediate)*. Chicago: Educational Teaching Aids, 159 W. Kinzie St.

Forte, Imogene, and MacKenzie, Joy. *Creative Math Experiences for the Young Child*. Nashville, Tenn.: Incentive Publications, 1973.

Frank, Marjorie. *Kids' Stuff Math*. Nashville, Tenn.: Incentive Publications, 1974.

Grime, Gary, and Mitchell, Don. *The Good Apple Math Book*. Carthage, Ill.: Good Apple Publications, P.O. Box 299.

Horn, Sylvia. *Patterns and Puzzles in Mathematics*. Chicago: Lyons and Carnahan.

Johnson, Hiram; James, S.; Barnes, B.; and Colton T. "Learning Centers for Mathematics." In *The Learning Center Idea Book: Activities for the Elementary and Middle Grades*. Boston: Allyn and Bacon, 1978.

Kaplan, Sandra N., et al. *Change for Children: Ideas and Activities for Individualizing Learning*. Pacific Palisades, Calif.: Goodyear Publishing Company, 1973.

Kennedy, Leonard M. *Models for Mathematics in the Elementary School*. Belmont, Calif.: Wadsworth Publishing.

Kennedy, Leonard M., and Michon, Ruth. *Games for Individualizing Mathematics Learning*. Columbus, Ohio: Charles E. Merrill.

Laboratory Mathematics: Teachers Management Guide and *Laboratory Mathematics: Math Lab Activities*. E.D.R.S., Anderson County School District No. 2, Honea Path, S.C.

Lerch, Harold H. *Active Learning Experiences for Teaching Elementary School Mathematics*. Boston: Houghton Mifflin Company, 1981.

Media for Education. *Monster Math, Dinosaur Drills Math Mazes, Nutsy Numbers, Special Math*, and other activity booklets. Los Angeles: Media for Education, 13208 W. Washington Blvd.

Moore, Carolyn C. *Why Don't We Do Something Different? Mathematical Activities for the Elementary Grades*. Boston: Prindle, Weber and Schmidt.

O'Neil, David, ed. *Gimmicks*. Des Moines, Iowa: Central Iowa Math Project for Low Achievers, 1350 E. Washington Ave.

Schuh, Fred. *The Master Book of Mathematical Puzzles and Recreations*. Edited by T.H. O'Beirne. Translated by F. Gobel. New York: Dover, 1969.

Sobel, Max, and Maletsky, Evan. *Teaching Mathematics: A Source Book of Aids, Activities, and Strategies*. Englewood Cliffs, N.J.: Prentice-Hall, 1975.

State of Illinois, Office of the Superintendent of Public Instruction. *Mathematics Aids, Bibliographies, Comments for the Teachers of Slow Learners*. Springfield, Illinois.

Sykes, Edna L. *Arithmetic Activities Handbook: An Individualized and Group Approach to Teaching the Basic Skills.* Englewood Cliffs, N.J.: Prentice-Hall, 1976.

Publishers

Educat Mathematics Resource Guide, a catalog of materials that are produced for mathematics education, is published periodically by Educational Materials Catalogs, P.O. Box 2158, Berkeley, California 94702. Items mentioned in the catalog are to be ordered from the listed publishers, not from *Educat*. The most recently issued catalog included materials marketed by the following publishers:

Action Math Associates
825 Monroe, No. 10A
Eugene, OR 97402

Activity Resources Co., Inc.
P.O. Box 4875
20655 Hathaway Ave.
Hayward, CA 94540

Alden Games
P.O. Box 2131
Sunnyvale, CA 94087

Alternatives in Math Education
61 Avenida
Berkeley, CA 94708

Boston College Mathematics
Institute
Boston College
Chestnut Hill, MA 02167

The Center for Open Learning
and Teaching, Inc.
P.O. Box 9434
Berkeley, CA 94709

Center of Innovation in Education
19225 Vineyard Lane
Saratoga, CA 95070

Comprehensive School
Mathematics Program
CEMREL, Inc.
3120 59th Street
St. Louis, MO 63139

Creative Computing
P.O. Box 789-M
Morristown, NJ 08108

A.R. Davis & Co.
P.O. Box 24424 E
San Jose, CA 95154

Intergalactic Publishing Co.
221 Haddon Ave.
Westmont, NJ 08108

Jacobs Publishing Co., Inc.
4747 N. 16th Street
Suite 100-B
Phoenix, AZ 85016

Key Curriculum Project
P.O. Box 2304
Berkeley, CA 94702

LOMA Co.
338 Flurnoy Ave.
Florence, AL 35630

The Math Group, Inc.
396 East 79th St.
Minneapolis, MN 55420

Math House
551 W. Surf St.
Chicago, IL 60657

May-Jay Productions, Inc.
P.O. Box 88
Hubbard Woods Station
Winnetka, IL 60093

Metric Genie, Dept. MA
P.O. Box 305
Corte Madera, CA 94925

Modern Math Materials
1658 Albermarle Way
Burlingame, CA 94010

N & R Products
621 Taylor Ave.
Alameda, CA 94501

Parks and Math Co.
954 Idlewood Drive
San Jose, CA 95121

Perelli-Pak
Box 31355 (R)
San Francisco, CA 94131

Stokes Publishing Co.
P.O. Box 415
Palo Alto, CA 94302

TEACHERS
P.O. Box 398, Dept. E
Manhattan Beach, CA 90266

T.M.T.T.
990 Asbury (D)
San Jose, CA 95126

Touch & See Education
   Resources
Dept. L
P.O. Box 794
Palos Verdes Estates, CA 90274

Walnut Publishing Co.
P.O. Box 1473
Burlingame, CA 94010

WFF'N'PROOF Learning
   Games Associates
1490-PO South Boulevard
Ann Arbor, MI 48104

William Kaufmann, Inc.
One First St.
Los Altos, CA 94022

Index

To Readers

We would like to know your reactions to this first edition of *Teaching Elementary School Mathematics: An Active Learning Approach.* Your evaluation of the book will help us respond to the interests and needs of readers of future editions. Please complete this questionnaire and return it to: College Marketing, Houghton Mifflin Company, One Beacon Street, Boston, MA 02107. Thank you very much.

Are you

A. a student preparing to teach?   Yes   No
   If yes, 1. during what college year did you take this course?
      _____ freshman _____ sophomore _____ junior
      _____ senior
   2. did you take a college math course prior to taking this course?   Yes   No
      If yes, what was the course title?

   _____

B. currently teaching at the elementary level?   Yes   No
   If yes, 1. how many years of teaching experience do you have?
      _____ 0 to 2 _____ 2 to 5 _____ more than 5
   2. at what level has the majority of this experience occurred?
      _____ primary (K-3) _____ intermediate (4-6)
      _____ upper

When responding to the following questions, please refer to specific chapter numbers, section headings, page numbers, and paragraphs (for example: Chapt. 1, Algebraic foundations, p. 14, para. 2).

1. Are there any terms or concepts that were not adequately explained?   Yes   No
   If yes, specify.

   _____

   _____

2. Are there topics that are unclear, need further explanation, or should be expanded?   Yes   No
   If yes, specify.

   _____

   _____

3. Are there points with which you disagree?   Yes   No
   If yes, specify.

   _____

   _____

4. Are there topics that are unnecessary and should be deleted?
   Yes   No
   If yes, specify.

   _____

   _____

5. Are there topics relevant to consideration in program development that should be added?   Yes   No
   If yes, specify.

   _____

   _____

6. Did you have difficulty with any of the mathematical content?
   Yes   No
   If yes, specify.

   _____

   _____

7. Were any illustrations in the text too complicated to understand?   Yes   No
   If yes, specify.

   _____

   _____

8. Were any suggested activities that you completed inappropriate
   for your study of teaching elementary mathematics?
   Yes   No
   If yes, specify.

   _____

   _____

9. Any additional comments, suggestions, or reactions?

   _____

   _____